# Out of the Blue

*Art Stephenson*

SIFAT

A SIFAT 40th Anniversary
Publication

# Out of the Blue

Copyright © 2019 by Arthur G. Stephenson
All rights reserved
ISBN-13: 9781799138907

All Rights Reserved. No part of this publication may be reproduced, stored in a retrieval system, or transmitted in any form or by any means, electronic, mechanical, recorded or otherwise, without the prior written permission of the author.

Order copies of this book from Amazon.com or from:

SIFAT Publications
2944 Country Road 113
Lineville, Alabama 36266
sifat.org

*All proceeds from the sale of this book go to the work of SIFAT*

Printed in the United States of America by
Kindle Direct Publishing

Cover background artwork by Hannah Stephenson

*For our children, grandchildren, great-grandchildren and generations of children to come.*

*May you all find a life of love for God and others.*

******

# Table of Contents

Chapter One
**Call from NASA – 1**

Chapter Two
**Life on the Move – 7**

Chapter Three
**We are Not Alone – 19**

Chapter Four
**Love of My Life – 27**

Chapter Five
**Douglas – 41**

Chapter Six
**Family Times – 49**

Chapter Seven
**Hiking – 63**

Chapter Eight
**The Church, The Body of Christ – 83**

Chapter Nine
**TRW – Part 1 – 91**

Chapter Ten
**Mid-Life Crisis – 103**

Chapter Eleven
**TRW – Part 2 – 113**

Chapter Twelve
**Oceaneering – 127**

Chapter Thirteen
**MSFC Introduction – 147**

Chapter Fourteen
**John Glenn's Return to Space – 159**

Chapter Fifteen
**MSFC Management Challenges – 169**

Chapter Sixteen
**Events Surrounding Chandra Launch – 197**

Chapter Seventeen
**MSFC Space Program Challenges – 221**

Chapter Eighteen
**Columbia – 237**

Chapter Nineteen
**MSFC Education Programs – 249**

Chapter Twenty
**Back to Industry – 255**

Chapter Twenty-One
**Supporting Angels – 269**

Chapter Twenty-Two
**Titles or Testimony? – 279**

Chapter Twenty-Three
**Giving Back – 285**

# Acknowledgements

Without the encouragement and help of Sarah and Ken Corson, founders of Servants in Faith and Technology (SIFAT), the story of my life up to now would never have been written. Most of us don't think about recording our experiences growing up, our transition to adulthood and then our time raising a family and conducting a career. I am very glad Sarah and Ken encouraged me to pass on some of my memories to our children, grandchildren, great grandson, and generations to come. After I decided to write this book, Sarah and Ken kindly coached me on how to self-publish and answered my many questions. Sarah spent hours and hours reading and offering suggestions on punctuation, grammar and guiding me in this sometimes difficult process. I even learned what a "split infinitive" is and how to correct it! Ken graciously agreed to write the book preface. I can't adequately express my thanks to you, Sarah and Ken, for your loving support.

Thanks to Loa, my loving wife of 55 years. She was always there to help me with spelling when the computer did not give me the answer because I was so far from even being close to the right spelling. Thanks for listening to my trial compositions and offering advice. And thanks, Loa, for giving me the time to do this, always understanding and positively supporting this effort.

Our artistic granddaughter, Hannah, graciously agreed to provide the *Space Galaxy* background art for the book cover. Thank you, Hannah, for creating such a beautiful representation of God's Universe.

Thank you, John (our son), for finding time in your very busy schedule to take a walk with me to listen to what I was struggling to communicate in the book and affirming my direction with it.

A special thank you to our daughter, Kristin, for creating a very detailed three volume scrapbook chronicling my five years at NASA's Marshall Space Flight Center. Without these detailed records and pictures, I could not have accurately shared many of my experiences at NASA. Also, thank you, Kristin, for reading the manuscript and offering suggestions for improvement.

And thanks to our family *computer guru*, Mark, Kristin's husband, for always being ready to help conquer my seemingly unending computer challenges.

Art Stephenson
February 2019

# Preface

Between the covers of this book, we have a first-hand account of some major events of humankind's pioneering venture to the moon and beyond into space. For anyone interested in space travel or in history, this book is a gold mine! But it is much more! In the midst of serious, heavy circumstances, the story shines with inspiring faith and trust in God. Art Stephenson's Christian witness and reliance on God in good and bad times is expressed sincerely. This thread runs throughout the book and throughout his life as well. This autobiography is captivating from the start when he introduces his family, his growing-up years, his relationships and feelings. It carries the reader on into the major events of his professional life which also are some of the major events of his generation.

Perhaps Art is best known for being the Director of NASA's Marshal Space Center in Huntsville, Alabama, though he has worked in many other space programs and companies. But to us at SIFAT, we know him as a committed Christian, who works long hours to help those in need. Since 2008, he and his wife Loa have come on many trips to SIFAT's International Headquarters in Alabama giving their time to help in whatever need we have. They have also gone to Ecuador each year since 2013 to help us work among the children of several slum areas. Today, Art serves on SIFAT's Board of Directors. He also chairs the committee that helps SIFAT's graduates with "seed" money for their own community projects.

In reading his autobiography, one realizes that his dad must have been an extraordinary man too. Art reflects many qualities of his dad to his generation in more than mere DNA. His father was a pioneer in the atomic age. Now Art has been a pioneer in the space age. What a legacy!

As Art recounts the major events of his life, we find his values, his faith shining through all the while he is dealing with bureaucracies, celebrities and confronting and solving human and technical problems. We see the nitty gritty of management, technology, and again the weight of dealing with multiple bureaucracies all with more detail than we could have imagined. *Out of the Blue* is rich in historical information, facts, events, people.

His story starts with an introverted boy who had to move around a lot because of his father's work. He constantly had to find and make new friends. He recounts how God helped him overcome his fear of speaking in public and develop special skills that others later acknowledged. Thus, they placed him in leading roles to help guide one of the highest and most meaningful tasks in human history--- our voyage beyond the confines of earth into space. This book tells that story in rich, meaningful detail.

Engineers are not always noted for having great writing skills, but Art's communication skills are excellent. He describes events as though they happened yesterday. He places the reader right in the middle of some of the greatest events of our generation and we experience it through his words as if we had been there.

It amazes me to find a man who came to wield such influence, power and authority to be so humble, compassionate and caring. His modesty, humility, and gentility are part of his Christian character, and circumstances show his backbone, wisdom, insight, and persistence too. I am glad that his story is not locked up only in his memories. His story is a part of our time and part of the higher accomplishments of our nation and of our species. I am so glad that he has shared it with us all and that he is allowing SIFAT to share it with the world.

Ken Corson
SIFAT Founder

# Chapter 1

# Call From NASA

*"For surely I know the plans I have for you, says the Lord, plans for your welfare and not for harm, to give you a future of hope. Then when you call upon me and come and pray to me, I will hear you. When you search for me, you will find me; if you seek me with all your heart."*
--- Jeremiah 29:11-13 (NRSV)

The call from the National Aeronautics & Space Administration (NASA) Administrator's office was a total surprise to me. Joe Rothenberg, Associate Administrator for Human Space Flight, was on the other end of the call. His words came out of the blue. "Would you like to be considered for the position of Director of NASA's Marshall Space Flight Center in Huntsville, Alabama?"

At the time I was President of Oceaneering Technology, a sector of Oceaneering Inc. This company is primarily an offshore oil field services company that had ventured into supporting NASA. I was responsible for overseeing the company's work for NASA, the U.S. Navy and some financially challenging, fixed price contracts for the entertainment business. Our NASA work involved design and development of tools, toolboxes and restraints used on Shuttle flights by astronauts when they worked outside the Shuttle Orbiter to perform tasks such as repair of the Hubble Space Telescope. Also, we were NASA Marshall Space Flight Center's contractor operating their Neutral Buoyancy Facility used to train astronauts for "zero G" external shuttle operations (*Extra Vehicular Activity*). Our NASA work also included design and development of galley equipment for the International Space Station. For the Navy we were responsible for all search and recovery operations requiring deep dive robotically operated vehicles. Both of these divisions included very interesting, additional unique products we designed and manufactured. For the space launch industry, we built "blankets" or heat shields for the aft end of launch vehicles. We made diapers for women pilots flying the supersonic SR-71 aircraft on long duration flights. For the entertainment parks at Disney World we built dinosaurs for the Dinosaur ride and at Universal Studios sharks for the Jaws ride. In short, I was in my dream job.

My response to Joe was not well thought out. I said, "Joe, you've got to be kidding. I know something about Marshall Space Flight Center (MSFC) having worked as a contractor supporting MSFC while at TRW Inc. (which stands for Thompson, Ramo, Wooldridge), and now Oceaneering. Center Directors are grown from within MSFC, not from industry and, besides, my current work is primarily with NASA's Johnson Space Flight Center (JSC) in Houston, which unfortunately is a rival to Marshall in some sense and I don't think I would be well received at Marshall." There was a long pause on the other end of the phone. Then Joe said, "I understand. No problem. We are putting together a list of potential Center Directors for Marshall and your name is on the list if you want it to be. If not.... OK."

Some six years before this call I had received a call "out of the blue" like this one from Oceaneering and my initial response was a similar one --- "You've got to be kidding." I caught myself and responded back to Joe, "Hey, I am open to considering it. Where do we go from here?"

There would be a lot less money working for NASA but this was not a concern. Maybe there was an opportunity to make a difference for the better working for NASA at MSFC. Certainly, having worked on projects with MSFC as my customer, some ideas occurred to me that would be useful to implement at Marshall.

The next thing I knew I had flown to Washington DC and was sitting one on one with the NASA Administrator, Dan Golden. I had worked indirectly for Dan while we were both at TRW and so we knew each other. By this time I was excited about the possibility but also, being an introvert like Moses, I was somewhat hesitant. We talked about a lot of things but as we concluded the meeting Dan said, "You realize you will be responsible for all of the propulsion elements of the Shuttle Space Transportation System including the Orbiter main engines (3), the External tank (the source of main engine fuel) and the Solid Rocket Motors (2). A spec of metal in the wrong place in one of the main engines is the number one threat to safety during launch." (The solid rocket motors had already killed the "Challenger" crew six years earlier). Dan went on to say, "You may someday be accountable for the deaths of some of our country's most heroic and famous men and women astronauts. My questions to you are 1) can you handle this grave responsibility? and 2) what do you need to be successful in this job? Don't tell me now. Come back in a week after thinking about it and give me your answer." I agreed and as I headed for the Washington National Airport to fly home, my intense prayer was, please God, I need some very clear sign from you on this one. Your will be done, not mine. I had learned that life for this introvert could not be lived, particularly in high profile jobs where I was expected to be in front of people, without God at my side, lovingly reassuring me when challenges presented themselves.

So, I went home to Houston. The following week my left shoulder and arm went numb. I knew, this time, it was not a heart attack like I feared the other time it happened. I knew it was simply stress --- overload --- fearful thinking. Some wise person had told me once, "Worry is the misuse of the imagination; it is thinking about what you don't want to happen; it is something 90 percent of the time you can't do anything about." Yes, I was thrown into a state best described by that wise person's statement. After much prayer and thought I concluded, as I had in many previous risky and sometimes crazy job changes as well as personal crises, that my answer to myself and to Dan is, "Yes, I can handle this grave responsibility but not alone." To be successful I would ask for Dan's support for Marshall Space Flight Center and for me in this role. Much more important though, I knew, once again, I needed God to have my back, to know deep down He wanted me in this job. I did not know how it would turn out and certainly understood I could not do this out of my own strength. I would be totally dependent on Him.

A week later, as Dan had decreed, I was on a plane to Washington DC and NASA Headquarters to deliver my answers to Dan's two questions. I was confident, ready and honored to assume the leadership of one of NASA's largest, most important Centers.

---

On a Saturday morning, 4 ½ years after accepting Dan's offer to lead Marshall, I was at home relaxing, doing household chores like most non-working Saturdays. The phone rang and I heard my Deputy Center Director, Dave King's voice, "Have you been watching the TV?" I replied "No." He said, "You better turn it on.... any news channel will do. The Shuttle Columbia is breaking up over Texas...."

---

The story of my life that led me to this "Columbia moment" and beyond is the story I have attempted to share in this book. It is the story of a very shy, introverted boy who, with God's grace, found a way out of that lonely place. I am still an introvert and always will be. When I was young, seeing a stranger walking on the sidewalk toward me, I would switch to the other side of the street. Although I overcame this fear and response, when I encounter someone now when walking, a thought still enters my mind to switch to the other side of the street. When people read my resume it gives the wrong impression that my professional life was just one up after another. My personal and professional life, like most everyone, came with wonderful ups and very hurtful downs for me and my family members. I have tried to openly share the highs and the lows with the hope that maybe something I say will help those who read this book.

I don't think my story is one that is unique to me. For most people I know, life comes with great sorrow, disappointment, and some tragedies and, fortunately, with the best of times too. We all make mistakes. We all suffer the consequences from choices we make. Not all of us have the most important things in life and I have been blessed to have two of the most important ingredients. Those two are: 1) having a loving family and loving friends who have been there for me and, most important, 2) a faith in God, Jesus Christ and the Holy Spirit that has led and sustained me in the best of times and the worst of times.

Stephenson Family (2017) Left to Right; Front Row: Paul & Marinah, Scott & Hannah, Blake & Jack; Back Row: Mark & Kristin, Loa, Arthur & Art, Amy & John

# Chapter 2

# Life on The Move

*"I have learned that if you must leave a place that you have lived in and love and where all your yesteryears are buried deep, leave it any way except a slow way, leave it the fastest way you can. Never turn back and never believe that an hour you remember is a better hour because it is dead. Passed years seem safe ones, vanquished ones, while the future lives in a cloud, formidable from a distance."*
--- Beryl Markham

By the time I was 17 we had lived in 10 different houses in six cities in four states and I had gone to eight schools. We moved a lot. My father was never in the military so I can't say I was a "military brat." My father was a very intelligent physicist and engineer, and this opened doors and career opportunities for him. Unfortunately, or fortunately this caused us to move a lot.

I was born in New London, Connecticut when my father was working as a civil servant on submarine sonar technology for the U.S. Navy. Our moves from there until I left for college were to Los Alamos, New Mexico, to Mt. Tabor, New Jersey, San Diego, California, Torrance, California, and Palos Verdes Estates, California.

My father loved the ocean and the mountains. From the time we moved to California when I was nine until I left for college, we lived near the ocean with only a short 2 hour drive to the mountains. Around home the ocean was the big draw for our family. I swam in the ocean, nearly year-round, "free diving," body surfing and then board surfing. As a family we spent many Sunday afternoons picnicking and swimming with masks and fins at La Jolla Cove in San Diego. My summers in San Diego were spent body surfing and collecting and cashing in soda bottles to buy snacks. When we moved to Torrance, until I went 100 miles inland to college, I spent my summers board surfing.

My parents' housing selection pattern, each time we moved, was to rent a house when we first moved to a new

From left to right: Art, brother Carl, sister Lynn in La Jolla

location and then, after looking around for nine months to a year, to buy a house. It made life difficult for us kids because we typically had to change schools after one year in each new location.

When I was two years old in 1944, we lived in Los Alamos, New Mexico. My father was working on the atom bomb, one of the Oppenheimer team members. I can only remember one thing and that was I wanted to have more rides in that army jeep my father brought home one day to have lunch. When he drove off, headed back to work, I cried for a long time. He had been "recruited." The Army came to him when he was working for the Navy in New London, Connecticut and said, "You can go to the front line in Germany with the Army or you can go to a classified place we will not say where." It was obvious where they wanted him to go. He joined a lot of smart physicists in New Mexico. I regret never talking to him about this work before he died. My mother said he was very concerned about the deaths and destruction that could result from the use of this bomb and left after two years before the work was completed. The debate on the use of this bomb in Japan is a very heated one. I prefer to think historians had the right interpretation who say the bomb saved many lives. The Japanese people were not ones to surrender and it took not one but two bombs to get them to do so. It was believed an invasion into Japan to end the war would have claimed many U.S., ally, and Japanese lives.

    My father was near "ground zero" when the first bombs were tested in White Sands, New Mexico. This caused an early death from the radiation he was exposed to. He died from brain cancer at the age of 54 when I was just 31 years old. Fortunately, we were able, during my years after college, to develop a good adult-to-adult relationship. I had a good relationship with my father until I entered high school. After that, breaking free of his dominant nature was difficult for me and we clashed too many times. I am sure I was a typical teenage disaster in his mind. I wanted to be right about just one thing, but it never seemed to come out that way. He always had a better understanding of just about everything and I could see that he was actually right on anything we debated. Frankly, my father was so smart I never did win a debate with him until one day when I was a professional aerospace engineer/manager, he said, "You know more about that than I do." I was shocked! This was the day we became equals and I inwardly rejoiced! A smile comes to my face when I remember the one or two times after that when he asked for my advice.

Speaking of smiles there is a story I must tell about my father and me doing our respective jobs. I was working in the space sector of TRW (Thomson, Ramo, Wooldridge). My father was working for Aerospace Corporation that provided technical program oversight on Air Force space programs. I became a first-line supervisor pretty early in my career, not because I was a top-notch engineer but because I was able and liked doing things supervisors needed to do; things like planning, organizing, staffing, integrating, directing and controlling program resources. Most engineers at TRW, and in aerospace companies in general, would far rather do technical work than management tasks. A first-line supervisor at TRW was responsible for the work of about 15 to 20 engineers and technicians. My team was working on a classified program for the Air Force. I was asked, along with other team leaders on the program, to brief the top Aerospace Corporation customer and his team. The top customer was my father. That day came and there he was front and center in a packed conference room reviewing the program status. For sure I was not going to argue any point he made when it was my turn to brief. I went through a series of projected charts explaining each one as my father took it in but made no comment. We were having a difficult time achieving the desired hardware performance. I had a chart that was created to show the steps we had gone through up to now. As I was briefing this chart a smile came over my father's face. He said, "Looks like you are going in circles." The room erupted into laughter and I was the brunt of my father's jab/joke. I looked at it again and he was right. The chart showed steps that flowed in a circular pattern. As I recall my response was to acknowledge his legitimate point and laugh along with everyone else. Over my many years in the space business I have briefed company Presidents, military Generals, NASA Center Directors, the NASA Administrator, U.S. Senators and Congressmen, and the President's Science Advisor. Never have I had an experience like the one with my Dad that one and only time I briefed him in a professional setting. I would not have wanted to be invited to brief him again. Who knows what he would have come up with another time?

For 10 years during the time I was working in the same profession, and before he died, my father was always willing to listen to my challenges at work and could shed very useful light on those challenges. I was blessed to have his advice any time I asked. I knew he loved me, and I wished we could have had more time together. My mother lived until 92 and there was never any doubt she loved me. I miss both of my parents.

I was blessed to have such loving parents who taught me the importance of a relationship with Christ. Both were committed United Methodists and instilled the value in me of going to church every Sunday. Worshiping God was as important as breathing. They constantly encouraged me and always seemed to hold the belief I would succeed in life. That kind of encouragement made me want to fulfill their perception of who I could become. It seems simple but I wonder why all parents don't do what mine did --- encourage their children all of the growing up years until they leave home.

During my elementary and middle school years we lived on both coasts --- New Jersey while my dad worked on special electronics for Bell Laboratory and then in San Diego, California, where he worked on sonar for submarines as he had in New London, Connecticut. Then in 1955 we moved to Torrance, California, and my father joined Ramo Wooldridge Corporation working on Missile defense for the Air Force. This led to a role in the development of the first one of the space pioneers and was there when the "Space Race" with the Soviet Union began. Sputnik was launched in October 1957 causing great concern in the United States as it beeped in orbit around the earth.

In May 1958 my father came home and announced we were moving to the "Big Island" of Hawaii for the summer and fall. He was responsible for the installation, checkout and operation of a satellite tracking ground station on the southern tip of the island.

South Point, Hawaii Satellite Tracking Station
(Pacific Ocean in the distance)

This ground station was set up to send commands to one of the first U.S. satellites after launch to place it in orbit around the moon. Two truck transport trailers were outfitted in California and shipped to the South Point of Hawaii where they were connected to a large antenna mounted on top of a block house. This was a wonderful adventure. My task was to plant grass around the trailers and block house. The Army guys let me ride in their helicopter as it was used to calibrate the ground station antennas. I jumped off the South Point cliffs into extremely deep water near the site and free dived with my dad and other ground station workers. I learned to drive and obtained my Territory of Hawaii driver's license. They allowed a 15-year old to have a license. My dad taught me how to do four-wheel slides around corners on remote dirt roads. Years later I told my dad I nearly killed myself and a college buddy with this knowhow some years later driving down a windy road in the San Jacinto mountains. I dove with sea turtles and spear fished at a black sand beach near our home nearly every day. The black sand beach attracted tourists who wanted to take my picture at times when I came out of the water with a fish on the end of my spear. They thought I was Hawaiian, with my very dark suntanned skin.

Life can be fun, and it can be dangerous. I want to tell you a true story that brought this fact home to me at the age of 15. When we were in Hawaii, I came home one day after school to an empty house. Right after I arrived a car came speeding into our long dirt driveway. My father was away on the Mainland in California at the time. His deputy came rushing into the house wanting to use our telephone, as no phone was available at the ground station site, which was 25 miles away. At the ground station the only communication mechanism they had was a Teletype and it was only connected back to the 48 states. He used our home phone to call the Air Force station on the other side of the island and asked them to send aircraft to search for two of his men who had been swept out to sea at South Point.

South Point has severe currents that come from Japan and go back to Japan at that point. My mother often spent time collecting glass balls that came from Japanese fishing nets and landed on the beach near South Point. This is where I sometimes jumped of the cliff and free dived in 180 ft. deep water with my dad and others who worked at the ground station. We were always aware of the danger of this current and were careful not to go out too far from the cliff. It was and is an amazing place. One day one of the fishermen fishing from the top of the cliff hooked into an eight foot

Blue Shark bringing it to the surface right after we had climbed out of the water. But I digress.

Art returned to Ka Lae Point cliffs in 1997 where he, in 1958, jumped off the cliff to Free Dive

One of the two men who had been swept out to sea was not a strong swimmer and as he swam away from the cliff, he found he was not able to swim against the current to go ashore as everyone else could. He started drifting farther and farther from the cliff. Another one of the ground station crew swam out to him and decided to go with him as he was unable to pull him back to the cliff against the current. Two other men who had been swimming with them reported the situation to the deputy station manager back at the ground station. When the station deputy arrived at our house it had been over an hour since they had drifted out of sight toward the horizon. The Air Force immediately responded with search aircraft and miraculously they found them miles out to sea. The airplane crew later reported they saw a dangerous

40-foot, White Shark circling around the two men. A life raft was dropped to the men and later a helicopter came along and rescued both men. The deputy manager was not someone I knew very well but we both were in shock standing there after he had made the call. He did not hang around, but it seemed to me he was praying for their safety. The Air Force told the deputy on the phone there was little chance they could find two men in such a big ocean. When the news of the rescue came, we all were so thankful to God for this miracle. I remember talking to those two men not long after this ordeal and they both said they were fighting back thoughts of losing hope out there in that vast ocean. I thought, *How could anyone in that situation, not being able to see land anymore, keep up hope without believing in a God who promises to be with us always?*

Since we were in Hawaii when my sophomore school year started back home, I attended a local high school and experienced what it means to be a shunned minority as I was the only white person in the school of 200 students. At first I was the center of attention because other students wanted to know more about mainland youth ways such as the type of music we listened to and dances we danced but after a short time they made it clear I was not welcome in their circle of friends. Out of this experience I developed a personal sense of the prejudice and unjust ways of people toward minorities. This was a sad realization that shaped my thinking and still raises angry feelings when I see this so often in our world today.

I had a lot of time to myself that summer and fall in Hawaii. Every day I walked down to the very rough coast we lived next to and pondered the power of the ocean and its Creator. The hand of God in nature was obvious to me. It is easy for me to praise God any time I am in a place where nature is prevalent but also just by looking at the magnificent mature trees on our residential Houston street as they lose their leaves and are reborn every spring.

I wonder if this constant movement from house to house and school to school instilled in me a belief that I would be OK on the other side of each change. After all, even though it was hard, I always found life bearable after each move or new school and often enjoyed the adventure of learning about a new place. Moving from the east coast to "paradise" in California and spending five months in Hawaii were opportunities I thought were special. I lost friends in each place we left behind and, although difficult for me, found new ones where we moved only to have to say goodbye once more. This experience reinforced my introverted ways and being alone was lonely but OK too. Teachers called me a day dreamer. I found a personal relationship with God and Jesus Christ who never left me like so many friends did without a choice. As I entered the professional work place after college, I was not afraid of taking on the risk of change. I made numerous job changes throughout my career. But I had a sense with each job change that God was leading me and would always be there in good times and bad times. As I look back over my life, I can say this truth was obvious. It is much easier to see God's hand in the rear-view mirror.

By the time my wonderful wife, Loa, and I bought our first home after living in two houses and two apartments in our first three years of marriage, I was ready to stay in our new house for a very long time. Work changes were happening over the next years within the same large company, but I took refuge in not moving from house to house like I had experienced all my life. With the joyful births of our daughter Kristin followed by our son John our family grew to four in the first house we owned in Cypress, California. After 15 years in that house Loa, Kristin, and John took me aside and said, "We are ready to move somewhere else. We have lived here long enough." I was surprised but they gave me no choice. We were going to move.

We moved 10 miles from the inland city of Cypress to Seal Beach. Life in this beach city was a welcome change. We thoroughly enjoyed living a block away from the beach, a block from Seal Beach pier, and a block off of Main Street. We joked that we could buy everything we needed on Main Street except underwear. I found myself, once again, in awe of the power of God's Ocean as we experienced two "100 year" storms in our first year in Seal Beach that destroyed the town's ocean pier and flooded and battered homes along the beach. Fortunately, our home was a block away from the beach and was six feet above sea level, so we did not experience any damage from those storm's powerful waves driven by high winds.

Again, I was ready to stay put and we enjoyed ten great family years in this new home. John grew up surfing on Seal Beach like I had in my teens in San Diego and Torrance and Palos Verdes Estates. Kristin and John finished their high school years in Seal Beach and both went off to college from there. I would have gladly stayed in Seal Beach forever but about the time Kristin was getting married and finishing her master's degree and John was nearly through college with his B.A. degree, I got an unexpected "out of the blue" call from a friend, Mike Gernhardt, who was Vice President of the Oceaneering Space Systems in Houston, Texas. I had worked with him on a proposal to NASA I led for TRW and we had developed a friendship and respected each other's professional acumen. He asked me to consider taking his position with Oceaneering as he was leaving. He had been accepted into NASA's astronaut corps. I said, "Mike you've got to be kidding. After 28 years at TRW I am only four years from having retirement options to consider. If I leave now, I will have to pass up any near-term retirement options." I hung up the phone and prayed and thought about this offer for about an hour. I had just been handed another high stress 24 X 7 difficult NASA proposal to manage. I called Mike back and said I would make a trip down to Houston to consider the possibility. When I went home that night and told Loa about this unexpected call she didn't hesitate. She said, "Let's go!"

From a job standpoint I never did settle down. The longest job I had during my career was six years. I worked for TRW for 28 years but was able to make job changes within this large company not requiring us to move during those years. After TRW, I worked for Oceaneering for six years, NASA for five years and 3 ½ years for Northrop Grumman. After retiring from Northrop Grumman, I consulted with aerospace companies for seven years. All in all, I worked in the space business for 50 years. After buying our first house in Cypress, California, during those nearly 50 years, we lived in a total of seven houses, much to my liking, compared to the 10 houses we lived in during my first 17 years.

Art (6), mother with Carl (2), Aunt Holley standing, Lynn (9), and father in Mt. Tabor, New Jersey (1949)

## Chapter 3

# We Are Not Alone

(My Struggle to Break Free from Isolation)

> *"We know that in everything God works for good with those who love him, who are called according to his purpose."*
> --- Romans 8:28 (RSV)

For as long as I can remember my family attended church every Sunday morning without fail. As children and youth my older sister, Lynn, my two younger brothers, Carl and David, and I always attended Sunday school and Sunday evening youth activities. I was taught that Jesus loved me and is always with me. At the age of 12, while attending a revival meeting with my mother, I went forward at the end of the service to commit my life to Christ. Jesus was my friend. The Holy Spirit showed up at youth retreats when we all had a sense of God's very real presence. Being a shy, introverted person, I especially appreciated knowing that I was not alone. This belief has sustained me all my life and I have turned to my friend Jesus and routinely asked God to guide me when I struck out so many times in new directions in my personal life and professional life. I am convinced that without this love and support my life would have been much different. I would have hidden in my shell and found a safe place to exist and missed out on so many experiences and opportunities. I thank God for leading me to this realization early in life.

    I have already said we moved a lot. Just before I started 9th grade we moved from San Diego to Torrance in the Los Angeles basin and rented a house. I attended Torrance High School in 9th grade. Once again, true to form, nine months later my parents bought a house in Palos Verdes Estates and moved the summer before I started 10th grade. In the fall, on the first day of school, I got on the bus and rode to Narbonne High School without knowing anyone. The summer and fall after 10th grade was the time we were in Hawaii and when we returned I had to re-enter high school several months after the year had started. I was in a catch-up mode but the worst thing to me was I was not able to try out to play on the high school basketball team, something I had dreamed about doing. There would be no basketball team play for me in high school. All the way through high school I essentially had no friends at school. I ate lunch alone every day. The only time I felt good about having friends was when I played and lettered on the high school tennis team or competed successfully on our swim team. I did not socialize with my sports friends as they had their groups and did not invite me to join them. I don't think it is fair for me to blame them. An introvert sometimes waits to be invited. I was afraid to ask girls for a date, fearful of going to any of the dances, and only had one date during the four years of high school. Even in MYF (Methodist Youth Fellowship) I was afraid to approach girls and, as the church my parents chose to attend did not have kids that attended my school, I did not know the other teens in MYF. They had their cliques and did not invite me to join their group. Being socially awkward I found a sport that I could do alone and that was surfing. I loved to surf. My only friends were a couple of guys I surfed with and surfing became my life throughout my high school years. One summer my father said, "You have to get a job," so a surfing buddy and I said we would start a business making custom surfboards. Fortunately, my father thought that was enterprising and approved. Every day we went surfing in the morning and worked on building surfboards in the afternoon. We sold two surfboards that summer.

I enjoyed playing on the tennis and swim teams in high school. I played on the tennis team three years. A high point in tennis was winning first place in the high school league doubles competition my senior year. My parents didn't see me play in any tennis events in high school, but I did not expect them to come. Tennis did not draw many spectators in those days. In addition to tennis, I was on the swim team my junior year. Because I was playing on the tennis team at the same time as swim team workouts, I only went to swim meets. The swim team coach approved of my missing workouts because almost every time I competed in the 50-yard sprint I won the race. I had decided on a whim to try out for the swim team before the start of the competitive spring swim season. When I went to the tryouts, the only race I tried out for was the 50-yard race and surprisingly I won it. I reasoned my speed must have come from my body surfing and board surfing days that required moving quickly in the water to catch waves. Before you think this is so great, I will say I was competing on the B swim team not the A swim team. The A swimmers were faster. The good thing was our 4 X 200 meter relay team won second place in the Los Angeles City wide "B team" final competition race. We raced successfully in three elimination races to qualify for the race final. Compared to most youth sports these days this was not much of a feat. The great thing for me was my father was there that night to see us place second out of eight teams in that final race in the 1932 Olympic Swim Stadium. When our son John competed in baseball, soccer, swimming and water polo, I tried my best to make it to his events because I knew how glad I was when my father saw me compete in that race.

I assume every teenager experiences stress from parents, school, and peers. I know I did especially since I felt so often alone and isolated. There were many times when I felt this weight on me but did not know how to get rid of it. Some kids do destructive things, especially these days with drugs and alcohol. In my days we had alcohol, but I had no interest in that. Besides my parents' not approving alcohol, I just did not like the taste. Some students in my school bought motorcycles and rode in a crazy fashion. Maybe that helped them deal with the stress I am talking about. I know several classmates died from motorcycle accidents. One thing I wound up doing was shooting baskets in our driveway at a goal mounted on the garage. I would shoot baskets until I was about to drop. This seemed to help some. The second thing I did, especially when I was really angry, was take my tennis racket into my room and use it to beat my pillow on the bed. Something I noticed about myself back then (and now) is I get angry when things are not going my way. I try to say to myself, "Selfish you, get over it! Honor others' desires and needs; don't insist on your own way!"

My parents always assumed their four kids would go to college so I assumed I would. Both parents graduated from a small liberal arts college and so they recommended I pick a small college. My father went with me to attend high school student day at three small liberal arts colleges near Los Angeles. The one I really liked was the University of Redlands. After the U of R rejected my application, my dad and I met with the Dean of Admissions to understand why I had not been accepted. The Dean told me my high school grades were not up to par (I had a 3.4 out of 4.0 GPA and the University of Redlands was accepting only students with GPAs 3.9 and above) and I had met the U of R minimum threshold score for only one of the three college entrance exam areas. I re-took the entrance exam and sent those scores to the U of R and once again I was rejected. This time I had met two of the three acceptance thresholds but still fell short on the third one. I re-took the entrance exam again and personally carried the results of this third set of tests to the Dean of Admissions, 100 miles from home. By this time the Dean and I were getting to know each other pretty well. He looked at the test results and said, "You still fall short of our threshold on one of the three test areas." I must have looked pretty sad and disappointed. After a long pause he said, "I give up.... you can come to the University of Redlands." Sometimes persistence pays off. One thing was very clear to me --- I was absolutely the worst student in my entering freshman class of 400 students. I knew I would have to study harder than any other student to keep from being thrown out of school at the end of my freshman year --- something I was not going to let them do.

*Note: Funny thing* --- Years later the President of the University of Redlands called me when I was Center Director of NASA's Marshall Space Flight Center in Huntsville, Alabama, and asked me to come to the campus for their annual alumni awards ceremony. They had decided to give me one of two "Alumni Career Achievement Awards" for that year. It was an honor to accept this award. I resisted the temptation to say, in my short acceptance speech, that I only was admitted after applying three times where upon the Dean of Admissions threw up his hands and said, "I give up, you can come."

As I prepared to go to the University of Redlands I don't know where this thought came from, but I believe it was a whisper from God. I had never heard of the "Act as if" principle before but learned about it years later. It occurred to me that no one at the University of Redlands would know that I was such an introvert, no one would know I had only one date in high school, and no one would know I did not know how to dance. I decided I could be any person I wanted to be. I could act as if I were someone else – someone I wanted to be.

Just knowing what to say to a stranger, particularly girls, was difficult for me. My older and wiser sister, Lynn, helped me with this. When I asked her how to start a conversation with a girl she said, "Ask a question that will reveal something about that person or person's interests, then ask more questions about them and their interests. People love to talk about themselves and things they are interested in."

The summer after high school graduation I found a dance studio near home and took private lessons to learn to dance. When I got to the University of Redlands, I forced myself to be (act) outgoing, introduced myself to anyone I came in contact with, and learned to initiate conversation using my sister's suggestions. At the first freshman dance I asked a young lady named Phyllis to dance. I had learned the box step at dance school. When I started to dance with her, of course, I started stepping in a square box pattern. She looked confused and stopped me, saying in a caring way, "What are you doing?" (I have shared this story many times with youth groups I worked with over the years wanting them to realize the impact they can have on the life of an introvert.) After I explained where I was coming from Phyllis very kindly said, "No problem, all you have to do is hold me just so, [as she demonstrated], and walk around the dance floor in time with the music." Phyllis literally held my life in her hands. She could be kind and help me get past this insecure and difficult place or she could have sent me running away from girls and dances for who knows how long. It was not long before I asked Phyllis out on a date and then asked her for several more dates. Frankly, I was ready to propose marriage. She finally took me aside and said, "I like you and have enjoyed our time together, but I want to date other men so let's just cool it, OK?" I was a bit heartbroken but managed to move on. I was no longer afraid to ask other women to go out on dates with me. Thanks to Phyllis I was finally able to bridge a cavernous gap between girls and myself. I could be a friend with the opposite sex! I did not have to be alone any more, apart and isolated from one half of the population.

Now I knew not only did I have God and Jesus who are with me all the time but also, I could be a friend to guys and gals. God intends for life to be abundant for all of His children. That includes a rich relationship with Him and also with others. He wanted a man and a woman to become one in marriage, something I knew I wanted very much. Now I was in a place where I could find the "Love of my life" and not be alone going forward.

******

# Chapter 4

# Love of My Life

*"Being deeply loved by someone gives you strength, while loving someone deeply gives you courage."*
--- Lao-Tzu

In my sophomore year at the University of Redlands one of my three roommates, Fred Robinson, was dating a beautiful freshman girl with an award-winning smile. Fred introduced me to Loa one night when our paths happened to cross under a streetlight on campus. I thought, wow, Fred is a lucky guy. A few weeks later Fred broke up with Loa. He felt so bad about it knowing that Loa was having a difficult time after his decision to break up. He dared me to ask her out. That was the easiest dare I have ever accepted. She said yes to my invitation on Valentine's Day, 1962, to go on a double date with Fred and his date. Fred and I had fun creating a unique date plan. Fred drove. We picked up the girls who were friends and headed for a local outdoor, drive-in-theater. Before we got up to the pay station, we stopped the car and asked the girls to get into the trunk of the car, as we could not afford to pay for more than two people. Of course, they refused. When we drove into the theater Fred parked the car in the last row facing away from the screen and we slid over to the girls, but they called our bluff surprising us by sliding our way and we boys quickly abandoned our joke.

That night after dropping the girls at their dorm, I told Fred, "Loa is someone I could marry" and thanked him for giving me the opportunity to date her. Over the course of that school year Loa and I became friends and then became more than friends. Loa did things like doing my laundry. I loaned her my car, even though the front driver side door regularly flew open on right turns due to a latch I was not able to fix. One time Loa was driving with some girlfriends and they were all surprised during a right turn when the door swung open and Loa casually reached out, grabbed the door and pulled it back in without taking her eyes off the road. We introduced each other to our parents. My parents told me she was too good for me and I was surprised when I realized they were serious. The only absolute requirement Loa said I had to meet was being a United Methodist. Fortunately, I qualified!

The summer of 1963 between my junior and senior year, and between Loa's sophomore and junior year, we were married in the United Methodist church in Safford, Loa's hometown in eastern Arizona. Fred was the best man. My other two roommates, Larry Spencer and Bill Hendrick graciously made the journey to Arizona to witness the wedding and Larry sang a solo for us.

Loa and I drove my 1954 Ford back to California with a water bag hanging on the front bumper. This was something everyone did in those days to deal with overheating engines on the hot desert. It was not unusual to see people regularly stopping by the road, hoods up, waiting for their car radiator to stop boiling so they could add water and be on their way.

We, of course, did not have air-conditioning and when we drove through Yuma, Arizona in the late afternoon with the windows down the temperature was 120 degrees. To this day we say we have never been hotter. If we are in a hot place, we just remember Yuma and tell each other, "This is not hot compared to Yuma."

Our honeymoon was supposed to be for a week in my parents' friends' cabin in the mountains east of San Diego, but after three days Loa was too eager to set up our house in Redlands, so we headed there ahead of schedule. I had tossed a bunch of furniture into our apartment before going to Arizona for the wedding and Loa had not seen our new home yet and was anxious to settle in our nest or should I say her nest.

Our life in Redlands that year was financially challenging, but we never complained. The apartment we rented had cracks in the walls with light and air streaming through. Yet we were very happy to be together and teamed up to face a new life together. We were on a tight budget and so the rare dinner out was walking about a mile to a downtown Redlands restaurant where we could buy a short stack of pancakes for 35 cents. Loa was really my helpmate. My grades went to all A's my senior year and she helped me apply for a post-graduation job by typing 100 letters we sent to potential employers. 1964 was a time when entry-level aerospace engineering jobs were few and far between. Being from a liberal arts university majoring in engineering was not attractive to aerospace employers. Only one job offer came my way and I thanked God for that one offer. When I interviewed with Litton Industries Inc., a military electronics company in California's San Fernando Valley, fortunately they asked, "Outside of engineering skills, what other skill might you bring to this job?" My answer was, "I believe I have an ability to write." They immediately hired me. Engineers are notoriously bad writers. Little did I know they needed engineers who could write, to talk to test equipment designers and write procedures to use with the test sets to check out the military combat jet computer. The company had a government contract to design and manufacture these computers.

Five months after I started at Litton, the company lost the computer contract and long lines formed as people who had been laid off stood in line to collect their severance pay as they processed out of the company. I quit after the third round of layoffs knowing I was next because I did not want to have "layoff" beside my first job description on my resume. My next stop was Space Technology Labs where I had worked as a summer intern between my college junior and senior years just before our marriage. Space Technology Labs (later known as TRW) would not hire me after graduation because of their policy to only hire people with experience. Since I had five months of experience with Litton now, I could be hired. I was fortunate to get a job designing digital test equipment to be used to test the Abort Guidance System on the Apollo Lunar Lander Vehicle.

Through all of this turmoil and job changes Loa was a trooper finishing her college education and earning her bachelor's degree in education at California State University, Northridge. This was not of her choosing but was conveniently located in the San Fernando Valley near the apartment we rented not far from Litton.

Throughout my working years Loa stood by me, did a great job raising our kids when it seemed I was too busy at work to be there for them. After the kids were out on their own, she backed me up through thick and thin and in times when I was dealing with hard situations like having to lay people off or when the tragic Columbia shuttle accident occurred. Once when we were living in Seal Beach Loa told me the kids asked, "When is dad coming home?" They thought I was on a trip out of town. I was working on a proposal to the government requiring what seemed to be 24 hours a day, seven days a week. I'd been getting up before they did and coming home after they were already asleep.

We were in Houston and I was working for Oceaneering Inc. when, "out of the blue," came the call for me to go to Huntsville, Alabama, to lead Marshall Space Flight Center. Loa did not want to make that move. We had two grandsons, ages one and three she cared for regularly while our daughter, Kristin, worked part-time and son-in-law, Mark, worked full-time. Loa said, "I know how much you want to take this new job and I, of course, will go with you but it will be very hard to leave Kristin and Mark's two boys, Paul and Blake." We agreed she would return to Houston almost once per month for all the time we lived in Alabama. Even so, she cried nearly the whole way as we drove our two cars the 750 miles from Houston, Texas to Huntsville, Alabama. She actually did return to Houston almost once per month for all the time we lived in Alabama. I have to say Mark is an absolute saint for allowing his mother-in-law to spend so much time in his house sleeping on the foldout couch bed in the living room.

Life as wife of the Marshall Space Flight Center Director is not an easy one. To begin with, my days were long and most days I came home with a briefcase full of stuff I needed to work on that evening. There were times when I had to be away for days on end. Then there were the many events she was expected to attend even if she really did not want to be there. When I travelled, I usually rode on the Marshall airplane with the NASA team. If she was going to the same event, like a Shuttle launch in Florida, she had to fly commercially as only civil servants could fly on the government airplane. She always kept a positive attitude through it all.

Loa never complained about the pull on my time from my working world. Who could ask for a better life mate? As some women say in the South, we are "bestest friends." There is no doubt I will never make up for the times I worked away from home leaving her to deal with the home "fires" without my help.

A day before my 60th Birthday I was in Florida supporting a shuttle launch. Loa had invited family, friends and relatives to come to Huntsville, Alabama, to attend a surprise birthday dinner for me. Without my knowledge, my mother, sister, aunts, uncles, best friends from California and our two kids and their families from Houston were already in Huntsville. In addition, she had invited my Marshall executive committee staff and their spouses to attend the party. The restaurant reservations were set, the cake ordered, and everything was in place for this big surprise. We were having difficulty getting the shuttle launch off due to weather or a hardware issue; I don't really recall the exact reason. I called Loa that day before my birthday after another aborted launch and said I would not be coming home as a result and would have to miss being there for my birthday. There was a long pause on her end of the phone and then she started crying. She had to tell me who was there from out of town for the special surprise birthday party she had arranged.

Of course, although difficult, I found a way to escape my duty to support the launch and came home. She still insisted on blindfolding me in the car, so I did not know the location of the party. As I was led blindfolded into the restaurant, everyone shouted out "Surprise!" It was a great evening. As people shared cards and gifts Loa presented me with a scrapbook album she had created depicting my life history including pictures from my childhood family, our family and my professional life. She had even included my school report cards that did not show such great grades. This is just one example of how, over the years, Loa has made our kids and me feel special.

When we moved to Alabama, we bought a house in a beautiful valley northeast of Huntsville with forested hills and farms in the bottomland. I told Loa I wanted to buy a motorcycle as this was a great place to ride on backcountry, paved roads. She said, "Over my dead body." A year later I made the same statement and she said the exact same thing. One year later the subject came up again and this time I said, "I am going to buy a motorcycle." Much earlier in our married life I did own a motorcycle when we lived in Cypress, California. The problem with owning a "bike" there was you had to drive 50 miles just to get out of the city where the riding was good country riding. Loa and I had taken long trips on that motorcycle as far as places like Flagstaff, Arizona and Northern California to the Sierra Mountains. On these rides we were accompanied by friends. When we went to Arizona our good friends Roger and Georgia Klinkers rode their motorcycle and Bob and June Diets road their motorcycle. These were great adventures and Loa only complained a little about the uncomfortable seat behind me. When our son, John, got to the age of nine and took too much interest in the motorcycle, I sold it. I did not want him to grow up wanting to ride a motorcycle based on my belief teenagers did not have enough driving experience to know what to look for/anticipate in traffic and thus teens were more vulnerable to what could be very severe and life-threatening accidents.

Getting back to my buying a motorcycle, two members of my staff at Marshall entered the picture when they heard I wanted to purchase one. Jim Kennedy, Director of the Engineering Directorate, and Dave Bates, Chief Financial Officer, both were motorcycle owners and devoted riders. Jim had a BMW and Dave had a Harley Davidson. They had a bet between them on which type of motorcycle I would buy. Loa and I went looking at and trying out the two types of motorcycles. Loa thought I should get the BMW and I liked the Harley Davidson. She said the BMW matched my personality better. I kind of liked the sound of the Harley bikes. One day I came home and told Loa I was getting a Harley Davidson Softail Classic bike. Dave Bates had come to me and offered to let me buy a bike he had on order for nearly two years. He really wanted to win the bet. I knew it took a long time to get a new Harley at that time and you had to pay over list price to get one. When he sweetened the deal by letting me get it at list price, I accepted his offer. Dave had ordered this bike in Montana where the dealer, due to poor sales in the winter, let people buy them at list price. Dave offered to go get the bike in Montana and trailer it back to Alabama and deliver it to my home. Pretty good deal. I still owe Dave something in return. Loa and I enjoyed riding that bike in the green hills and valleys of Alabama. Maybe I enjoyed it more than she did. As I drove it less and less, I was reluctant to have her ride on it with me due to my concern about being aware enough and skilled enough to deal with the challenges of riding safely "two up."

There is a saying amongst motorcycle riders that says, "Either you have gone down, or you will be going down." One afternoon I was riding along a two-lane road in farming country and I came up behind a slow-moving pickup truck towing a work type trailer. The closer I got to him, he started slowing down. I figured he would certainly know I

Harley Davidson Softail Classic with Loa and Art

was behind him due to the sound of my loud exhaust pipes. As he continued to slow down, I thought that was my cue to pass him on the left. As I got next to the trailer wheel, he abruptly turned left toward an obscure opening in a field fence. I slammed on my brakes and started sliding sideways leaning to the right and as the back of the trailer passed me my front wheel barely missed the trailer. I whipped around behind and to the right as I miraculously regained control and passed the truck and trailer on the right. The driver, who never did anything to acknowledge me, calmly continued into the field through the fence opening. This is one of those times when you just say, "Thank you Lord and Thank you Lord Loa was not riding with me." I enjoyed many country rides with that motorcycle. When we moved back to Houston, I sold the motorcycle not wanting to ride it in traffic again like I had in California. Loa was a good sport in letting me have these rides, but I think she always breathed a sigh of relief when she heard the loud noise of my motorcycle with its *Screaming Eagle* exhaust pipes approaching the house. I never did "go down" other than tipping the motorcycle over while parking it after a long, all day, tiring ride.

    I would like to say one more interesting thing about motorcycles and that is the influence one has on one's offspring. Two weeks after I bought my motorcycle from Dave, our son John called us to say he had bought a Harley Davidson too after hearing I had one. I thought, well at least he has been driving for 20 years now and knows something about what drivers might do. After that John and I had some fun Alabama rides together. When we moved back to Houston, John still had his motorcycle and he also had a family with two young kids. He is a pastor and visits hospitals and had been exposed to tragic effects from life-changing motorcycle accidents. He sold his motorcycle after we talked about the need to remain in one piece for the benefit of his family.

    During our many years together, Loa and I have tried to do something special when it came to our wedding anniversaries. We sometimes failed to do so when work interfered. I remember some wonderful times like when we were in Germany on our 15th anniversary and we went to a hotel and restaurant for a very special dinner --- a dinner only to be experienced in Germany. The restaurant food was exquisite. We decided to spend that dinnertime talking over the worst and fondest memories of our marriage and we grew closer as a result.

    Another very special time was on our 50th anniversary. We were in Hawaii on the island of Maui and as usual when we are there, we had dinner reservations at our favorite restaurant "in all the world" --- Mama's Fish House. When we got there, I surprised her by checking into one of

50th Wedding Anniversary Dinner at Mama's Fish House

their cottages on the beach for the night. They only have four cottages on the beach as I recall. Our cottage opened up on Mama's Fish House's beautiful grounds and private beach. We had a wonderful dinner walking a few feet to the restaurant from our cottage via the beach. The next morning we walked out onto the beach with no one around. The restaurant is not open for breakfast. We sat on a bench looking out on the crystal-clear ocean waves peacefully breaking toward shore and realized this was a time we would never forget, and I know we never will. It does not get any better than that.

In 1997 Loa and I were vacationing in Fraser, Colorado near Winter Park. In the middle of the night Loa woke up with a severe headache and upset stomach. Her thinking and speech were adversely affected. I quickly drove her to the only medical facility in the area in the town of

View of the beach from our Mama's Fish house cottage

Grandby. The nurse there called a doctor and got him out of bed. When he arrived and looked at the situation, he immediately arranged for Loa to be taken by ambulance to a Denver hospital. I drove on ahead of the ambulance worried and constantly prayed asking God to keep her safe and cure her all the way to Denver, an 85-mile drive. When they assessed Loa's situation in the hospital emergency room the doctor came and told me she had bleeding in the brain and he thought she needed immediate surgery. Alone and praying without ceasing did not adequately describe my situation. The emergency room doctor then told me that an outstanding neurologist and brain surgeon was on his way and he would make the final decision on whether or not to proceed with surgery.

I was with Loa when the surgeon came to us after looking at the test results. Loa was unable to speak. He said he thought the bleeding had stopped and that it was in a very delicate spot in the brain in her speech center explaining why she could not respond to verbal questions. He recommended just waiting to see if the bleeding would start again before operating. Over the next four days with numerous tests no additional bleeding was observed. The doctor said he thought it best to return to Houston and seek the advice of a surgeon there. Kristin and John had dropped everything and flown to Denver to be with Loa and me. The doctor said, the only thing Loa might need is a speech therapist to which Kristin responded, "I am a speech therapist." When we got back to Houston, we saw a surgeon who said he would operate. We scheduled the operation but then I insisted we get a second opinion. The second doctor said he would not operate due to the risk of permanent loss of speech. By this time Kristin had been working with her mother and her speech was improving as the blood clot from the bleed dissipated. We decided not to have the operation and the only lasting impairment was her reading speed. Previously she had been a speed reader but after this episode, she read a little faster than me. Her speech was totally restored within several weeks, with just occasional difficulty with word-finding.

  Two more strokes in the same area of her brain have taken their toll on Loa – one in 2011 and one in 2018. Both caused her reading speed to be reduced and now she is a very slow reader. Her love of reading has not diminished, and she patiently reads more books per month than I do.

  God is Good, no doubt. Brain hemorrhaging can be fatal. We thank God often for sparing Loa. To talk to her, one does not notice any disability. She has not lost any physical capability so often experienced by stroke victims.

  This year, 2018, we celebrated 55 years of marriage. We keep saying to one another, where did all that time go? Yes, we have had our share of difficult times as all couples have. Each time we found a way through it and came out with a stronger, deeper relationship. Lately, we say things to each other like, "We need two brains to manage at this age." We complete each other's sentences and know what the other is thinking before they say the words.

In the family in which I grew up, we routinely shared this prayer at mealtime: "Father of all, all that we have is from you. Take our thanks and bless us, that we may do your will." This has been and still is a family prayer for us. Loa and I often thank God for our health and know we are called to help build His Kingdom on Earth with the resources He has given us.

*God has certainly blessed my life by giving me Loa who is the "Love of My Life."*

## Chapter 5

# Douglas

*"We never truly get over a loss [of a child], but we can move forward and evolve from it."*
--- Elizabeth Berrien

At 3 P.M., December 12, 1966, I was becoming and a little concerned. I had been sitting in the "father's waiting room" waiting to hear the good news about the birth of our first child. (You probably know in those days fathers didn't go into the delivery room.) Finally, a nurse came in and asked me to come into the hall. The doctor wanted to talk to me. He proceeded to tell me the impossible....our baby boy, although completely healthy in his mother's womb, had died less than 10 minutes after birth. In the next moment Loa, happy as could be, was rolled out of the delivery room in front of me with a big smile on her face.... She didn't know.... They had rushed the baby away when they realized something was wrong, but they had said nothing to her. I had to tell her what had happened, and she went from being the happiest I had ever seen her to the depths of despair.

There are times like this when most of us want to curl up and die. I surely did. I was alone as they took Loa to a recovery room under a nurse's care. My father, who was working at the time, dropped everything and came to the hospital to do what he could for Loa and me. The question came, "Did I want to see Douglas' body?" Dad went with me to see him. Of course, this was very hard to do. Douglas looked as natural and normal as any new born. He had a beautiful face and a healthy head of dark hair, a trademark of Stephenson babies. Dad and I cried together. I think the only other time I saw my father cry was when he left our family in New Jersey to travel to work in San Diego, California, knowing he would be away from us for two months and possibly longer. I could not have gone to see Douglas alone. Having my father with me meant the world to me. We all need that kind of support at times like this.

As my father had, Loa's mother, Agnes Sutorius, responded. She dropped everything and flew from Arizona to Los Angeles to be there for Loa. She arrived before we left the hospital. We went home to a house that was ready for Douglas. The nursery room was beautifully furnished and one of the hardest things was dismantling it. Agnes stayed with us and provided loving support until after Christmas.

Loa, more than anything, wanted to be a mother. After I had obtained a paying job following graduation and we managed to buy a working car (unlike my college car) and a piano (Loa's choice), we were more than ready to have a family. Somehow it took us a couple of years before Loa became pregnant with Douglas. Oh, how I had wished we had gone home from the hospital with Douglas. Leading up to his birth all the doctor's visits and tests gave us confidence he was a perfectly healthy baby. No issues whatsoever. Our first-born son died because the heart valve that pumps blood to the lungs was not developed properly. He was perfectly healthy while in the womb, as this valve was not called upon to operate prior to birth. When he was born this valve was required to open and close as the heart beat circulating blood to the lungs.

With today's technology doctors would have detected this faulty valve and been able to immediately operate inserting an artificial valve to give him a normal life. Two of my elderly friends just had heart valve replacement and they were home within a few days after their operation. The death of our first child caused Loa's and my "world" to go from "life is good with good things always coming to us and always will" to major devastation. Neither of us had experienced personal tragedy before. Growing up we both had attended church every Sunday, gone to college, gotten married, and I landed an engineering job right out of school at a time when jobs were scarce. Life was just like it was supposed to be. Now we were asking BIG TIME, "Why me, why us, God? I had given my life to God when I was 12 but did I fully grasp what that meant? This was a major wake up call.

As I look back on the time when we lost Douglas, that experience could have resulted in my moving in one of two directions – toward God or away from Him. I could have sought a deeper relationship with Him, or I could have rapidly come to a point where I had no use for God. Who was this God who would allow such a thing to happen to us? We had done no wrong, had we?

Our response, I believe, depended on our relationship with God at that time. If one has a view that God is a God who is angry, critical, judgmental, a police enforcer, a distant God, then you might not seek such a God. If one sees God as a warm, loving, patient, forgiving, understanding God who wants a close and personal relationship with us, then you are more likely to seek out such a God. In our case the latter was true. Our parents and those saints that had loved us enough to teach us about the love of Christ and his Father in Heaven brought us to this understanding of God.

My response to this loss was to revert to the way I dealt with life in Hawaii during those many lonely days when, at 15, I would go down to the cliffs below our house and contemplate life while watching magnificent waves crash into the cliffs. So, I went to the ocean cliffs of Palos

Verdes where we were living at the time and just sat for hours asking God to show me the way as I cried and wondered what life ahead would be.

A lot of weeping, soul searching, and asking God tough questions turned us back to the church we had never left but now we came with a new perspective. We turned to our local church to put our lives back together. As a result, we became very involved and focused on a life that was connected to Jesus and those who saw Him as their guiding light.

Loa and my relationships with Christian people and God grew rapidly. Soon after Douglas died, we moved into our new house in Cypress. We found a small, very friendly church and joined a small group in our church that met weekly to pray together and support one another. The pastor, Hal Edwards, hearing our story, quickly recruited me to lead the youth program with another guy in his 20's like me who cared deeply about young people. I joined Roger Klinkers who became one of my best friends and remains so today. We had the challenge of leading games and worship for sometimes as many as 100 youth each Sunday evening. Then we offered to have the kids come to our homes on alternating Wednesday nights at one another's house, where we sang, and wrestled with many theological questions they raised that frankly Roger and I had not thought through. We would respond where we could but had to say at times, "We will get back to you on that one. Come back next Wednesday." When you are faced with this kind of questioning there is no alternative other than to seek answers for yourself. If you want to deepen your faith, try working with kids that can ask the most difficult questions. I began to seek God through daily devotions, reading books and listening to sermons in a new way. My introverted ways had to be set aside as I had learned to do in college, and I thanked God for the ability to do so. This experience with youth was where I began to be a leader for the first time. As the years went by leadership opportunities emerged first in the church and then in my profession. My leadership training truly began in the church, not at work. When you are an introvert like me, it seems to me, it is much easier to stand up and speak before loving Christian friends than to do it in front of professional groups. Through this new experience in the church and leading our youth program I was inspired to begin a daily devotional time first thing every morning. From that time on I have had a goal of spending time with God and Jesus every morning reading Bible scriptures and wise Christian writings and spending time in prayer. During those quiet, searching times I have often felt the presence of, and guidance from God. It comes via thoughts entering my head to call someone or do something. Sometimes nothing really pops up and that is OK because this time of centering on God has been a very real blessing in so many ways. I miss this time when I don't take time to be with God in this disciplined way. Of course, the goal is to turn to God throughout the day. I remember, when we had drinking fountains at work in the hallway outside the restrooms, I would try to use drinking water from the fountain as a time to remember God and ask for his guidance.

    I found having a routine was important and I have tried to have that routine over these many years after Douglas died. The routine I am talking about comes in two forms.

    The first routine has been to have a place somewhere in the house where I could sit by myself and practice the second routine, my devotional time, that I will describe below. These days I enter a short hallway in our house that divides in two directions – one to the right, my office, and one to the left, my devotional chair in our den. My goal is to turn left every morning where I feel God is calling me, but it is tempting when things are pressing to turn to the right where daily, worldly tasks await. Now that I am retired my daily task more often than not is associated with tasks I do in support of a Christian outreach mission. In my working years most often a "right turn," so to speak was to deal with a work issue or home issue before heading to work.

The second routine was to follow a process for my devotional time that was the same every day. This has changed over the many years but always involved reading scripture, reflecting on that scripture, and praying. For the last 15 years I have been blessed to use a daily devotional book called *A Guide to Prayer for All Who Seek God* by Norman Shawchuck and Rueben P. Job. This devotional, published by Upper Room Books, presents a chapter for every week of the year. Each chapter begins with scripture followed by wonderful writings by "tall" Christians throughout history, people like Mother Teresa, Henri Nouwen, and Dietrich Bonhoeffer. After reading and contemplating these writings there is a scripture that is suggested for every day of that week. Next, the devotional suggests a consistent prayer pattern: thanksgiving, petition, intercession, praise and offering, followed by a time of silent reflection, listening to God, and journaling.

Would all of this have happened if Douglas had lived? Would I have started seeking God by adopting a habit of daily devotions and reading Christian books? Maybe through some other process. I certainly don't know but I think God can use tragedies or other experiences in our lives to give us options that could, if we choose, lead us to a decision in life that moves us toward Him. I believe in what Methodists call Prevenient Grace. This is the concept that God is constantly wooing us to accept His loving, forgiving Grace. He seeks to have a closer relationship with us. Out of our tragic and very sad loss of Douglas came a dramatic good in our lives and that good was to seek a deeper relationship with God and, in response, a deeper relationship with and love for all people.

Every parent gets the question, "How many children do you have?" For years we responded by saying, "Two." I guess the pain of losing Douglas was one we did not want to relive in the telling if we said, "Three." A few years ago, we talked about it and decided to no longer do that. We now say, "Three - two living and one in Heaven." We know Douglas is with Jesus and the living God in Heaven. We are looking forward to meeting him some day and giving him some hugs and kisses we never were able to give on this side of Heaven.

******

# Chapter 6

# Family Times

*"At the end of your life, you will never regret not having passed one more test, not winning one more verdict, or not closing one more deal. You will regret time not spent with husband, a friend, a child, a parent."*
--- Barbara Bush

When Douglas died, we were house-sitting for a colleague of mine for six months. Before that we had spent three months living in my parents' house as they took a combined business and personal trip around the world. Our task was to oversee my youngest brother, David, who was in seventh grade. Before that we lived in an apartment in Torrance for a year and before that a year in an apartment in the San Fernando Valley. Moving around was consistent with my life history but I was looking forward to living in one place for a long time. While house-sitting we started looking for a house we could afford and wound up buying a new house in Orange County in the city of Cypress. When we moved to Torrance, had I started taking flying lessons and obtained my private pilot license. Our last flight was over our house under construction looking down on where the money I was spending on flying would go. What an exciting time. And not long after we moved into our new house Loa became pregnant.

With great joy we welcomed our daughter, Kristin Lynn Stephenson, into our family. When we took her home from the hospital, we placed her in her crib, covered her up, and as she slept, Loa and I looked down at her in amazement and said to each other, "What do we do now?" A little more than two years later we joyfully welcomed our son, John Richard Stephenson, into our family. Of course, Loa read every child-raising book on the market and she became a model parent. Each of us had our own views on how to raise children based on how our parents had raised us. My father like his father was one who did not hesitate to spank us when we got out-of-line. My mother would often threaten us with, "Wait until your father gets home." As our children reached an age where they found ways to do things that upset us, Loa let me know that spanking, as a way of discipline, was not going to be practiced in our home. Although against my natural urges, I learned Loa's better way and saw how effective her methods were. Our children were fortunate to be raised by a very loving and persuasive mother. They wanted to please her and for the most part they pleased both of us most of the time with little discipline required.

When I was growing up between the ages of 5 and 9, we lived in a beautiful little town in New Jersey called Mt. Tabor. For vacations we often drove up to Bay Field, Ontario, Canada to my mother's childhood retreat home called Holley Lodge. It was named after my grandmother's maiden name. My memories of that home away from home were real treasures --- fishing, swimming and watching sunsets over Lake Huron. I wanted this kind of experience for our family so, soon after we figured out we could afford it, we bought an acre of beautifully forested land in the San Jacinto mountains east of Los Angeles near a town called Idyllwild. This property was just a two hour drive from home. Three years later after saving enough money, we hired a mountain contractor to build "Holley Lodge" on our land.

Holley Lodge 2 in Idyllwild, California

This became our weekend retreat get-a-way. We fondly referred to this second Holley Lodge as our "cabin." I decreed we would have no telephone, no TV and no radio. My family never forgave me for nixing the telephone. That was too much isolation. I wanted no calls from work, and I will admit that I was totally selfish on this point. Guilty as charged. We played games together, took hikes and sat in front of a roaring fire in the fireplace on cold fall and winter evenings.

As I think back on those times now many good family experiences come to mind. Without a retreat place like Holley Lodge we would have missed this very important time together.

What parents say and do with their children has a big effect on them, their life values and how they see life. When I was in second grade, living in Mt. Tabor, my older sister, Lynn, and I walked about a mile each way through the woods every school day to our elementary school. One autumn Saturday afternoon a friend and I decided to go to our school, what for I have no recollection. When we got there we decided to open one of the windows to our second-grade classroom and climb into the classroom. Not knowing why we had done this, just to do something, we stole some chalk from the black board, what for I have no idea. After we exited the classroom thinking we had committed the perfect crime, never to be found out, my friend said he had some matches and we should set some leaves on fire creating a small fire. I recall I hesitated when I thought of my father teaching me about the dangers of fires. I reluctantly went along with the idea and before long we had a little fire going next to the woods. We kept adding leaves to the fire. About this time some older kids some distance away on the playground saw what we were doing and started running in our direction yelling at us to stop. Frightened, we ran toward home leaving the fire behind. As I approached home, I heard the volunteer fire department fire alarm calling the firemen to action. At home I ran upstairs to my bedroom and closed the door hoping upon hope those older kids did not identify us.

That night the one and only small-town policeman came knocking on our front door and I knew then I was in big trouble. I could not hear the conversation downstairs but after a long while I heard the front door close and then my father came up stairs. He came into my room and calmly shared what the policeman had said about the fire. Of course, I was bracing myself for the worst licking of my life, but he surprised me. He told me how disappointed he was in me.

He said he thought I knew better than that, never expecting me to be so careless with a fire. He wondered aloud why I would do such a thing. Then he left the room. I was in shock realizing he was not going to give me a big spanking or restrict my playtime in some big way. My father miraculously never talked about that time again. The way he handled that situation had a major impact on me. I can honestly say thereafter I always wanted to please my parents and so did my best to avoid any possible bad behavior. Sure, I did things I should not have done after that but not conscientiously or deliberately. When I went to school the next Monday, I saw about an acre of woods that was charred and burned to the ground. Boy, was I regretful. Kids knew what I had done but avoided talking about it, thank goodness. I don't think anyone ever knew we had gone into our classroom and stolen chalk and neither of us was ready to tell anyone. I guess we all have our childhood secrets. Interestingly, my father continued to discipline his children by spanking, not realizing, I guess, the way he had treated me that day was so effective. I suppose my setting a forest fire was so far beyond belief he was moved to treat me differently that day. I think our Father in heaven is hurt by what we do or fail to do and is deeply saddened. I don't think He strikes us down in response to our bad behavior, even unbelievable bad, bad behavior. His response is to give us another chance.

  When Loa and I built Holley Lodge number two we had in mind not only spending family time there but also offering our mountain home to others. The first weekend we moved in we asked the members of our church adult support group to bring their families to our new mountain home for the weekend. Many slept on the floor due to a lack of available beds. We had a great weekend together. Over the 25 plus years we owned Holley Lodge many Christian youth and adult groups held retreats there. Families retreated there to have time in the mountains away from the hustle and bustle at home. Sharing this blessing God had given us was important, we believed. We asked people to write about their experience at the end of each visit in our "Holley Lodge Log." I always looked forward to reading what they wrote and was amazed and pleased with the good they shared that came from being there.

John was three and Kristin was five when we built Holley Lodge. They grew up spending many weekends in the mountains. One of the things I wanted to do was to have time with each of them just with me for a weekend once each year. This was particularly important to me since I spent so much time working away from home and I thought it would be good to concentrate on each of them for this time. I will never forget the first one-on-one Holley Lodge trips, first with Kristin and later with John. Kristin at the age of seven proudly became the "mother" fixing lunch and dinner for the two of us. She organized our entire weekend. She took on the role of running the household. We played games of her choosing and went to bed when she decided. As much as I could I tried to make it her weekend.

For his weekend with me John wanted to take hikes together on Saturday. But on Sunday morning, being four years old, he woke up in the morning looking for his mother. We had to cut that second retreat day short. We left for home right after breakfast. We surprised mom as she came out of the 11 A.M. church service that morning and John could not have been happier to see her. We took more of these trips over the years and I think they were special because of the conversations I was privileged to experience with both kids as we drove to and from the mountains and throughout the whole weekend together.

One of John's and my favorite things to do besides hiking in the mountains that surrounded our place was to go and sit on "our special rock" a short distance from our cabin. This special rock had a great view of the surrounding mountains and the town of Idyllwild in the valley below.

John was always a thinker. He would ask life-searching questions as we sat on that rock. From the time he was two years old he would ask thoughtful questions, especially when we took walks together. The rock became "our rock." Several years ago, while consulting with Northrop Grumman in Redondo Beach, California, I had a free weekend and so I drove up to see our cabin even though we had sold it years before. It was fun seeing the improvements the new owners had made but the best thing was walking out and sitting on John's and my rock. Of course, memories of sitting on that rock came rushing back. How great it felt to have that solid foundation to anchor such good memories of times with John.

When we moved to Seal Beach and John became a surfer, he and I took several one day or weekend surfing trips south along Southern California beaches. These were special times where we bonded doing things he and I both like to do. I believe as parents God calls us to find things our children are interested in and spend time with them pursuing their dreams. Is this not a good definition for friendship?

In 1978, I was offered a short-term five-month consulting opportunity working for a German company in Bachnang, Germany. Our family moved to a small German town 30 kilometers from Bachnang where no one except children spoke English. They were learning English in school. We rented the top floor of a house. The landlady and owner occupied the middle floor and the lower floor was rented to people who came and went. Kristin was nine and John was seven. We enjoyed getting to know the owner and her two girls and the kids bonded with her girls teaching each other their respective language while playing together. One daughter later came and lived with us in Seal Beach for a summer. We learned the age-old truth that to really know someone you have to live with and be with them.

Over the years our children were growing up, our family took many great vacations including rented pop-up tent trailer trips, rented motor home tours and flights to beautiful places in many states including Hawaii. No doubt these were very memorable times as a family. However, as we look back over our times together, all four of us have said we would pick Germany as the best and most significant family time. In Germany we ate dinner in old castles, drove

Ice cream hit the spot in front of the Notre Dame in Paris

to spectacular towns along famous rivers, visited the Black Forest, and visited medieval towns along the "Romantic Road." We travelled to Munich and took the nearby gondola up to the Zugspitze mountain peak and watched people skiing in the warmer summer sun. I was required to work 40 hours per week on average so I would work 50 hours/week for four weeks and then we could spend a week on tour around Europe. During these week-long vacations we travelled to Switzerland, Austria, Italy, Lichtenstein, The Netherlands, France, Spain and England. We traveled by train on the *Orient Express* to spend a week in Paris and, when Loa was desperate to speak English to someone other than the family, we flew to London for a week.

Life was different during this time in Germany. I usually rode the train to work but sometimes rode my bike. Our children played with German children and readily picked up their language. We would look to them to help us communicate with clerks in stores. I had planned to learn some German at the company where I worked, Telefunken,

Breakfast on the Italian Riviera

but the employees wanted to practice their English when communicating with me.

    For one-on-one time with Kristin and John, I took each on a train trip to a town up or down the track to have lunch there and buy them a gift. Walks in the beautiful German hills near our home were very enjoyable. Through all of these family experiences we drew closer as we met the challenges of living in a foreign place. Everywhere we went we learned something new. Just going to dinner at a local restaurant in our little town was quite an experience. The way the meals were served was different and the food was new to us. We enjoyed hearing a large men's choir in the restaurant bar singing beautifully as we ate our meal in the adjacent room, something we could never experience back home. We learned how kind and friendly people are all over Europe. Because the children were missing the first month of school they studied with teacher, Loa, during the summer. Being on a tight budget we had planned ahead and shipped camping gear along with my bike and other things to Germany. Having this camping gear, we camped across Europe when we were traveling by car. This too was a new experience as we discovered Europeans have different ways of camping. One late night we were in our tent sleeping and a bus pulled up and people poured out and began setting up their tents. The surprising thing was they proceeded to pitch their tents all around us as close as six inches from our tent!

    Kristin and John married perfect mates and have kids of their own. We are blessed to have five wonderful grandchildren. Kristin married Mark Parkinson and John married Amy Sorrels. They could not have made better choices and we are so proud of our two kids and their mates. Kristin and Mark have three boys, Paul, Blake, and Jack and John and Amy have Scott and Hannah. Paul has a son named Arthur. If you want to feel old become a great grandparent. As our grandkids were growing up, we all have joined

Family in Telluride, Colorado celebrating our 50th Wedding Anniversary (left to right): Blake, Scott, Mark, Amy, Hannah, John, Loa, Kristin, Paul, Jack, Art

together on Caribbean cruises, Disneyland visits, Hawaiian vacations and Colorado trips. We celebrated Loa and my 50th Wedding anniversary with our family a few weeks ahead of the actual date. We rented a seven-bedroom house with room to spare for everyone in beautiful Telluride, Colorado. This was a special time for us as Loa and I re-stated our marriage vows in front of the whole family presided over by our son and pastor John.

After we moved to Texas from California, we picked Colorado as our new mountain destination like so many other Texans. Loa and I bought a 1/22 share in a little three-bedroom mountain home in Fraser, Colorado. We managed to trade our time with other partners in the house to give us a one-week trip to Colorado in the winter and another in the summer. Now we were able to travel to Colorado with our adult children and grandchildren although we did not have room for everyone if they were to all come at the same time. Our view from our little Fraser house was a dirt road that ran by in front. One day I was complaining about our view with John's wife, Amy. She looked at me and said, "What are you going to do about it?" By this time, I was working at Northrop Grumman, having left NASA and I was making a lot more money in industry. Within three days we bought a quarter share in a beautiful three level, four-bedroom house with a great view overlooking the ski slopes of Winter Park resort. Quarter share translates to having one week a month at the house. Our family has enjoyed going to Winter Park ever since. We have room for all of Kristin's five and John's four but rarely has everyone been there together. It is our hope that this third "Holley Lodge" will be a place of happy retreat for our family for years to come.

    I still seek one-on-one time with each of our two children, their spouses and our grandkids. One way I do this is by going to a Houston Texans home football game with each one each year. I have two season tickets. We have good talking time on the way to and from the game but once the game begins, I am not sure I am very good company as I am

Holley Lodge 3 in Winter Park, Colorado

way too serious about the game. I need to work on being a better companion during the game. My excuse is it is so hard to talk with all of the noise. What other place is amenable to a "high 5" after the Texans score a touchdown! There are 10 home games each year, so this is just the right number of games to allow me to take each one to a game including little great grandson, Arthur, in the future.

Since retiring I have gotten more involved in Non-Profit Christians organizations. One such non-profit is Servants in Faith and Technology (SIFAT). I will speak more about this organization in a later chapter but for now I will say being associated with SIFAT has changed my life and deepened my faith in Christ. I mention it here because we have had the joy of going to Ecuador on SIFAT sponsored mission trips with members of our family. I have led our church SIFAT mission team to Ecuador the past five years and Loa has gone each time. A few years ago, Kristin went with us to Ecuador and this coming summer John, Amy, Scott and Hannah will be joining our team. Kristin is going with us too. To serve Jesus by serving "the least of these" in Ecuador is a real privilege and doing this with family members is extra special for Loa and me.

One thing I have tried to impress on our family is the importance of a strong Faith in God and a partnership with Christ. I know I fall far short on this, but I have tried to do this by the way I have lived my life. Talking about it is not so useful, I think. Loa and I are 75 and 76 now and we are hopeful we will experience the joy of seeing our grandkids marry spouses who have a high priority of seeking a strong relationship with God. Hopefully we will be able to see many great grandkids grow up in the Christian Faith.

******

## Chapter 7

# Hiking

*"Now I see the secret of making the best person. It is to grow in the open air and to eat and sleep with the earth."*
--- Walt Whitman

There is something about walking or hiking with someone to whom we have developed or wish to cultivate a close relationship. Sitting down to meals together one-on-one is another good way to do this but I say walking or hiking is better. Why? There are no distractions interrupting the conversation caused by servers or overhead TVs or other restaurant patrons. Show me people who walk or hike together and I will show you people who are good friends.

When I was 10 my father took me on a three-day backpacking hike in the San Jacinto Mountains 100 miles from San Diego. We hiked up to the mountain peak camping overnight on the way up. After reaching the summit (nearly 11,000 ft elevation), we hiked down the backside of the mountain and found a campsite there for our second night before heading back to the car on the third day. We covered 25 miles and endured a 5,000 ft altitude change up and back down. I discovered how hard backpacking can be. As we hiked along the trail hour after hour and sat in front of a fire warming ourselves each night, we talked about things that we would never, ever have talked about in any other setting. At home with my mother, older sister and younger two brothers any meaningful conversation was impossible it seemed. Doing things together like free diving off the coast of Point Loma, San Diego or hiking trails and camping is where my relationship was built with my father. At home the radio, TV, chores and homework interfered with having any good talks.

My father was an Eagle Scout, so our family vacations were camping trips, first in tents and then in a little travel trailer. One summer we took six weeks and camped our way from California to the East Coast, north to Buffalo, New York, then to Bay Field, Ontario to Holley Lodge, then back across the northern part of the country back home to San Diego. Many times we headed for the California Sierra Mountains. Yosemite was a favorite place for us. We went to Big Sur in Northern California a number of times. And then there was camping closer to San Diego in the local mountains and desert. We were always taking walks and hikes on these trips.

The summer I was twelve I was invited to join a great adventure. My father and two men he worked with at the Navy Research Laboratory in San Diego decided to climb Mt. Whitney, in the California's Sierra Nevada Mountains. This mountain is the highest peak in the lower 48 states. For several weeks before the day came to drive to Mt. Whitney my dad would get me up at 5 A.M. to "fast walk" for miles up and down the hills of Pt. Loma. Back then no one worked out like they do today. As time went on my dad added the requirement to carry a loaded 45 lbs. backpack during these morning walks. We were going to get prepared for this hike of all hikes.

When the big day came the four of us drove up U.S. Hwy 395 to the desert town of Lone Pine on the eastern side of Mt. Whitney. We looked up at that mountain and made some comment like, "Boy, aren't we glad we are driving up to 8,000 feet before we start our climb!" The shortest and most popular route to climb Mt. Whitney is an 11-mile trail from Whitney Portal, 13 miles west of the town of Lone Pine. They say ice axes and crampons are needed in the spring and early summer, but technical climbing equipment is not usually necessary between mid-July and early October even though it will snow up there in mid-summer. The elevation at the trailhead is 8,360 ft. The elevation at the summit is 14,505 ft. While I had climbed before with an elevation change of 5,000 ft. on Mt. San Jacinto, hiking to the nearly 15,000 ft. high Mt. Whitney peak was going to be a different experience. No one in our group had climbed that high before and we had no idea how we would handle 45 or 50 lbs. backpacks at high elevations. Our plan was to camp on the way up to the peak to acclimate to the elevation before moving higher. The first day out we would camp at Outpost Camp at an elevation of 10,400 ft. just 3.8 miles up from the parked cars. The second day was to be a real challenge. Day 2 was to be a 14-mile hike. Leaving early, we would hike to the pass, or what is called the Pacific Crest, at about 13,500 ft. elevation, leave our packs there and climb the last 2 ½ miles to the peak (1,000 ft. elevation climb) without the backpacks. After reaching the summit we were planning to hike back down to the pass, pick up our packs, and hike down the backside of the mountain into the inner Sierra Nevada Mountains to spend two days at several remote mountain lakes rarely visited in those days. We would camp at about 10,000 ft. elevation for those two days. We were excited about fishing for Golden Trout that exist only near timberline (roughly 10,000 to 11,000 ft.). On Day 5 we planned to hike back up over the 13,500 ft. pass and down to our waiting car. Day 5 would require a hike of 17 miles but what the heck, the last 10 miles were all downhill. All in all, our plan was to be gone five days hiking about 35 miles, excluding day hikes around our campsite on Days 3 and 4.

Day 1 was harder than I thought and I was happy to get to Outpost Camp and shed my pack. Backpacks in 1954 were not the modern backpacks by any means and did not put the bulk of the pack weight on one's hips, which is the case these days. Most if not all of the weight was carried on the shoulders. Some of us including me were using World War II Army backpacks.

We had a fifth member of our team, a Labrador dog who was full of energy and made us look pitifully slow. He would run way ahead and then turn around and run back to us as if to say, come on, you are moving too slowly. He explored above the trail and below the trail. I wanted to figure out how he could carry some of my load but did not suggest that to his owner.

That first night we were introduced to the most amazing moonless dark sky. The stars were from horizon to horizon and could not have been brighter or more beautiful.

Art on the Pacific Trail on the way to Mt Whitney Peak

Early the next morning with the sun barely over the eastern horizon, we mounted our packs and started up. The going was tough but we did pretty well given the extremely rocky trail conditions. We made it to the pass at about 2 P.M., dropped our packs and headed for the peak. The trail was about four feet wide and in places it dropped 2,000 ft. to the west and 3,000 ft. to the east. It felt like we were walking on the top of the world with most of the Sierra Mountain peaks now below us. About a half mile up the trail from the pass I started feeling sick to my stomach and a bit dizzy. As we went higher my condition got worse. Only a mile from the peak I was ready to stop but after a talk with my dad I kept going and was glad of it. We made it to the top and signed the register. Looking over the register for that summer we could find no one close to the age of 12. This was a proud moment for me. I made it!

Bob, Dad, Fred, and Art and our friendly companion at Mt. Whitney Summit

Heading back down to get our packs, I was amazed at how my sick feeling dissipated and went away as we descended. By the time we got to our packs I was feeling nearly normal again. It was getting on in time so we headed down the trail at a fast pace. Our dog started to slow down considerably and his running and roaming had disappeared. Upon inspection his feet pads were blistered and bleeding. His master had planned ahead bringing little leather booties --- one for each foot. The dog seemed to give a big sigh of relief when the booties were tied onto his four feet and we headed down the trail. For the rest of our days hiking that dog went nowhere without his booties and he considerably reduced his roaming tendencies.

As we descended the long trail my father had a great idea. We could save a lot of down and up climbing and shorten our hike to our lake destination if we just left the trail and followed the map contour line around the mountain. Contouring means keeping at the same elevation working our way along the mountain to our desired destination. So, we headed off the trail descending to the contour of the destination lake and following that elevation around to the lake. Not long after our decision to follow the contour to the lake, the sun set and we found ourselves feeling our way along the mountain with flashlights. The going got very tough with drop offs we had to work our way around. We finally made it to the lake late that night and agreed leaving the trail was a poor decision. Several days later as we were hiking on Day 5 back to the Whitney pass on the trail this time, we looked at where we had descended and could not believe we had done it. More than 100-foot drop offs seemed to be everywhere.

Throughout the hike together there developed a distinct culture within our group that was foreign to a pre-teen. Every time we needed wood for a fire, or the dishes needed to be washed, everyone eagerly volunteered to do the task. At times it seemed we were fighting in a friendly way to do the tasks. I, for the first time in my life, saw what great teamwork and genuine helpmates looked and felt like. Each time a task was identified all four of us eagerly volunteered to do it. Maybe this is what heaven is going to be like.

The fishing was unbelievable. It seemed that every cast resulted in a fish on the line. The fish were beautiful Golden Trout true to their name. They were not really big but plentiful and they took to the lures without hesitation. One afternoon Bob and Fred, my dad's friends, decided to hike about three miles up to a lake above us. My dad and I hung around camp and of course I was enjoying the fishing there. About dusk the two came back and Bob was holding a trout by his side with the tail hitting the ground. They eagerly told us the story of how the fish had hit the line and fought like the devil. When it was within reach, the fish got off the line in shallow water. Bob was not going to lose this fish, so he dove at the fish and managed to grab it and capture it getting completely soaked in the process. Back at camp they were eager to measure the fish. When we did it was 21 inches in length. That night the fish was our dinner and the four of us could not finish all the meat from that one fish.

After two great days at our lake campground having seen no one, we packed up and headed back toward the pass. We thought it was hard going up but I have to say the worst part was going down from the pass to the car. My feet had developed blisters and it seemed, based on the pain, there were blisters on blisters although that was not true. Going down the rocky trail was much harder than going up on Day 2. The dog and I, with our poor feet, were really glad to get back to the car.

As we drove down into Lone Pine late on Day 5, I knew exactly what I was going to have at the restaurant --- the best cheeseburger and milk shake I had ever eaten. I really did not want any more "dried, just add water and boil" type food.

The first summer after we were married, I talked Loa into going with me on a three day, 15-mile backpack hiking adventure out of Tuolumne Meadows in Yosemite National Park. I was convinced my new bride would love it. She had never been on such an adventure and she was not so sure. The first day out was an eight-mile, 2000 ft. climb up the mountain to our first campsite. It was a struggle for her all the way until she could see the campsite from about half a mile away. When she did see it, she took off and I could not keep up with her. When I did catch up to her she was lying on the ground on her back and said something like, "Never again." A year later I talked her into a two-day backpacking trip in Kings Canyon National Park with a co-worker and his wife. It was to be a wonderful hike getting to know new friends. I told her it was much easier than the difficult hike we had experienced in Yosemite. She reluctantly agreed to go. After we got back to our car and headed home, she was clear as a bell as she said, "Never again!" Then, when our two kids were around ages seven and ten, being a slow learner, I convinced Loa to take an easy family backpacking trip from the top of the Palm Springs Aerial Tram that runs up the side of San Jacinto Mountain from the desert near Palm Springs. I told her the trail would be pretty much level with very little elevation change. I was not quite correct on this although it was only about a three-mile, 800 ft. climb to where we camped. When we got to the campsite and set up, we had a simple dinner without bothering with a fire for cooking (my idea) and in the morning we had cold cereal and milk mixing powder in water for breakfast. The "Never again" statement came right after Loa asked, "Where is the hot coffee?" Three times and I was definitely out. That was the last backpacking trip for Loa after this very clear third strike.

  Through all of these hiking experiences Loa and I agreed on one thing: God has given us all a beautiful earth and seeing the mountains the way only hiking and camping can reveal is a wonderful testament to that truth.

Hiking above the Palms Springs Aerial Tramway. It is easy to see who likes hiking with a backpack.

Today, in our mid 70s, we love to go camping in our little 17-foot "Casita" trailer with all of the creature comforts. We typically spend two months out of every year travelling around our beautiful country this way. No more backpacking for Loa or me. We discovered fairly early in our marriage we have a lot in common in our views about what is important in life, about our values, about family and faith. We also discovered we have differences like she is not a fan of watching sports on TV, in person or in any form. She skied for a while to satisfy me but happily quit before too many ski trips. She does not like to play golf or any sport. What we found is consistent with a statement we discovered sometime early in our marriage and that is, "Love does not consist in gazing at each other, but in looking outward together in the same direction." (Antoine de Saint-Exupery) We found that

Loa with our Casita Trailer in Big Sur, California

identifying goals or projects we could strive for or do together brought us together. Examples of this were our children, Holley Lodge, family vacations, good causes, church activities to name a few. This kept us looking in the same direction. When we only "gazed at each other" this only served to identify our differences. I think it took about 40 years of marriage for us to see we just aren't going to change each other. After really buying into this we quit trying to make the other someone they are not and accepted the good in each other rather than struggling with our differences.

During John's growing up years he and I took a number of backpacking trips and day hikes in the San Bernardino and San Jacinto mountains not far from home. We also went on a number of backpacking trips in the Sierras. I wanted to do this because my time with my father was so special. I knew that if John and I did the same type of thing the result would be the same. We would have a life long bond from conversations we had on the trail and sitting in front of a warm fire at night. We could look at the bright moon and stars and fully connect with this great God we worshiped on Sundays in church. We could look over mountain valleys together and fish in streams knowing "whose we are." And all of that was exactly what happened. We shared things on these hikes we would never have shared back home. John found a love of nature just like I had with my father.

Art & John heading out on a Sierra Nevada Mountain Trail

There was a funny but dumb thing I did with John one time on one of our hikes. I said, looking at a topographical map, "Hey, we can save miles and eliminate elevation changes if we just contour around this mountain rather than follow the trail." Like the time on the backside of Mt. Whitney, this was a bad decision. We finally found our way but got lost for some time in the process. Amazingly, I had forgotten what should have been a lifelong lesson from the Whitney hiking trip --- Don't ditch the trail and try to contour around mountains you are not familiar with. There was another good reason not to leave the trails in both cases and that was personal safety. On Mt. Whitney, as we hiked down the back side of the mountain and as the sun set we got into some really tough terrain, scaling down steep places where we should have been on ropes to ensure if we fell it would not result in injury. The same thing happened on John and my off-trail trek. We were in places scaling rock-faced steep cliffs where we should have been on ropes for safety reasons.

On a Yosemite two-night backpacking trip late one summer, John and I headed into the mountains and before long, as we went up the trail, a light snowfall greeted us. The snowfall increased until I became a bit concerned about getting to our campsite before the trail became too tough to hike on or follow. We hurried along and were able to put up our tent in a driving snowstorm. The next morning we woke up to a beautiful clear day with our tent completely covered with about 8 inches of snow. We decided to cut our two-night trip short and headed back down the trail to our car.

When we walked up to my Toyota MR2 sports car, a little two-seat car, I was astounded to see the driver side window completely blown out with glass everywhere inside the car. John later told me I said, "I can't believe there are vandals in Yosemite!" Nothing seemed to be missing but we decided to go to the Ranger Station anyway and report this break-in. When I shared what had happened with the ranger the first thing he said was, "Did you have food in the trunk?" I said yes. When I was growing up we were instructed to lock food in the trunk so the bears would not get into it. He then said, "Was your back seat torn up?" When I told him no he said you were lucky. The ranger proceeded to tell me bears are smarter these days. They smell the food in your truck, break the glass, crawl into the car, shred and tear out the back seat to get to your food in the trunk. Then I recalled seeing the back seat of the car next to ours in the parking lot with a torn up back seat. I wondered at the time why the owner would drive a car in that condition. Then I thought about our

MR2 with the mid-engine between the inside of my car and the trunk. The bear had smelled the food in the trunk, knocked out the window and then could not smell the food inside our car and had walked away. The mid-engine had saved the day for us. Then the ranger said with a smile on his face, "If you think the car next to yours was in bad shape (with a destroyed back seat), let me tell you about another car/bear episode." He was laughing now. He said, "One time a bear got into a car the same way. He was a really big bear in a small car. He got into the glove compartment and found Ex-Lax and proceeded to eat it. Then he could not get out of the car and did everything he could to get out thrashing everything in sight. The Ex-Lax did its thing. When the owner got back to his car there was the bear inside his car. You could smell the car a mile away. I dared to ask the ranger what happened to that car? He laughed and said it was "totaled." They had just towed it to the dump.

When John was still in high school Loa's mother, who worked for the National Park Service in Loa's hometown, Safford, Arizona, sent us a notice for youth to join the Student Conservation Association (SCA) and work for a summer maintaining trails in different National Parks and National Forests. We thought it was a great opportunity and asked John if he were interested. He was and for two summers he worked for SCA. Between his high school junior and senior years, he worked on trails in the backcountry of Grand Teton National Park. The summer after graduating from high school before starting college he worked in the Sawtooth National Forest in Montana.

John took up serious rock climbing in college attending Colorado College in Colorado Springs. One summer when he was at home, he suggested the two of us do some rock climbing together. I had gone rock climbing once with John when he was in high school. That was our first time and we did some simple climbs under the supervision of a knowledgeable guide. So, I was really green when it came to rock climbing. John suggested we go to Idyllwild (where our cabin was located) and climb a world rated big rock towering over the town of Idyllwild. He picked out the easiest route to the top. Mind you he had never climbed Tahquitz rock before and now he wanted me to follow him up this very vertical rock. From its base to the top this rock

Tahquitz Rock in Idyllwild, California

rises about 750 feet. We started out just fine. John climbed ahead of me and did the difficult work securing pitons he clipped his climbing rope through as he went up. I removed them as I passed them. I secured him with a safety rope as he climbed and he did the same for me as I climbed. We climbed the whole day getting into some routes we had to back out from. The ground looked a long way down to me, but John pressed on. We finally made it to the top as the sun was setting. A beautiful view from there but not much time to enjoy it. The route down was around and down through the forest with no trail. That decent in the dark may have been the most dangerous part of our time climbing and hiking that day. I was struck by the level of trust I had given John as he led me through that experience. I was glad he knew what he was doing or at least I hoped he knew what he was doing. He later told me there were a couple of places going up the rock where he wished he had chosen a different way and he was not in his comfort zone while in those situations. I was glad he waited until later to tell me that.

In my 70th year I had a great idea! I would go with 15-year-old grandson Blake, Kristin and Mark's second of three boys, on a backpacking hike on the Appalachian Trail. Blake loved the outdoors and loved camping. Together we went to REI, an outdoor hiking gear and clothing store, and bought all of the latest camping gear. I had not backpacked

Art & Blake ready to begin our 3 Day adventure on the Appalachian Trail.

since going with John some 20 years earlier and everything had changed. We were now equipped with a new lightweight tent, new cooking stove, new sleeping bags, and new backpacks that place 90% of the weight on one's hips. Great stuff. This was going to be easy. I studied up on hiking the Appalachian Trail and found a nice, three-day, 23-mile hike in North Carolina. Loa, Kristin and Jack, Blake's younger brother, were staying in a nice "Bed and Breakfast" while Blake and I went on our adventure.

They dropped us off, wished us well, and assured us they would meet us three days later at a specific time 23 miles up the trail at a remote rendezvous point where the trail intersected with a dirt road. We were not sure cell service would be available so agreed not to depend on that. We would be out of communication for three days. Was this a good plan? What if they could not find the rendezvous spot or we were late getting there and we had no way to communicate? People used to deal with this all the time before cell phones. I did when I was younger.

Blake and I headed out with great anticipation of seeing the vast, near and far Smoky Mountains along the trail. The trail was through thick woods and we soon realized there were few vistas to take in. We saw trees and more trees mile after mile. While the backpacks were optimized for comfort, I found my older body was straining way more than I remembered with the horrible old backpack technology. We found that watering holes were sometimes hard to find or dried up and camping was only at very specific spots as there was no cleared level ground along the trail. The first day was enjoyable as we did see a couple vistas, and everything went according to plan. We saw very few people. As I had anticipated, we had great conversations just like the times my dad and I and John and I hiked. We talked about things we never would have found a way to talk about at home. On the afternoon of the second day rains came nonstop. Our feet were soaked in our new hiking boots that were not waterproof. Somehow my left foot went numb and has never been the same since that day. We found we had to hike much farther than we had planned to search for a place that was cleared and flat enough for a camp. This was a strain for me, not so much for Blake. We had walked eight miles the first day and 12 miles the second day. I had planned on a nice easy eight miles per day. At the end of the second day we only had three miles to go on Day 3. I will admit I was very happy to come to the end of our journey that third morning. We arrived early and relaxed until, right on time, Kristin, Loa and Jack came driving up in a cloud of dust to meet us. We were very glad to see them.

My goal is to find adventures with each of our grandkids. Paul, Kristin and Mark's oldest son, became very interested in the space program. Both Mark's dad and I were making a living in this field. When I discovered Space Camp in Huntsville, Alabama, soon after moving to work at the Marshall Space Flight Center, I encouraged Paul to attend Space Camp as soon as he was old enough to attend (age nine). Paul and I toured the U.S. Space and Rocket Center in Huntsville where Space Camp is held, and we toured Space Center Houston together only two miles from where he grew up. When he turned nine, he went to the week-long Space Camp in Huntsville and loved it. For the next eight years he attended Space Camp every year. After several years attending, Paul could have taught the courses at Space Camp.

Jack, Kristin and Mark's youngest son, found a great love for golf, playing on his high school golf team through high school. He rapidly passed my abilities on the golf course even though I had played golf since I was 12. Of course, I went with Jack's parents to as many high school golf tournaments as I could to watch him play as one of the top golfers on his team. When Jack was in his final high school semester last year, he and I went to witness the ultimate golf tournament, the Masters in Augusta, Georgia.

Left: Loa & Art with Paul at one of his USSRC Space Camp graduations
Right: Art and Jack at one of Jack's high school golf tournaments

    What a day that was for both Jack and me. We walked and talked our way through the day observing the best golfers in the world compete from sun up until sun down. Figuratively speaking, Jack thought he had died and gone to heaven and I enjoyed being there with him just like I enjoyed being with the other two boys during their special events.

    I treasure times spent with all of our five grandchildren. Loa and I took Scott and Hannah, John and Amy's two kids, to tour our nation's capital last year. We had a great five-day tour around Washington DC and President Washington's Mount Vernon home. I look forward to one-on-one time in addition to Texans football games with both Scott and Hannah down the road. As one gets older you realize you can't do things you did when you were younger. Sadly, backpacking is no longer something I feel I can do. I am sure there are many guys that still take

Art & Loa with Hannah and Scott in the U.S. Capital Building next to Statue of Stephen F. Austin of Texas

backpacking trips at my age but things now are different for me. I am spending a lot of time doing what I can for non-profit Christian organizations I am passionate about that are busy helping others have a more abundant life, as Jesus asked us to do. Now, in an attempt to deepen relationships with friends and family, I have to revert to sharing meals at home or in restaurants. As I said earlier, walking or hiking is a better way to build relationships but we all must adapt to what works in the time and place we find ourselves.

\*\*\*\*\*\*

## Chapter 8

# The Church, The Body of Christ

*"On the most elementary level, you do not have to go to church to be a Christian. You do not have to go home to be married either. But in both cases if you do not, you will have a very poor relationship."*
--- R. Kent Hughes

When Loa and I lost Douglas, as I said earlier, we turned to God and to our church. Our pastor and friends took us into their loving arms. They cried with us and did what they could to support us in our time of grief.

Our pastor, Hal Edwards, asked me to co-lead the church's youth program on Sunday evenings. At the same time, I was getting involved in leading the youth program, Loa and I joined a church-sponsored small group or what was called back then, a "Koinonia Group." This was a group of 12 or so adults who came together weekly to share their lives with one another, pray together, and support one another in the good times and the rough, not so good times. Truly, we experienced the Holy Spirit's presence often in this group. The people in our group became best of friends. Our lives centered on the church and these friends. We worshiped together, served others together, went on retreats together and regularly brought our families together for social activities. Our kids grew up together with our friends' children and they became best friends in many cases as well. With this kind of support, Loa and I had the kind of caring friends who stood by us as we worked through our grief from losing Douglas.

Small Koinonia Groups took off in our church and I began leading more than one group per week. I was asked to train others to lead these groups. Being an introvert, all of these up-front leadership roles in the church were the best training any emerging leader could have. I don't know if I could have led people at work if I had not been in leadership training at church.

Several years passed and our new pastor, Bob Diets, asked me to join him in leading a youth program at a United Christian Ashram week-long summer retreat held at a camp facility in the town of Idyllwild, in the San Jacinto Mountains about three miles from our cabin. We seemed to continually be drawn back to these beautiful mountains. The United Christian Ashram, still functioning today, is a family retreat so there is a children's program, a youth program and an adult program. The youth join the adults for worship but also have their own activities including support group gatherings and campfire time together each night. Leading the youth at Ashrams drew on my experience leading the Sunday and Wednesday night youth meetings back home. I was particularly inspired by the talks or sermons during adult/youth worship given by outstanding Christian leaders that first Ashram and many Ashrams thereafter. I looked forward to each worship service message. The founder of the United Christian Ashrams, E. Stanley Jones, was what was called the *Evangelist* at the first Ashram we attended. He was very clear about what this non-denominational Christian retreat was about. He simply said, "Jesus is Lord. Keep your eyes and thoughts on Jesus and all else comes behind that." Various denominations of the Christian movement can clash on style, sacraments, etc. but Brother Stanley focused on this one common truth in his preaching - *Jesus is Lord.* We had Methodists, Presbyterians, Lutherans, Baptists

Episcopalians, and you name it, and we all got along beautifully. This, I thought, was a glimpse of one week in Heaven.

The Mission of the United Christian Ashram is: *To inspire the transformation of all persons to be followers of Jesus Christ, and thereby discover, renew, and deepen relationships with God, ourselves, and others.*

Our family experienced the Christian Ashrams in varying ways. It had a lasting impact on all four of us. Not only was I profoundly moved by the experience of these week-long camps, I began to buy Christian authored books sold at the book table. These books changed my thinking and met a need I had to find answers to my questions as well as those our youth were asking about God and Jesus Christ and living a Christian life. I read books by E. Stanley Jones, who many say was one of the greatest $20^{th}$ Century Christian writers. I read books by Keith Miller, Bruce Larsen, Cecil Osborne, Carl Olsen, Elisabeth Kubler-Ross, Leo Buscaglia, Paul Tournier, Gordon Hunter, Thomas A. Harris, and many others. I could not get enough from reading these books and I read Christian authors non-stop for many years. Every time I went to a Christian conference, I was one of the first to buy books.

As time went on, I became the *Church-in-Action Hour* leader for the Christian Ashrams in Idyllwild and I also led other Ashram *Church-in-Action Hour* sessions held in other places in the state of California. Typically, I was leading as many as 150 people gathered in groups of four or five for an hour of sharing together. For an introvert this helped my self-confidence, but I must say, as I did all of my career leading people, every time I had to self-talk myself into believing I could do it, asking God for His support, before I stepped out in the moment to do it.

John and Kristin started going to Ashrams when they were very young and grew up attending them each summer. When John was 15 he committed his life to Christ at an

Ashram and felt the call to be a pastor. Years later, he would say, after resisting that call, he came back to it and entered the ministry in his 30s. He is now the senior pastor of a large United Methodist church in Richmond, Texas. John's wife, Amy, is the perfect preacher's wife, standing by him all the way.

My own involvement in Christian service in our church caused me to ask myself, when our children were yet young, "Am I in the right profession? Should I quit my job in the space business and become a full-time pastor?" I was really enjoying the Christian leadership roles I had been given and the studying and reading I was doing. Over a period of several years I wrestled with these questions. I would do what I always had done and that was to go off by myself and pray and ask for God's guidance in this regard. Then one day I was up in the same San Jacinto Mountains I had gone to since the age of 10, alone meditating in that beautiful setting and the answer came to me. I heard God saying, "You can be a Christian leader right where you work, where you pray, and where you play. You are to take my Word and be a Christian in your work place. You can be more effective for me in being a lay leader than in being a pastor." I shared this "answer" with my pastor at the time and he said, "Amen. Pastors are expected to care for people but your witness as a lay person can be so powerful." I have found his words to be true. Having had the privilege to participate in a number of *Walk to Emmaus* weekends where lay people present 10 of the 15 talks, I experienced how powerful a lay person's witness can be when they share themselves and their faith in God.

Our family has always been very active in church wherever we lived. For many years Loa was one of the church secretaries in our church in California and she has been a choir member as long as she could before her strokes slowed her reading speed to the point she could no longer participate. Our two children, Kristin and John grew up involved in the children's and youth church programs. Now please let a proud father brag on his kids a bit. For many years our daughter Kristin and her husband Mark have been leaders in the church where Loa and I attend. Kristin has been one of the lead singers in our Contemporary Service band since the initiation of that service 15 years ago. Interestingly John and Kristin were a part of the very first Contemporary Service band at our church --- Kristin singing and John playing the bass guitar. Later on John led that Contemporary Service as an associate pastor for several years before moving to lead his own church. Kristin has served as President of the United Methodist Women at our church. Kristin and Mark have led their Sunday school class for years. And Mark has chaired various church committees over the years. We are also very proud of John's wife Amy.

Kristin leading worship singing

She keeps the home functioning and supports John in his ministry leading his church. Needless to say, Loa and I are very proud of our family in many respects and it warms our hearts that they are leaders in the churches they attend.

I used to be known in my own right in churches we attended but now at our church I am the father of Kristin, the father of John or the father-in-law of Mark. Since John was an associate pastor at our church and moved on to lead other churches, I must get asked once a week, "How is John doing?"

I am convinced our children and their children will do far more than I have done to help build God's Kingdom here on earth. What better outcome could there be for a Christian father or mother? Truly, we have been blessed with a wonderful family.

John Leading Worship

From our first introduction to Koinonia Groups we found ourselves involved in a sharing and caring group in every church we attended since. When we attended Trinity United

Methodist Church in Huntsville, Alabama, we started a small group with four other couples and met every week until we left Huntsville after five years. Even though we left, this group has continued to meet together over the last 12 years, studying and praying together and offering support for each other. As I write this Loa and I are starting what is now called a *Life Together Group* at our church in Houston, Clear Lake United Methodist Church.

After my retirement my focus has been on helping where I can with Christian outreach organizations that our church supports. I will talk about these outreach organizations in Chapter 23.

******

Chapter 9

# TRW – Part 1

*"In the game of cards called life one plays the hand one is dealt to the best of one's ability."*
--- Anthony de Mello

When I quit my job at Litton Industries in 1964, five months after I started there, I called my father and asked him if he could help me get an interview at Space Technology Labs (STL) where I had worked as a summer intern the year before. Because I now had "experience," a requirement to be hired at STL, I hoped they would hire me. While no one ever told me if it were true or not, I believe my father's call or calls to a friend or friends at STL opened a door for me. He had worked there before Aerospace Corporation split off from STL and he had accepted a job with Aerospace Corporation. I received a call and invitation to interview from a first line manager in the Digital Test Equipment Department at STL. Not long after that I was hired. My first job was to design test equipment to test the "Abort Guidance System" on the Apollo Lunar Lander. This system was to be used if, in the process of descending to the moon, the astronauts decided to abort the landing and return to the Command Module in orbit around the moon. The only time the Abort Guidance System was used was on Apollo 13 when the spacecraft was behind the moon and the astronauts fired the "Lunar Descent Engine" to leave moon orbit and returned to earth.

How exciting to work on the Apollo program. I thanked God for this opportunity. I so much more liked working on the NASA Lunar Lander program than working on a combat jet fighter computer program at Litton. From this time on I knew, if I could choose, I would prefer to work on NASA programs. This bias did not keep me from working on many top secret and special access, classified programs over my years at TRW (formally STL) but when I had the opportunity, I chose to work on NASA programs.

Less than one year after I joined Space Technology Labs the parent company, TRW, decided to have all subsidiaries carry the name TRW (Thompson Ramo Wooldridge).

Grumman Aircraft Engineering Corporation was responsible for the Apollo Lunar Lander. I will never forget

Buzz Aldrin removing the passive seismometer from a compartment in the bay of the Apollo Lunar Lander.
--- Credit: NASA Photo

going to Grumman's plant located on Long Island, New York, to teach technicians how to use the test equipment we had designed. While there I had an opportunity to view the first Lunar Lander (called the Lunar Excursion Module back then) in the final stages of assembly in a large "clean room." A clean room is a room that has air flow systems that minimize dust in the air. Workers in the clean room wear white smocks, gloves and booties. It has the appearance of an operating room and is actually cleaner. It was amazing to think I was looking at the first human piloted vehicle that would land on the moon. Goose bumps formed on my arms and the back of my neck as I looked at white smocked men and women technicians working around the Lander through the plate glass viewing window.

This year, 2019, we will celebrate the 50-year anniversary of humans landing on the moon. All of us who were alive in 1969, can remember exactly where we were when the world watched Neil Armstrong take the first step onto the moon. I was 26 years old. Our daughter, Kristin, was only 7 months old. Loa and I were at a gathering of our church youth group for this occasion at the home of one of our youth. We all watched in awe, witnessing this historic event on a black and white TV. What an amazing thing to experience --- a most memorable moment in our life time. This was just 11 years after my family was in Hawaii where my father's team set up the ground tracking and command station to communicate with America's first spacecraft.

The work in the Digital Test Equipment Department was a lot of fun. In those days there were no computers we could buy. Spacecraft were full of custom designed hardware driven by custom designed software. The Digital Test Equipment Department had designed and built *digital cards* comprised of *gates* and *flip-flops*. We were tasked with designing special purpose test sets using these gates and flip-flop building blocks to perform test functions on the Abort Guidance System. We designed *counters*, *registers* and *decision logic* to accomplish the test functions we desired. We designed and built special test sets from the most fundamental building blocks found in today's computer, circuits that perform as *gates* or *flip-flops*. It is interesting to note that our cell phones today have more computing power, by far, than the entire Apollo spacecraft.

After two years on the Apollo Program, I was asked to go to another program and do, what I thought, was the very same kind of design work I had just finished. This sounded boring to me. Been there, done that. I decided it was time to try working in another engineering discipline and transferred to the Radio Frequency (RF) Laboratory. This Lab was responsible for the design of spacecraft receivers and transmitters used to communicate with ground stations on earth like the one my dad's team installed on the South Point of the big island of Hawaii. My co-workers in the Digital Test Equipment Department thought I was crazy and said so. They said, "No one goes over there from here. What we do is precise and predictable; what they do over there is approximate and a kind of voodoo." My first job in the RF Lab was to design a logarithmic amplifier. I won't put you to sleep explaining what a logarithmic amplifier is, but it was definitely challenging. The fun part was I was using design tools I had learned in school. The technician assigned to work with me knew far more than I did so he was not only my technician but also my secret advisor. Interestingly, he had served as my father's technician on the first satellite receivers STL produced. Small world.

Over the next few years I worked on classified satellite receiver design and manufacturing programs. After that period, I was promoted to the position of Section Head, TRW's title for a first level design organization leader. I had 25 people reporting to me when I first assumed this position. Soon after that the Apollo Program ended and funding for space programs was cut across the space industry. I was faced with having to lay off 10 people cutting my staff to 15.

This was a very hard time for me as everyone in my section was a talented, hardworking employee. I had just stepped into this new job and the first thing I had to do was the last thing I wanted to do. I asked God for wisdom and strength to make the right decisions. This was a time to show mercy to those we had to let go. There were far too many going away lunches where we did our best to honor these talented folks.

When I joined NASA to become the MSFC Center Director, media writers and reporters asked me what was the most significant accomplishment of my career? My answer was successful flight of the phase-lock receiver on the Pioneer 10 spacecraft my TRW section team designed. This spacecraft was the first spacecraft launched from earth to leave our Solar System. It was powered by four radioisotope thermoelectric generators since solar energy using solar arrays was not an option as the spacecraft moved away from the sun. While undergoing a final thermal vacuum test the spacecraft flight receiver lost lock which means it malfunctioned. Over the next two months we tried and tried to replicate this failure without success. It just kept working the way it was supposed to work. There is always a possibility that the test set had a momentary glitch and not the flight receiver. We just did not know. At that point I was called into a top program level meeting to address what we should do as the spacecraft launch date was fast approaching. The conclusion from that meeting was to launch the spacecraft with that mysterious receiver.

Launched in 1972, Pioneer 10 was still receiving commands from earth via that on-board receiver and returning signals to earth 30 years later in 2002. Soon after that, the spacecraft was commanded to shut down as power levels faded. I felt it was a special privilege to work on the first human created object to leave our Solar System.

Artist's impression of a Pioneer spacecraft on its way to interstellar space.
--- Credit: NASA

After being promoted to Department Manager of the Telecommunication Department, for the next six years my department of about 60 people designed and developed receivers for numerous TRW spacecraft and the Shuttle Orbiter S-Band Transponder receiver. When in orbit Shuttle astronauts communicated through this transponder. Interestingly, we had to achieve performance greater than theory at that time to avoid derailing trains in Europe that used S Band signals to switch train tracks. Obviously sending an S Band signal down toward earth at power levels needed to communicate was an issue for the trains.

Being a part of the development of both the Apollo and Shuttle programs were opportunities I cherished. Well after the Shuttle Transponder program was completed, I drove out to Edwards Air Force base on the California desert east of Los Angeles to witness the first piloted low altitude

Shuttle Orbiter drop test. It was carried aloft by a big Boeing 747 aircraft to about 30,000 ft elevation and then released to glide unpowered to a landing on Edwards' runway. The Orbiter always returned from space unpowered. What a thrill it was to be there with so many people who had worked on the program cheering as it rapidly descended, landed and rolled down the runway in front of us.

Enterprise takes flight for the first time in August 1977.
--- Credit: NASA Photo

Having led small groups in our church, I decided to offer a secular version of this experience to some people at TRW. Five men started meeting during lunch a couple times a month. We shared our life challenges and supported one another. We avoided work topics and focused on our personal lives. We all seemed to look forward to these sessions. After a year or so we hit on the idea of inviting our spouses to join our group once a month on a weekend night at one of our homes. Until I left the division we continued to meet at work and with our spouses outside of work. Everyone enjoyed getting to know the others. More than 35 years later we still exchange Christmas cards with one of those group members, Teresa Leone.

After six successful years as a department manager, I asked to be given an opportunity to be promoted to the position of Assistant Program Manager on one of the large division programs. Upper management had promised this promotion to me after five years in my department manager position but asked me to continue in my current job for a sixth year. When it became apparent they did not plan to honor this promise when the sixth year was nearly over, I started to interview with other companies. After having two job opportunities in hand I went back to upper management with an ultimatum – either honor the commitment they had made, or I was going to accept a position with another company. In hindsight this was the wrong thing to do. It was all my idea. I had not consulted God in prayer. I felt they had made a commitment they were not honoring. Throughout my career when I tried to shape the next move on my own, without asking God for his guidance, I found, without exception, it did not work out well. When opportunities came to me unexpectedly, "out of the blue," things worked out very well. I believe God blessed these unexpected opportunities. It seemed the opportunities I accepted after prayerful consideration led to situations where I was there to uniquely love and support the people I was responsible to lead.

Presented with my ultimatum, upper management responded by saying they did not want me to leave. It was a nice feeling to think they valued my contribution. They offered me the opportunity to go to Germany to consult with a German company for five months. As I shared earlier this turned out to be a wonderful family experience. They said when I returned they would honor their prior commitment.

After our experience in Germany when I returned to work, my manager put me in an office with nothing to do. It was heart breaking. After a week the message without saying it was --- leave. The person who replaced me to lead my former department blamed me for many issues that he perceived I had not handled well. Without going into them, I do admit my old organization was dealing with some very challenging situations, but I believe, if I had remained, we would have, as always in the past, worked our way through them.

It was very hard to be indirectly told I had failed. The new Vice President of my division, the same person whom I had worked for and who had promoted me to Department Manager, did me a favor and found a temporary job for me within the division so I had time to look for another job inside and outside the company.

Through a period of much prayer and patience I was eventually offered a job in another division of the company with a promotion. I had been in the Electronics Division that designed and built subsystems for spacecraft. My new position was titled Advanced Systems Manager in the Spacecraft Division. This division used subsystem components my prior division and other companies designed and manufactured for spacecraft. This was a great opportunity to expand my knowledge and experience.

When I was managing my department in the Electronics Division, we won several competitive contracts for other space companies responding to their requests for proposals. My new position was all about bringing in new work for TRW and, much to my liking, this work was associated with NASA. I was given responsibility to pursue all new TRW human space flight work within the Department of Defense (DoD). Since there was only one human space fight vehicle in the United States---Shuttle--- I was asked to win competitive DoD Shuttle payload contracts. Payload, in this case, can be explained by thinking of a commercial truck. A truck is paid to haul goods from one place to another. So, if the truck is hauling furniture, for example, the payload is the furniture because the truck company gets paid to deliver the furniture. Launch vehicle companies are paid to deliver satellites to earth orbit so the satellite is the payload. The Shuttle Orbiter was like a truck. It had a big compartment that can be opened in space to deploy a satellite the Orbiter had carried to orbit. The DoD was interested in conducting space instrument testing in the Orbiter bay so the instruments would be the payloads. My job, therefore, was to identify and organize a proposal effort to win DoD Shuttle Orbiter payload contracts. Frankly winning this type of work was considered unlikely. No one at TRW thought the DoD would issue a request for proposal for this type of contract.

I started making calls on Air Force Captains and Colonels down the street from TRW at Aerospace Corporation. After a lot of digging I found an Air Force Captain who was not getting much attention but he had the job of looking into flying Air Force instruments and experiments in the external bay of the Shuttle Orbiter. Over the next two years this effort mushroomed into a large competitive DoD procurement. I found myself in charge of TRW's Space Vehicle Division efforts to win this contract which would be the biggest unclassified program the company could win in that calendar year. Four other companies entered the race to compete. The program was called the "Sortie Support System" or like everything in aerospace, known by an acronym, SSS. The Air Force customer created a request for proposal calling for the design and construction of a structure and supporting electronics to accommodate instruments and experiments that would be mounted in the Shuttle Orbiter's open bay (doors open to space). I assembled a small team that grew to 50 people to plan our approach and write our proposal to the government. We visited U.S. and European companies to assess their ability to provide structural and electronic components for this new system. We conducted studies to optimize the system concept we would propose to the government and then selected the supplier companies we intended to buy components from should we win. The effort grew to 90 people in the final stages of the proposal. For most of the last six months before we turned in our proposal to the government most of my team worked six days and often seven days a week nearly every waking hour.

As we approached the time to submit our proposal TRW's senior management attention peaked. Deke Kendall, who had managed a major spacecraft program, replaced me as the program manager. This was to be expected. He was a great guy and I loved working for him. One day he came to me and said he had been asked to brief the program to the company President and CEO. He asked me to join him and give the major part of the briefing as I had the knowledge of the program, having led the effort for two years. The two of us went to the President's conference room and, as I was briefing the president, he began to ask very detailed questions that I was unable to answer. I had many people working the details as I was coordinating the overall effort. The culture at TRW at that time was based on the premise technical knowledge was the number one trait top-level managers needed to have. Organizational and people skills were way down the list of priorities at that time. Bottom line, I essentially failed the test, a test I did not know I was taking beforehand.

A week later Deke came into my office and said he really felt bad. He had been told to remove my name from the program management team we were to propose to the Air Force. I would not be given any role on this program I had brought to life for the company. As he left, I closed the door sat down at my desk and wept. I can't remember any time before this that I had wept over a work situation but now I did. I was asked to continue to lead parts of the proposal and I did until the proposal was sent to the Air Force customer.

Six months after we submitted our SSS proposal the government cancelled the procurement without having picked a winner.

Disappointments and failure at times are part of what happens in the business world. What is important is how we respond to those situations. Because of my faith in God and my belief He had a plan for me, I was able to move beyond SSS determined to take on the next challenge, still wanting to make a difference.

# Chapter 10

# Mid-Life Crisis
(A Time of Learning)

*"There is a tipping point in midlife, a midpoint in your journey, a day when you feel that middleness of having equal parts past and future, of the life that you've lived and the life that you will live, of what is done and what is still possible."* --- Michael Lipsey

I worked at TRW in Redondo Beach, California for 28 years before leaving to go to Oceaneering in Houston, Texas. About midway in my career at TRW I reached a point or condition in life some people call the *Mid-Life Crisis*. I was told this was a condition mainly attributed to men. Loa certainly did not share this experience. I think I was a good husband and father. I was an active participant in our church. I enjoyed my work and my family. I was running in 10Ks and participating in half Triathlons (swim, bike, run). After we moved to Seal Beach, I swam to the end of the city pier most weekday mornings year-round. Loa and I had our Koinonia Group. We had our mountain home. We had good friends. So, why this feeling of discontent? Why was I asking myself, "Is this all there is?" Maybe God was moving me in a new direction. I did not know.

A good friend, Dick Kichline, and I, on occasion, ran together and played tennis together. One of these times he told me about a course he had taken that he felt greatly benefited him. It was called *Successful Life Course*. I asked some questions and the more he talked, the more I became interested. The only U.S. Congressman elected from districts in two different states, Ed Foreman, taught this course. He was an impressive, dynamic and entertaining speaker. He teamed up with a vibrant woman to conduct a Friday night through Sunday weekend life changing course. I signed up. I came away from the course with tips, ideas, and techniques to lead a successful, positive life. At the course I was introduced to the "Act as if" principle I used without knowledge of this principle back when I entered the University of Redlands. I learned a wide range of good ideas at this course including, for example, a memorization technique and an improved time management technique using a simple visual listing method. I came home a more positive person with useful new techniques to apply in life. The course is no longer offered but before it was terminated at different times Loa, Kristin and John as well as our oldest grandson, Paul, attended the course. I think it had a positive impact on all of us. I will share how I used some of these new techniques at TRW later on in this book.

Attending the Successful Life Course opened me to try some other life altering courses. One of these was a course in Los Angeles conducted by Tony Robbins. Tony had a unique way of looking at life and was a real showman. Many of my friends and particularly my wife, thought I was nuts for going to this course. The first night, Friday night, in front of 200 attendees Tony helped a few people with phobias to overcome their fear of a particular thing or experience like snakes and driving. He helped them see they could change the way they thought about this situation and escape their phobia hang-up. We saw people transformed in real time. For example, a lady deathly afraid of snakes, after a half hour, let a snake be dangled around her neck. I don't think this was a set up but who really knows. Then into the evening he took us all outside to view a big bonfire telling us to take it all in without explaining why. His life learning methods were very specific with steps 1, 2, 3, etc. I found some of these methods useful and was glad to learn them. About 11 P.M. he continued talking about overcoming fear and to demonstrate that he proposed we all walk across a 2200-degrees Fahrenheit bed of coals resulting from the bonfire we had observed earlier. He said we needed to be in the proper, very positive *can-do* state of mind to avoid being burned before we made this eight-foot walk across the coals. I managed to walk that walk in bare feet without getting burned as essentially all of the 200 people in attendance did except those who opted out or were denied the opportunity by one of Tony's staff. A staff member could deny a person if that person was considered to not be in the right state of mind after being asked some questions. When I got home that Friday night and crawled into bed at 2 A.M. Loa said, "You stink, you smell like smoke" and I told her I was around a big bonfire. It was some time before I risked telling her what I had actually done. After we finished walking on the hot coals, Tony said this experience was not to impress anyone, but rather to convince us we are holding ourselves back in life because of our fear of failure.

 I learned some useful ideas and techniques from both Tony and Ed Foreman and still use them today. While the Tony Robbins course was considered a far-out proposition by some, when I announced that I was going to go to a Forum Seminar, over two consecutive weekends, Loa knew I had really gone off the deep end. The Forum came out of the Est Seminars created by Werner Erhard in 1971. These seminars were set up to "rip people's masks off so they could see who they really are" or at least who other people said they are. It was too extreme and for some people it was destructive rather than enlightening as intended. Est was replaced with the Forum. It was a kinder and gentler approach. Like the Est seminars, the Forum seminars were conducted over two weekends involving a total of 40 hours. There was a convener who presided over the sessions. About 120 people sat down on the floor in a large room and were witnesses to an interview process with someone volunteering to be the subject for that particular session. The session topic was dealing with a difficult life experience like divorce or a difficult parent. Participants put themselves in the shoes of the person being interviewed and learned from observing what that person experienced. The overall premise of the Forum was nothing is really what you see or experience because everything is tainted by your "rose colored glasses" formed by your unique life experiences. Each of us views the world through "glasses" formed by our culture, up-bringing, parent and peer influence, religion, ethnic origin, life experiences, etc. We don't realize everyone else comes from a different place than we do. This was a valuable realization for me, not learned by being told, but by experiencing, first hand, how others saw life in these Forum sessions.

  The summer between my freshman and sophomore college years (1961), before I met Loa, I worked as a lifeguard at a Los Angeles city swimming pool. All of the lifeguards were white. There was a black "towel boy" named Fred working in the men's dressing room. At lunch we played basketball and he joined us and outplayed all of us white guys. I took a special interest in him remembering my isolation while going to high school in Hawaii. We became friends. One day Fred invited me to go to an Ella Fitzgerald concert in downtown Los Angeles. When the day came to go, we heard Ella had cancelled her concert due to voice issues. Fred invited me to spend the evening with him anyway. We went to what later became the infamous Watts burg where he lived. For the next six hours I saw a lot of people but no white people. We went to his home where I saw wall-to-wall beds. No one was at home. When I asked where everyone was, he just said out on the town. We went to a walk-up window food place to eat and then to a nightclub. I would have felt insecure, but Fred was a big strong guy. That night my eyes were twice normal size as I took it all in. Why do I tell this story? I share it to say Fred and I could have lived on different planets. That is how different his life experience was from mine. The only way I could even begin to understand the way he experienced life was to walk in his shoes. Those six hours were just the beginning of *walking in his shoes*. I would have had to move in there and live in his neighborhood for a couple of years to begin to understand what he was dealing with in life. That was the lesson of the Forum. Four summers later the Watts Riots took place in Fred's neighborhood. I wish I had remained in contact with Fred as I would have liked to know, from his perspective, what happened before, during and after the Watts riots.

It was not long before I walked away from both Tony Robbins repeat course opportunities and Forum continuing seminars. Everyone was encouraged to attend supplemental seminars/workshops --- one after another. They both took on the characteristics of what I believed was kind of a cult. People got so excited about both experiences and wanted more so they kept showing up week after week, month after month encouraging others to do the same. Although I gained from attending, I felt these experiences were not of Christ and actually caused people to worship Tony and Forum leaders. They pulled people away from recognizing and worshiping God, creating another kind of religion. I wanted to focus on Christ and concluded Christian conferences were for me.

On the other hand, I learned useful insights from both the Tony Robbins and Forum experiences. I did not regret going to either experience. I took away what I found to be helpful and rejected those ideas that did not fit my life values based on Christ's teachings. Tony put some handles on dealing with life situations effectively. The Forum taught me the important point that what I see is not what others see. We all operate, the Forum stated, thinking if only everyone else acted out of the way I see the situation whatever it might be, the world would be better. In the fall of 2018, as I write this, our country, most people believe, is a very divided country. I think we are seeing high fences between people. People are not willing to compromise their position and wanting everyone to see things the way they do. This, in my opinion, divides rather than unites. We need to start with things we agree with and look for ways to respect our differences.

I know during my mid-life crisis time, it was hard on Loa. She worried about what I might become. Recently we were talking about this period in my life. She paid me a nice compliment. She said back then, in the end, she was confident I was well grounded in my Christian faith and would not go off the rails, something she feared at first. She also said she observed in me an ability to find what was good in experiences that included good and bad ideas and take the good ones and reject the bad ones. I appreciate the confidence she had in me and am glad I did not do more destructive things while I was facing my mid-life crisis.

We lived in Cypress and then Seal Beach, both about a one hour drive each way to TRW in Redondo Beach during rush hour. Therefore, I had a lot of time to myself in the car as I commuted to and from work. I decided rather than listen to music, talk shows or the news, I would listen to motivational speakers on cassette tapes. I listened to Ed Forman, Earl Nightingale and Dennis Waitley among others.

Earl Nightingale talked a lot about what he found in Napoleon Hill's book, *Think and Grow Rich*. Although I bought and read Napoleon's book, since I did not have a goal of growing rich, I lost interest in the book but the following statement by Napoleon profoundly hit me: "What the mind of man [or woman] can conceive and believe, it can achieve." I was struck by the idea that if I could conceive of a goal or outcome and come to fully believe in that goal or outcome, then I could achieve it. The key word here is *believe*. You really have to believe it is possible.

In the book of Mark, Jesus says, *"Have Faith in God. Truly I tell you, if you say to this mountain, 'Be taken up and thrown into the sea, and you do not doubt in your heart, but <u>believe</u> that what you say will come to pass, it will be done for you. So, I tell you, whatever you ask for in prayer, <u>believe</u> that you have received it, and it will be yours."* The apostle Paul says in Philippians 4:13, *"I can do all things through Christ, who strengthens me."* It seems to me we have to be careful about what we ask for because we might get it, but at what cost?

The following statement by Earle Nightingale also has had a profound impact on me: "You become what you think about." Therefore, if one thinks constantly about money then everything is about having more money and what one needs to do to get more money. If one is thinking only about golf, golfing becomes one's life priority. I once met a guy who talked about golf every time I saw him. I brought up the subject of church and asked him where do you go to church? (In Alabama the question is not "Do you go to church?" It is, "Where do you go to church?") He said he attended church for years and enjoyed it very much, but he no longer goes to church as he is committed to play golf every Sunday morning. The apostle Paul said in Galatians 6:7, *"What you sow, so shall you reap."* This is so true.

An example of how an awareness of these ideas has affected my life and the life of my family occurred one day when I was meditating on the beach for a six-hour period. My daily devotional guide encouraged the reader to take a block of time one day every year to assess one's life goals in relation to the teachings of Jesus. We were living in Cypress about six miles from the beach. As I sat on the beach looking at the homes that lined the beach, my mind wandered to thinking about how nice it would be to live right on the beach in one of these million-dollar homes. What could be better than having a view of the ocean and sunsets every day? The seminars I had attended included the importance of personal goal setting. Thinking of Napoleon's statement, "What the mind of man can conceive and believe, it can achieve," I said to myself, "I believe I could earn enough money to enable our family to move into one of these million-dollar homes." Then I thought, to achieve this goal I would have to focus on Nightingale's statement, "You are and will become what you think about." This million-dollar house goal would require I focus on and do the things necessary to achieve this goal. And that would be money --- making lots of money. I would have to figure out how to "climb the ladder" at work more aggressively and/or buy a business outside of work like a fast food franchise to increase our income. I could borrow on the equity in our house and buy a franchise. It would consume all of my time. What would that cost in terms of relationships with my family and friends? How would this impact my involvement in things that had been so important to me: my church, my small group, helping others, and my Christian walk? It was easy for me to answer that question after thinking about the alternatives and the impact of setting a goal to own a beach front home. The answer immediately came to me: The negative impact on my family and on my life would be too great. No, I chose to live in a place and have a standard of living that does not pull me away from these most important things or values in life. That day was a significant day for my family and me. As a result, we froze our standard of living and rejected adjusting our lifestyle to fit my income as it went up in the following years. Admittedly we had a comfortable standard of living at the time, so this was no great sacrifice. Since that day we have not aspired to acquire more material things in life, freeing us to give more to others in need. What a joy this lifestyle has been for us.

I think John Wesley, founder of Methodism, confirmed this lifestyle when he said, "Earn all you can, give all you can, and save all you can." As for earning all you can,

I think he was talking about doing this without taking advantage of others and having an objective of helping "the least of these" rather than surrounding yourself with more and better material possessions.

I am reminded of the words in Matthew 6:19 and 6:21: *"Do not store up for yourselves treasures on earth.... For where your treasure is, there will your heart be also."*

Denis Waitley, another motivational speaker I listened to as I drove to and from work, had a significant impact on our two children as we followed the advice he offered in the following recommendation: Go to Johnson O'Connor Research Foundation (JORF) and take their aptitude testing to find out what professions would work best for you. Denis spoke about being a parent and helping his children and grandchildren find a profession they not only could enjoy but also would feel very natural to them, increasing their satisfaction and success in that profession. The JORF solution he advocated aligned personal aptitude skills with professionals who are very successful and feel comfortable and pleased to be in their profession. These skills are basic skills a person is born with. They are not acquired skills. He pointed out that so many young people back into their professions by just following someone's advice. A friend could say, "Hey, you could get a job over here as they have an opening and the pay is good." I asked my dad what I should study in college and he suggested engineering. He said you did well in science and math in high school so go into engineering. In high school most of us took tests asking us what we liked to do, and the counselors used that information to suggest professions we might like to go into. Following these approaches for picking a profession often resulted in frustration and unhappiness in that profession after spending thousands of dollars to get the associated degree.

Denis Waitley gave high praise to the Johnson O'Connor Research Foundation (JORF). The testing they do combined with follow up counseling takes about one and a half days. Denis sent all seven of his kids to JORF. What he found was this process helped his kids know, before they went to college, what major fields would work best for them based on their inherent aptitudes. Consequently, they did not get through college, like so many do, and then find they did not like the profession they had trained to go into.

Our family found the JORF aptitude testing to be very helpful. Kristin and John took the testing while they were in high school. Today, Kristin, a speech therapist, and John, a Christian Pastor, could not be happier with the work they do, thanks to JORF. Loa and I took the testing when our kids were in high school too and the results confirmed what we had come to know from experience. Loa confirmed she never should have gone into teaching. She had taught for two years and quit after feeling uncomfortable with that profession. By the time I took it I was already in upper management and the tests confirmed my aptitudes were aligned with working with people more than doing technical engineering work.

I have recommended JORF to many people, especially to parents who are about to send their kids to college. I tell them they can spend thousands of dollars helping with tuition, room, board, and books and find after graduation their child has learned a profession they don't stay with because it is a big mismatch. If you want to learn more, Google "Johnson O'Connor Research Foundation." They have testing centers in most major U.S. cities.

In Chapter Nine I shared the first half of my experience working at TRW. It was very good experience but also included difficult times. As I look back on that time, I think God was with me. I also think he was with me during my mid-life crisis. The things I learned that I have shared in this chapter helped me as I faced new challenges at TRW and beyond.

## Chapter 11

## TRW – Part 2

*"When you are in the valley, keep your goal firmly in view and you will get the renewed energy to continue the climb."*
--- Denis Waitley

After we submitted our Sortie Support System proposal, I was asked to lead the division's efforts to win large space solar array contracts. When deployed on orbit these fold up arrays would be about 20 ft X 100 ft. During launch this array was to be stored in a box with the 100-foot dimension shrinking to one foot. There were two NASA customers, Johnson Space Flight Center (JSC) in Houston, Texas and Marshall Space Flight Center (MSFC) in Huntsville, Alabama. JSC planned to deploy their large solar array from the open bay of the Orbiter to provide power to extend the on-orbit stay time of the Orbiter. MSFC planned to deploy their large solar array on a space platform satellite being designed to accommodate experiments, sensors and other payloads. After two years working on solar array programs both were cancelled by the government. Once again, I worked on programs that went nowhere. I knew God had a plan for me. At times like these I recall historical figures like Abraham Lincoln who experienced tragedy after tragedy and failure after failure in life yet ultimately was in the right position to save our nation. Although my trials

Artist's rendition of MSFC's Power Platform that did not go beyond the design stage.
--- Credit: NASA Rendering

paled in comparison to his, maybe as Abraham was tempered, hardened and gained resiliency through these difficult times, God was using my disappointing experiences to do the same for me.

When the solar array programs fizzled, I was asked to head an Advanced X-Ray Astrophysics Facility space observatory design team working on an early study contract for MSFC. This program later became the Chandra X-Ray Observatory. TRW later competed for and won the contract to work with MSFC to design, manufacture and launch this observatory. Years later when I arrived at MSFC I found myself responsible for a MSFC/TRW team that was working through significant issues leading up to launch of this $1.5 B spacecraft.

After a few weeks trying to come up to speed on the Advanced X-Ray Astrophysics Facility program, I was re-assigned to lead an effort to win a spacecraft program overseen by MSFC called the Orbital Maneuvering Vehicle

(OMV). I was to spend three years leading the pursuit of this program and, after TRW won it, two years working on the program. The OMV was to do pretty much what its name implies. It was to move around in orbit servicing spacecraft, de-orbiting spacecraft that no longer functioned, and de-orbiting space debris. The first and most important OMV mission was to periodically re-boost or raise the Hubble Space Telescope orbit altitude as its orbit altitude decayed over time.

Right after I was given this new program to pursue, I visited the MSFC program office in Huntsville, Alabama. I went alone. I had no budget and no team at that point. I remember having a meeting with the OMV Chief Engineer who was responsible for all of the technical people on the program at MSFC. The first thing he said to me was, "Why are you here? We already have five well qualified contractors and three of them have funded studies underway." It appeared he was not interested in having another contractor waste his time. I told him TRW was definitely going to bid the next cycle of funded studies even though I had not talked to upper management about any win strategy and had not asked for funding to pursue the program. I did not lie about this as I really believed we would bid on the next phase of this contract and it was up to me to get the company positioned to have a shot at winning a contract in that next phase. I asked the Marshall OMV Chief Engineer to describe the most challenging issues on the program – the issues that kept him up at night. In addition to going over the program requirements in general and giving me a set of the program technical documents, he described two very big issues he was worried about.

I took those two major concerns back home and asked a group of the most creative people I knew across our division to come to a free lunch. I used a Successful Life Course technique to brainstorm and then poll the group on how best to address these issues. In a two-hour lunch meeting that group came up with what became the winning strategy that three years later landed a $300 M contract to build the OMV. Here are the issues the MSFC OMV Chief Engineer shared with me and the solutions we adopted in our lunch meeting:

1) The OMV was to be refueled in the Shuttle Orbiter bay with fuel brought to orbit by the Orbiter. A concern MSFC had was the danger of transferring this fuel from the Orbiter to the OMV in the Orbiter bay with humans a few feet away inside the Orbiter. This is a dangerous process if a leak occurs. All of the five other competing contractors were developing techniques to safely transfer fuel. Our team came up with a better idea. We proposed an approach that did not require any fuel transfer, rather we proposed the use of replaceable propulsion modules brought to orbit in the Orbiter. The modules would plug into the vehicle. They would have fuel tanks connected to the thrusters and engines used to maneuver the vehicle. We would use the Shuttle Orbiter robotic arm to remove the near empty propulsion modules from the vehicle and replace them with fully fueled modules. This would involve only disconnecting and reconnecting mechanical and electrical interfaces. There would be no fuel lines disconnected or reconnected and no fuel transfer from the Orbiter to the OMV. The Shuttle Orbiter would carry full propulsion modules to orbit and swap out the empty ones. This was a key discriminator that set us apart from our competitors.

2) There was a big concern about overstressing the Hubble Space Telescope during re-boost. Our team decided to propose a variable thrust engine that would very gently push the Hubble Space Telescope that was susceptible to even miniscule thrust levels.

This unique engine technology was only available from TRW, the company that had developed the variable thrust engine used by astronauts to maneuver the Lunar Lander during descent and landing on the moon. Neil Armstrong and Buzz Aldrin would not have completed their historic moon landing without having this variable thrust engine. As they descended close to the moon, they encountered large rocks where they intended to land. By varying the thrust of the engine, like a helicopter, they were able to maneuver the Lander to a clear area and land with only seconds of fuel remaining. We would adapt this unique engine technology to address the OMV very low and variable thrust level requirements.

The MSFC customer loved our two unique discriminators. TRW won one of the three preliminary design contracts that led to our competitive bid for the big prize, which was to win the competition to be the single contractor selected to design, develop, and manufacture the OMV. Winning this

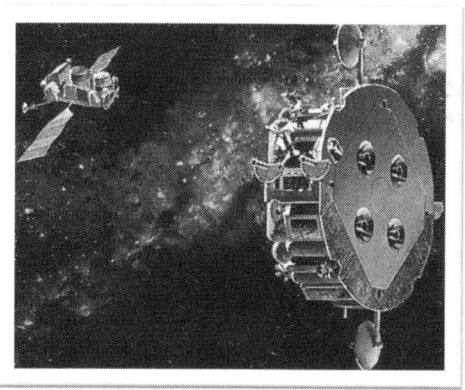

Artist's rendering of OMV maneuvering to dock and service a spacecraft.
--- Credit: TRW proposal to NASA/MSFC

Artist's rendering of OMV's Main Propulsion Module being replaced in the Orbiter bay using the remote manipulator arm.
--- Credit: TRW proposal to NASA/MSFC

competition was an uphill battle primarily because one of our competitors, Lockheed Martin, had already built a similar vehicle to re-boost the Hubble Space Telescope (HST) and it had already been launched into orbit and had undergone on-orbit testing. It had not actually docked to the HST. Our team was concerned that we could not overtake Lockheed Martin who had this major advantage.

To attack this doubt I hired Ed Foreman, from the Successful Life Course, to come to TRW and meet with our OMV team members and their spouses. We held a half day seminar and Ed effectively shared the positive and motivating techniques I had learned when I attended his Successful Life Course. Our team emerged from that seminar "fired up." We went on to do the extra mile things to produce an outstanding OMV proposal. Years later several of those attendees told me what a difference that seminar made for our winning team but also what a difference it had made in their family lives. Inviting the spouses, I was told was not acceptable company practice. I knew that but decided to do it anyway!

I led TRW's study and proposal team up to a couple of months before we submitted the final proposal. At that time, once again, the company replaced me as the Program Manager. This time I was included on the proposed management team as TRW's Chief Systems Engineer leading our system engineering team.

TRW senior management became more and more interested in this proposal effort as our final proposal submittal date approached. After we sent our proposal to MSFC we were required to orally brief our proposal to the government OMV contractor selection team, the Source Evaluation Board. When we went to MSFC in Alabama to present our proposal the President and CEO of TRW Inc. joined our team.

After pursuing this contract for three years we won the OMV design, development, and manufacturing $300 M contract! This was the first unclassified spacecraft TRW had competitively won in 10 years. Of course, this was an exciting time for me and was a time when I received more compliments from coworkers and upper management than any other time in my career.

As Chief Systems Engineer, I led a great team of system engineers on the OMV program for two years. The late decision to remove me as the OMV Program Manager was hurtful to me. Company management replaced me with a person who had not been a spacecraft program manager, the criteria I had been told would be used if I were to be replaced. This was one more disappointment for me, but I was willing to do whatever was needed to win the program. The new TRW OMV program manager and I got along well, and we became good friends.

After two years I was asked to leave the OMV program to become the first Director of Space Transportation and Servicing. Once again, I was tasked with winning new spacecraft programs. This time the first opportunity that surfaced was a contract Johnson Space Center intended to award. We won an early study contract and then a full design contract for a Satellite Servicing System. The ultimate contract was to design, develop and manufacture a kit to be placed on the front of the OMV that included a robot to service on-orbit satellites. After nearly two years we won the servicing kit contract. I was in Hawaii with my family on vacation when I got the call we had won the competition. We celebrated! Two days later I got a call informing me NASA had cancelled the OMV program. Several weeks later NASA officially informed us they would not be awarding a Satellite Servicing System (SSS) contract to TRW because the SSS was dependent on the OMV as its carrier vehicle. I had spent nine years pursuing these two programs and neither would be completed and launched to operate in earth orbit. The OMV was well along in development with all of the subsystem components entering the manufacturing phase when the program was cancelled.

At this point my small group went back to "square one" in pursuit of new contract opportunities. Based on our OMV expertise we went to Europe and sold a study contract to the European Space Agency. They were conducting early design studies on what later became the Automated Transfer Vehicle (ATV). ATVs performed supply missions to the International Space Station (ISS), transporting various payloads such as propellant, water, food, air, and experiments. These ATVs also re-boosted the station to a higher orbit while docked to the ISS. After offloading the payloads from an ATV it was stuffed with waste, undocked and re-entered the earth's atmosphere burning to destruction. We won the contract with ESA because the ATV, like the OMV, had to autonomously dock to the ISS and ESA was interested in understanding the OMV docking technology. Dan Goldin, the same person that later hired me to the position of MSFC Director, was the Sector Vice President at

Surrounded by the blackness of space, the European Space Agency's "Johannes Kepler" Automated Transfer Vehicle -2 (ATV-2) approaches the International Space Station (24 Feb. 2011)
--- Credit: NASA Photo

TRW for Space Vehicles and he was amazed we had won a contract from the European Space Agency (ESA). To our knowledge, ESA had never awarded a study contract to a U.S. company.

The American Institute of Aeronautics and Astronautics (AIAA) received an invitation from the Soviet Union in early 1991 to tour the Soviet Union Space infrastructure. The AIAA invited each of the major U.S. space companies to have one person from each company participate in this tour. I volunteered to be the TRW representative. The tour group was comprised of about 12 people, each from a different company. We flew to Moscow, toured Star City where the cosmonauts live and train for space flight and toured the unmanned spacecraft development center near Moscow. They gave us a tour of the

Soviet space station that was identical to the one in orbit. It was not a mockup and could have been launched into space. They also gave us a tour of their mission control center in Star City. Then they flew us aboard a soviet aircraft to Kazakhstan, a 2000-mile flight, to tour their launch facilities there. We went to the launch pad where Yuri Gagarin was launched and visited the nearby museum in honor of him. They said, "You should have been here yesterday; we had the 386th launch from off this launch pad." The representative from McDonnell Douglas, the company that builds the Delta family of launch vehicles, and the representative from Lockheed Martin, the company that builds the family of Atlas launch vehicles, were amazed at the robust and rapid launch capability of the Soviet Union. They quietly commented, "There is no way we can compete with these guys."

Soviet army generals hosted our entire tour. When we traveled by bus armed police escort vehicles with flashing red lights accompanied us. As our bus drove on one-lane roads in Kazakhstan, on-coming traffic drove off the road into the ditches as we drove by. I could tell when I returned to my hotel rooms during this tour my things had been searched. When I walked around Moscow's Red Square and looked into the stores on the square, I noticed the shelves were mostly bare. This was at a time leading up to the dissolution of the Soviet Union a year later and the economy was in serious trouble. It became apparent the Soviet Union was eager to sell the use of their space assets to U.S. companies. They did get the attention of many of the companies, but TRW was not one of them. Over the following years U.S. companies used Russian payload processing facilities to prepare U.S. satellites in Russia for launch on Russian launch vehicles.

Not long after I returned from the Soviet Union, I attended Dan Goldin's annual briefing to his sector senior managers. At the end of the briefing he presented his list of program priorities. The business I was managing was ninth out of 10 program business areas. His number one priority was a company effort to win competitive launch vehicle contracts and to compete with U.S. launch vehicle companies. TRW was not in the launch business but Dan decided we should be. TRW had teamed with Thiokol Propulsion to propose a launch vehicle based on a new Thiokol solid rocket motor. The Air Force planned to issue a request for proposals for multiple Medium Launch Vehicles (MLVs). The long running incumbent supplier for this Air Force launch vehicle requirement was McDonnell Douglas with their Delta 2 Launch Vehicle. Dan believed we could beat their price. After the briefing I went to my Vice President boss who reported to Dan Goldin and I told him I would like to work on one of Dan Goldin's top priority programs. He talked to Dan and the next thing I knew I was asked to lead the MLV proposal. The proposal team was working in Ontario, California, about 60 miles from our home. Loa and I moved to a company rented apartment in Ontario and dedicated the next six months of our lives to this proposal. Loa was hired to help with the proposal as an editor.

We had an uphill battle to replace the incumbent supplier, McDonnell Douglas. The Air Force depended on Aerospace Corporation to technically oversee all of their launch vehicle contracts. We set up and conducted over 130 hours of briefings on all aspects of our MLV design to Aerospace technical experts to give them confidence our new launch vehicle was technically viable. In the end the lead Aerospace manager for MLV told me we had thoroughly addressed all of the technical aspects of the TRW MLV vehicle design. This was a major accomplishment making our proposed launch vehicle design a viable contender.

Toward the end of our proposal effort Dan Goldin left TRW to become the NASA Administrator. He had been the champion for the effort to bid on the Air Force MLV contract. When he left, his replacement decided to cancel the effort. I received a call from the Vice President I reported to and was told to send everyone home. The company would not pursue the MLV program. I called a meeting and told the 80 people working on the proposal the company had cancelled our MLV proposal effort. Many of these people returned to their home organization and were given layoff notices. This was another very sad day for me. The team had worked so hard and long in support of this effort.

After this disappointment, I said to Loa, we are out of here, let's go skiing. Loa and I left town as soon as we could and drove to the Sierra Nevada Mountains where we skied for a week. We had a good time skiing, but I had a nagging feeling about what was next for me at TRW.

By this time people looked at me as one who had a good reputation as a proposal manager. Unfortunately managing proposals was a very demanding, high pressure, six or seven days a week job. Family life suffered and I was growing tired of going from one proposal effort to another.

When I returned to work the Vice President I reported to asked me to come to his office. He said I was to head up the technical proposal for a major program pursuit, the Tracking and Data Relay Satellite System (TDRSS). The customer was NASA's Goddard Space Flight Center in Greenbelt, Maryland. This system included not only multiple spacecraft but also the ground station. TRW's proposal team was already well underway and the final government request for proposal was not far off. It immediately hit me that this would require a massive technical learning effort on my part. I became very concerned about having enough time to come up to speed technically.

Two weeks later my concern had not abated. I was working under extreme pressure, mostly self-imposed. I was in meetings all day, every day, trying to understand what was required and TRW's design approach to address those requirements. Also, I was working to understand what TRW's design discriminators were, essential for winning any competition. As I drove home from work one day my left shoulder and left arm became numb and I was concerned I was having a heart attack. I decided to check myself into the same hospital in Long Beach where our two children had been born. Just outside the hospital emergency room door I called Loa and told her what I was about to do. She encouraged me to check in. The hospital acted like I was having a heart attack. They ran their standard battery of tests and found no evidence of a heart attack, but they kept me overnight. In the morning a doctor conducted a treadmill test and determined I had not had a heart attack. He concluded, after hearing about my work situation, my body was reacting to the stress I was experiencing at work.

  One week later I received an unexpected call at work "out of the blue" from Mike Gernhardt asking me if I would be interested in taking his job as Vice President of Oceaneering Space Systems in Houston. Adding to that discussion, it was apparent to me, after being in the hospital dealing with the physical impact of job stress and the continuing habit of management to assign me to stressful proposals, I had to do something different. Continuing with the status quo was not the answer. I really believe God presented an alternative path for me at Oceaneering. Going to Oceaneering, however, was a risky business move for me, but we boldly packed up our things and left California. For me that was after living there for 40 years, for Loa after living there for 30 years. We had to leave family, longtime friends, our beach home and Holley Lodge. It was not easy to do but by the time we headed for Texas (June 1992) we were excited to start a new life in the Lone Star State.

******

## Chapter 12

# Oceaneering

*"We are all faced with a series of great opportunities brilliantly disguised as impossible situations."*
--- Charles Swindoll

Not long after Mike Gerhardt's call in March 1992, I flew to Houston from Los Angeles to interview for the position of Vice President of Oceaneering Space Systems with John Huff, President and CEO of Oceaneering Inc. This company is a commercial offshore oil services company. Oceaneering owns and operates the world's largest fleet of deep dive, Remotely Operated Vehicles (ROVs) used to service deep-water offshore oil fields. It also provides divers for shallower water operations and sells products like subsea cables used for trans-ocean communications. Oceaneering has long been the contractor the U.S. Navy turns to for underwater search and recovery operations. Mike started out as a diver with the company and eventually became an Oceaneering Vice President. In 1988 Mike founded a new division of Oceaneering Inc., Oceaneering Space Systems, to offer products and services to NASA. He rightfully observed that NASA could benefit from Oceaneering's expertise in two ways: (1) astronaut training operations under water and (2) remote operation of International Space Station robotics. NASA trains astronauts to perform tasks in space outside the Shuttle Orbiter by putting them in space

Samantha Cristoforetti, an astronaut with the European Space Agency, performing an exercise in the Neutral Buoyancy Laboratory near JSC.
--- Credit: NASA Photo

suits in a swimming pool. They float like they would if they were in a spacesuit outside the Shuttle Orbiter or ISS performing installation or maintenance operations. Oceaneering divers had performed difficult underwater tasks in offshore oil fields for years much like NASA intended to perform on the ISS and already performed in the Orbiter bay. This experience could benefit NASA.

NASA's plans to remotely operate a robotic arm and a robot on the end of it on the International Space Station could benefit from Oceaneering's experience operating underwater ROVs. Mike reasoned that rather than NASA learning techniques the hard way, by trial and error, Oceaneering could bring its vast experience in the oil field diver and ROV operations to NASA. Indeed, NASA was interested in Oceaneering's offer to help. Mike assembled a talented engineering team and started contract work with NASA Johnson Space Center (JSC) prime contractors, Boeing, McDonnell Douglas and Lockheed Martin. I met Mike and his team when TRW was bidding on the Satellite Servicing System Contract to Johnson Space Center. They

Oceaneering tethered Remotely Operated Vehicle
--- Credit: Oceaneering Photo

joined our proposal team as a subcontractor offering their expertise in robotics.

After arriving in Houston, before my interview with John Huff, I went to the Oceaneering Space Systems offices and visited with Mike and his team and looked at their business potential. The 25 engineers, some former Oceaneering divers, and support staff that Mike had assembled were talented people. They were coming up with very creative astronaut tool design concepts that were well received by NASA. The NASA prime contractors were hiring Mike's team members to help with their space station operations work. My concern with the division was the lack of NASA approved/certified processes making contracting directly with NASA nearly impossible. NASA requires approved quality assurance processes, bonded stores for materials, procurement processes, accounting systems, etc.

When I had my interview with John Huff, I pointed out the very positive reception Mike's group was getting from NASA based on my calls to NASA and industry people

I knew who could comment on the reputation of Oceaneering Space Systems (OSS). I also told him my concerns about the lack of approved and certified processes. When John offered me the job, I told him I was interested but pointed out that to be a viable NASA contractor, Oceaneering's best approach would be to purchase a space company that already had the required certified processes and had existing contracts with NASA. I said I would come to Oceaneering if John would grant me permission to pursue the goal of acquiring such a company. John agreed adding one caveat and that was the purchase price for such a company would have to pass Oceaneering's return on investment criteria.

I was excited about the opportunity at Oceaneering, so much so that at my TRW going away luncheon, recognizing my 28 years with the company, I did something unusual. I briefed those in attendance like any other aerospace briefing with charts projected on a screen. This probably was the first and last time any going away luncheon included a briefing. I wanted my longtime friends to know what the company called Oceaneering's main line commercial business was and what the company was doing with the space division I would lead.

On the first day of employment in June 1992, I walked up to the steps leading in to Oceaneering Space Systems' warehouse office and shop in Webster, Texas and stopped in my tracks and seriously said to myself, "What are you doing here?" I had left a major aerospace company, approaching 50 years of age, where my future was secure to come to lead a group of 25 young people who weren't really in the NASA business yet. OSS was a "want to be" at best, dependent on the whims of some NASA's prime contractors. Little did I know the OSS business situation was about to go downhill.

I began my new job by visiting OSS NASA supporters and customers at companies that were subcontracting with OSS. Everyone gave me positive reviews. However, before long I was hearing about NASA altering the scope of the space station prime contractor "work packages." Within three months of my arrival the changing work content of the Johnson Space Center Space Station prime contractors' contracts (Boeing, McDonnell Douglas and Lockheed Martin) caused them to cut their workforce and the first people to be cut were their subcontractors. Suddenly members of my new team were being sent home. We appealed to NASA and they pushed back on the primes, in some cases, and the primes called some of our people back, but many OSS employees came home without jobs. Suddenly my new division was losing money.

One unexpected situation I found soon after I arrived was Oceaneering, being a commercial company, did not understand accounting and billing on "cost plus" contracts. "Cost plus" means you bill your actual costs plus you bill the profit margin agreed to by the government. I won't bother you with the details but what I discovered, with the help of an accounting consultant I hired to look at our books, was Oceaneering Space Systems was improperly billing customers. They were not doing this deliberately but just were doing it because of a lack of understanding about government contract accounting. We had to train the OSS accounting department in proper government accounting and billing processes. This reduced the amount of profit we were able to realize for the same number of billing hours.

Every month the company CEO required all of his division Vice Presidents to come to his office and talk one-on-one about their prior month financial performance. This was a commercial company on the New York Stock Exchange and the clear goal was to deliver profit. In Oceaneering's commercial business, profit was easily computed. It was simply income minus expenses. I had employees who were generating no income yet cost the company their pay plus their benefits. I was not ready to lay off people yet. My fourth month financial review was not a good meeting with John Huff. After a lot of leg work and pleading with NASA to help us keep work at the prime contractor companies, things got a little better and by the fifth and sixth months we were not losing money, but we weren't turning a profit either. Early in 1993, I told John I was working the acquisition angle pretty hard and had found a company that was a good match and hoped to help Oceaneering acquire it in the near future.

The most attractive company to acquire was ILC Space Systems located just outside the north gate of Johnson Space Center (JSC). It was a subsidiary of ILC Dover in the state of Delaware. (I don't know what ILC stands for. I looked the company up on Google and did not find an answer.) ILC Space Systems employed about 160 employees and it had NASA prime contracts. It also had subcontracts with NASA and DoD prime contractors to design, develop, and manufacture the following space hardware and sewn products:

- Tools, toolboxes and constraints used by astronauts when they performed tasks in space outside the Shuttle Orbiter or eventually outside the space station.
- Space Station galley components
- Refrigerators for space station experiments
- Sewn blankets used as engine heat shields on Atlas, Titan, and Delta launch vehicles
- Sewn products for various aircraft applications

In addition, ILC Space Systems operated MSFC's Neutral Buoyancy Simulator (NBS) in Huntsville, Alabama used to train astronauts planning to perform tasks external to the Shuttle Orbiter for activities such as repair of the Hubble

Space Telescope. When TRW was competing to win the OMV contract at MSFC, we took a full-size mockup of our OMV design and conducted tests in the NBS, demonstrating TRW's proposed propulsion module swapping was quite feasible.

When I arrived at Oceaneering, OSS had been competing with ILC Space Systems on designs for astronaut tools. NASA viewed merging the two teams positively. None of the other ILC products and services were competing with OSS. Therefore, a merger via an acquisition looked like a good match.

Three family members owned ILC Dover after the founder died --- the founder's son and two daughters. The son spoke for the two sisters. I contacted him and told him Oceaneering was interested in buying his division in Houston. He sounded like he might consider an offer. Through a lot of back and forth and two trips to Long Island, New York for talks in his office, we arrived at a point where we agreed we were too far apart on price and agreed to disagree. While this was going on the space station program survival became a political football due to cost overruns. Space Station Freedom was cancelled by the newly elected President Clinton and NASA was directed to come up with a smaller, less expensive space station design. Dan Goldin reached out to Russia with President Clinton's support and the new design was to incorporate Russian modules. In addition, Russia would have a control station as well as the U.S. An "up or down" vote in the U.S. House of Representatives was coming up in the spring of 1993 to decide whether or not to cancel NASA's Space Station program. The U.S. Senate supported this new space station program. The ILC owners became nervous as the House vote approached. Fearing the loss of ILC Systems' space station contracts they reopened the negotiations. Beyond the expertise of the employees, more than anything, Oceaneering was buying the future value of the space station contracts. John Huff asked me, "What is the likelihood of NASA's space station being cancelled?" I had been thinking a lot and praying about this situation and, after a short pause, I said, "John, no problem, it will pass." I was not just negotiating with ILC owners to buy their Houston division; I was also negotiating with John Huff. In addition to keeping his support in the face of the vote in Congress, John told me I had to commit to earning sufficient profits to pay back the ILC Space Systems purchase price within five years.

We settled with the ILC owners on a purchase price of $8M, less than half the price the owners had requested in the beginning. A month after we purchased ILC Space Systems the vote in the U.S. House of Representatives passed by one vote in May 1993. NASA's space station had survived!

Thinking we would be able to buy a company, I had read several books on conducting successful acquisitions and mergers and vowed to myself to follow the suggested best practices. Of course, before the purchase was agreed upon, we had spent a good deal of time talking to ILC customers to be sure they viewed this merger positively. They did. We had also conducted a thorough due diligence on the ILC Space Systems contracts and accounting records before we agreed to buy. We wanted no surprises.

Once the purchase was announced, the ILC employees were my number one concern. Hearing their division had been sold, the employees logically were worried about their future employment. Will they have a job? Will they be demoted if they are in a leadership role? The day we announced the merger, I held two All Hands meetings, one with OSS employees and one with ILC employees. To reduce or hopefully eliminate concerns about their employment, I told everyone they would know if they had a job with OSS or not within a week. Most were told within a day. I knew which employees I would not keep before making the announcement. As I recall only four ILC Space Systems employees were not hired.

One of those I would not hire was the President of ILC Space Systems. This was another negotiation I had with John Huff leading up to the announcement. Actually, this time it was a real debate. John kept the top management of companies he bought in the past. He reasoned that they knew their business better than his managers did although he had to put some of his managers into the organization to work through some issues. In particular he just liked to keep the top manager. He proposed the ILC President become my deputy. I had talked to NASA customers about this person and concluded this was not a good idea. I decided to tell John three things: (1) He had hired me to run his space division and thus I wanted his confidence to do that, (2) I felt the ILC President was not someone I would be comfortable having on my staff in any position, and (3) He needed to decide between my being the leader of this new division or the former President of ILS Space Systems. I would resign if he decided to keep him in any position. I had another reason for my position. I did not want any confusion about who was the go-to guy in the organization for managers reporting to the front office. I felt the deputy arrangement would have legacy ILC employees appealing to my new deputy while the legacy OSS employees would make their appeals to me. This would cause a split in the organization and not lead to the unity I was seeking for the new OSS team. John accepted my request to not hire the former president.

One of the challenges in merging two companies is to bring the two organizations and cultures together in a way that everyone would feel good about the resulting company organization and culture. I had done my best to understand how to address this challenge prior to the merger. First, I was able to form a new organization that kept all of the prior leaders from both entities in leadership roles excluding those

ILC employees we did not hire. As a new management team, we developed our mission statement and created the company values we would try our best to follow when making decisions. We shared the mission statement and values with all of our employees asking them for their feedback and then their acceptance. I shared with the management team that I intended to manage by our values and asked them to consider the values as guideposts when making business decisions. I asked them to hold me accountable to do what I said. When issues came up in staff meetings, I tried to ask how our values would influence decisions on those issues.

Some of the heritage OSS people came to the merger thinking that the ILC folks would be asked to operate the way OSS had operated which was an informal, unconventional approach. They had taken pride in doing things not according to the way aerospace companies did things. One day I ran into a situation where a heritage OSS person was upset at having to follow a particular formal process ILC had in place when we purchased ILC. I had to point out that we paid a lot of money for ILC formal processes approved by NASA and we would use them. We could consider improving a process, but we would have to get approval from NASA before we would follow a different process. A few OSS heritage people wanted the freedom they had at OSS and eventually some left the company.

As I mentioned earlier, during my last 10 years at TRW in the Space Vehicles Division, not a single thing I worked on found its way to space. After arriving at Oceaneering, I had the great satisfaction of again working on programs that put things we produced into orbit. Every Shuttle launch and many Delta, Titan and Atlas vehicle launches had Oceaneering Space Systems hardware or sew material heat shields on them. I was finally working on programs that developed and manufactured products that were launched into space. This filled a real void I had lived with at TRW for those 10 years. Thank you, Lord, for allowing me to be associated with programs that launched things into space again.

Since its launch in 1990 the Hubble Space Telescope had been orbiting the earth at roughly a 300 mile altitude but not producing clear images due to an improperly manufactured main telescope mirror. The main telescope distorted mirror problem was discovered after it was launched. After this discovery NASA had spent a number of years designing instruments to compensate for this misshaped mirror. The approach was to replace some of the instruments, like the Wide Field Camera, with redesigned instruments that would compensate for the mirror defects. Instrument replacement was to be accomplished by capturing the telescope with the Orbiter robotic arm and placing it in the open Shuttle Orbiter bay where astronauts would perform space walks to exchange the instruments.

The first Hubble Space Telescope (HST) servicing mission, in the fall of 1993, was very exciting for the new OSS organization. Within six months after completing the acquisition of ILC we eagerly awaited lift off of the Shuttle to make the needed HST repairs. ILC Space Systems had designed and manufactured a suite of tools for this mission and two toolboxes to house them that were mounted in the Orbiter bay. Heritage OSS engineers had designed and manufactured a couple of tools as well for this mission prior to the acquisition. I will not forget the long days and nights when the world watched the most critical components on HST being replaced by astronauts using our tools and crew restraints. I was excited because we had contributed to making a difference. Since this first repair mission HST has brought us images of amazing distant galaxies, nebulas, in some cases over 200,000 light years away. Over 10,000 galaxies have been observed in just one image. Mind boggling!

Astronauts, Musgrave and Hoffman replacing key
components to give HST clear vision
--- Credit: NASA Photos

Over the years Oceaneering Space Systems has been a key supplier of tools used on five HST servicing missions. Words cannot describe the images Hubble has given us of God's seemingly infinite universe.

Something new for me at Oceaneering Space Systems was getting involved in local area politics. I joined the Bay Area Houston Economic Partnership, an organization that engaged leaders from local companies, city and county governments and educational institutions to advocate for the benefit of our community. Our focus was to advocate for NASA Johnson Space Center programs in the U.S. Congress, which translated to jobs for our companies and community. In the process I learned about how to interface with our representatives in the House and Senate in

The star-forming region NGC 3603 contains one of the most impressive massive young star clusters in the Milky Way. Bathed in gas and dust the cluster formed in a huge rush of star formation thought to have occurred around a million years ago. The hot blue stars at the core are responsible for carving out a huge cavity in the gas seen to the right of the star cluster in NGC 3603's center.
--- Credit: NASA Photo

Washington D.C. Every year members of this organization went to Washington for three days of visits to our representative's offices and to receive briefings from people like the NASA Administrator, Dan Goldin. I also took some company issues with NASA to the local U.S. House congressman asking for his help in resolving them. He was able to get the NASA's Administrator's attention, opening the door for me to discuss those issues with Dan Goldin. In addition, I volunteered to be chairman of the local area United Way Campaign one year and this was a valuable learning experience for me as I interfaced with other Houston business leaders. These political and business

The Eagle Nebula's Pillars of Creation. This image shows the pillars as seen in visible light, capturing the multi-colored glow of gas clouds, wispy tendrils of dark cosmic dust, and the rust-colored elephants' trunks of the nebula's famous pillars.
--- Credit: NASA, ESA and the Hubble Heritage Team

experiences would be very useful to me in my future role as Director of Marshall Space Flight Center.

There are many OSS stories I could share but one in particular stands out. Some very smart heritage OSS members had started work on a liquid oxygen breathing backpack before I arrived at OSS. This technology involved storing oxygen in the very cold liquid state and converting it to gas to breath. John Young --- Gemini, Apollo, and Shuttle astronaut --- expressed interest in Oceaneering's liquid oxygen system and visited OSS several times to see the progress we were making. He was a very unassuming guy and was my number one astronaut hero. As I have said, I worked on the Apollo and Shuttle programs and to see him command the first ever, very risky Shuttle flight greatly impressed me. OSS employees would drop by my office and say, "Hey, John Young just left." I was inwardly upset they did not let me know he was there! Anyway, one time when I did see him on one of his visits, he told us he sure likes this design because it is not dependent on a pump that could easily have failed with the Apollo and Shuttle breathing systems. He said how embarrassing it would have been to die on the moon in front of the "blamed TV" when a "dumb pump" quit working.

My five years as Vice President of Oceaneering were a lot of fun. We had our challenges with contract performance in a few cases but in those cases, we were working on state-of-the-art, breakthrough technologies like the liquid oxygen breathing system. Customers knew we were working on difficult challenges and treated us like partners rather than a bad company. Our financial performance consistently met the annual goals John Huff set each year for OSS. While management teams in other divisions within Oceaneering did not get performance bonuses every year, I was proud of the OSS management team as they received bonuses every year during my five years. Before the end of our fifth year my commitment to John Huff to pay back the company's $8M investment to buy ILC Space Systems had been met.

During my time as VP of OSS I made significant efforts to acquire other companies. I went after three other companies and came very close to closing the deals on two of them. What I realize looking back on these three attempted acquisitions is how hard it is to complete acquisitions. Part of the challenge was getting past Oceaneering's very conservative financial criteria. Part of the challenge was dealing with company owners that wanted too much for their company.

At the end of my fifth year at Oceaneering John Huff asked me to oversee all of his government and entertainment businesses. He did not understand government contracting and did not want to know. The Oceaneering division in Maryland, called Oceaneering Technologies or Otech, employed 220 people conducting three types of businesses. One was support to the U.S. Navy providing deep water ROVs and divers. The second business was designing and manufacturing theme park entertainment rides. Oceaneering built the sharks for the Jaws ride at Universal Studios and dinosaurs for Disney World's Dinosaur ride. The third business was using robots to deal with radioactive waste at waste sites in Washington State.

    I had a particular interest in Otech because I knew they were the contractor the Navy and everyone else turned to when they needed to do underwater search and recovery of anything lost at sea. Otech had a fascinating history then and would in future years. When NASA's Shuttle Challenger exploded 90 seconds after leaving the launch pad, Otech recovered all of the pieces on the ocean floor off of Cape Canaveral. When TWA Flight 800 exploded after takeoff from JFK International Airport, the Navy was called upon to recover all of the debris across the ocean floor. Otech did this recovery. Otech was called upon for many other such operations. Years later after I left Oceaneering when Discovery Channel decided to recover Gus Grissom's Liberty Bell 7 Mercury Capsule in very deep water, Otech performed that recovery. And when the dive on the Titanic was performed Otech provided the Remotely Operated Vehicle.

    John asked me to manage the Otech division as well as the OSS division because Otech was losing money. My new title was President of Oceaneering Technologies. My first order of business was to investigate why Otech was not able to deliver a profit. It was puzzling because many of their contracts were "cost plus" contracts, which means they could bill the government what their actual cost was plus a fixed percentage for profit. What I discovered was Otech was bidding contracts proposing and committing to labor rates lower than actual labor costs in order to increase the probability of winning. Otech won contracts but then lost money performing on those contracts because they had committed to labor billing rates that were less than their actual costs. We simply had to change the way Otech bid on proposals to reflect actual labor costs. The other problem was they were bidding on fixed price contracts at costs they could not achieve. After we addressed the labor bid rates and the fixed price bidding practices, the financial performance greatly improved and my time overseeing Otech was a pleasure. The Otech people were dedicated to performing in an outstanding manner and they did just that.

One of the Oceaneering Space Systems heritage employees, Curt Newport, working in OSS's Washington DC office was passionate about doing something only Otech could do – find and recover Gus Grissom's Liberty Bell 7 Mercury Space Capsule. Gus was the second U.S. astronaut following Alan Sheppard to be launched into space. Gus's flight lasted only 15 minutes and successfully landed in the Atlantic Ocean. In rough seas the capsule door blew off unexpectedly and water started coming into the capsule. Fortunately, Gus was rescued by navy divers before his space suit filled with water. Before the rescue helicopter could lift the capsule out of the water it became too heavy to lift, from water rushing into it, and was cut loose and sank to the bottom of the ocean. This was the only Apollo capsule not recovered. Curt had been researching the location of the capsule reading up on the splash down location and interviewing everyone he could to locate the zone where it most likely could be found. He asked me to talk to John Huff, CEO of Oceaneering, about sending one of Oceaneering's search ships to the location zone he had identified hoping the ship's crew would find the capsule using their towed sonar instrument. John was not interested in doing this due to the high cost of an unfunded mission. My sense was that NASA would not pay Oceaneering for such a mission based on what

Sikorsky helicopter attempting but failing to recover the Liberty Bell 7 spacecraft
--- Credit: NASA Photo

they would consider an amateur's estimate of the location, so I did not bother to ask NASA for funding for this adventure. To his credit, Curt was persistent and kept track of the goings and comings of Oceaneering's search and recovery ships. On one mission he noticed they would pass very near the zone where he thought the capsule would be. He approached me again asking for the ship to be slightly diverted to search for the capsule. John Huff gave in to my request this time and approved the two-day delay it would take to troll over the area Curt had identified as the likely location of the capsule. At this point I felt I had to notify NASA. I called George Abbey, Director of Johnson Space Center, and informed him of this event. I also called the

NASA Administrator's office to let Administrator, Dan Goldin, whom I had worked for at TRW, know of our plans. We eagerly awaited the results of the search. They located an object that looked like the shape of the capsule, but it turned out to be a piece of an aircraft wing that matched the size and shape of the Liberty Bell 7 capsule. John Huff was not happy with this wasted effort. Curt left the company not long after that. The story, however, did not end there.

After I had moved on to Marshall Space Flight Center in Alabama, I heard the news that Discovery Channel, working with Curt Newport, had located and

Liberty Bell 7 recovered in 1999
--- Credit: NASA Photo

recovered the Liberty Bell 7 capsule. This capsule was raised on July 20, 1999, one day shy of 36 years after it sank to the bottom of the Atlantic Ocean. It was recovered from a depth of 15,000 feet, 3000 feet deeper than the Titanic. The newspaper I read reported Curt Newport, who had worked for Oceaneerng on the recovery of the NASA Space Shuttle Challenger, TWA flight 800, and the Titanic, commanded the expedition. I know Curt was happy and I would guess John Huff was happy as Discovery Channel hired Oceaneering to perform the Liberty Bell 7 capsule search and recovery.

    I was President of Oceaneering Technologies for less than one year when I got an unexpected call "out of the blue" from NASA asking me to consider the position of Director of Marshall Space Flight Center. My six years of experience with Oceaneering was a great training ground for me to be ready to take the reins of MSFC. As I said, I believed God was calling me to this new position. Why, I was not sure. The interview and subsequent hiring process took about five months. While I enjoyed my job at Oceaneering, I was honored to be considered and then hired for this important NASA position.

    As I think about it now, it is clear to me having positive relationships are at the root cause of things for me in my career. My relationship with Mike Gerhardt opened the door for me to come to Oceaneering. My relationship with John Huff opened the door for me to manage Otech. My relationship with Dan Goldin at TRW opened the door to be considered to lead Marshall Space Flight Center. And most important, my relationship with God and Jesus Christ, knowing I was not alone, gave this very introverted person the willingness to accept high profile, risky jobs I could never have imagined or believed I could or would accept. I thank God for giving me whatever courage I had to accept these jobs.

## Chapter 13

# MSFC Introduction

*"You cannot swim for new horizons until you have courage to lose sight of the shore."*
--- William Faulkner

Months after Dan Goldin offered the Director of Marshall Space Flight Center (MSFC) job to me, the day arrived when he introduced me to the people of Marshall. It took months to satisfy government hiring requirements. In addition, Dan wanted to introduce me in person at the Center so there was some waiting time for his schedule to accommodate him traveling to MSFC. In addition, U.S. Senators and Congressmen representing Alabama had to sign on to my being in this position. So, I waited patiently not knowing when the call would come for me to go to Huntsville, Alabama to be introduced.

With no forewarning, Dan called me one afternoon at 4 P.M. and told me he wanted Loa and me to be at MSFC at 8 A.M. the next morning. Dan asked me to check us into a hotel in Huntsville using Loa's maiden name. He did not want anyone to know he was going to introduce me as the new Center Director. He was concerned, he told me, that there were rumors that I was the one to assume this position. Loa and I rushed to make arrangements to get from Houston to Huntsville, Alabama by the next morning. We had to fly into Birmingham on the last flight and then drive

100 miles to Huntsville arriving at about midnight. Although this was stressful it was also exciting for me. My introverted self said, I am nervous, while my "Act as if" self said you can handle this.

The next morning when we arrived at Marshall's 4200 headquarters building lobby, we were greeted by Associate Administrator, Joe Rothenberg, the person who called me to see if I would be interested in becoming the MSFC Center Director. I would report to him in this new position. I took Joe aside and said, "This is all new to me. I would appreciate any advice you might offer." He responded by saying, "Be aware of the power you have in this job. People will listen to you and they will respond to what you say." He went on to exaggerate to make his point. He said, "If you say, I want a pink Volkswagen on the front steps of this building on Monday morning, it will be there." I appreciated this advice and over the next weeks and months I found this to be true and had to be careful with what I said.

When Dan landed at the nearby Redstone Arsenal airfield and came over to the lobby of building 4200, he took me aside and said, "I am going to talk about something" (I don't remember what that was) and then he said something he had not mentioned before. He said, "I will introduce you and then you share your vision for Marshall." Fortunately, I was prepared, having expected at some point before long, to be given the opportunity to share my vision.

Rumors were flying around, I was told, that if I were the one who came to Marshall, I was coming in to throw out the top management team and bring in my own leadership team. Certainly, I was not coming in to dismiss the leadership at Marshall. Most people at the Center believed the "Acting Director," Carolyn Griner, would be named the Center Director. Following my introduction, I was pleased to hear Dan say Carolyn had agreed to stay on as Deputy Center Director. She was a big help to me in understanding

Center processes and challenges over the next one and a half years before she retired from NASA.

My speech to the Marshall employees that day went something like, "I am honored to be here. I did not take this job because I wanted to make a lot of money. (They knew I had just left a job in industry where executives made much more money.) I did not take this job to be closer to my family, as they all live in Houston. I took this job for the same reason you come to work every day, because I want to make a difference." My sense was MSFC employees had lost hope to some extent and I wanted to help them have hope for the future. I went on to say I think the best days for Marshall are not behind us but are ahead of us and I talked about why I believed that to be true. Many employees thought times would never be as good as they were during Apollo days with Wernher von Braun as MSFC's first Center Director. My goal was to offer a message of hope. I introduced Loa and thanked her for her support, especially since she was leaving her two grandsons and family behind in Houston. I ended by saying I am very much looking forward to coming to Marshall and learning more about the great things you all are doing.

When MSFC had an All Hands meeting, the auditorium would only accommodate about 250 people, so the meeting was broadcast on Center-wide TV. This way the 2,700 civil servant and roughly 3,500 on-site contractors who supported Marshall could observe the meeting in the auditorium.

After the All Hands introduction and after seeing Dan Goldin and Joe Rothenberg off at the Redstone Airport, I went back to my new office and asked to see two people: The Chief Legal Counsel and the Director of the Customer and Employee Relations Directorate (CAER). Working for the government for the first time, I wanted to be briefed on legal issues I needed to be aware of to avoid saying or doing the wrong things. The head of the legal office, Bill Hicks, briefed me and after offering helpful advice he asked me if I had ever been sued on the job. When I said no, he said, "Well, you will be sometime in this job." Looking back on my five years at NASA now, I realize how fortunate I was not to have been named in any lawsuit. I wanted to see the Director of CAER, Tereasa Washington, to ask her to be sure and give me any advice she could offer now or in the future to keep me out of trouble with our contractors and NASA employees. I also wanted to thank her for helping me get through the government paper work, as she had been the person on the other end of the telephone, helping me through the required paperwork process during the months leading up to my coming to NASA. Following these meetings, I met with the press and they were eager to know everything about me, my family, and my years in aerospace. I was at MSFC for just that one day and then Loa and I returned to Houston to make arrangements to move to Huntsville in two weeks. Before we left Huntsville, we looked at houses over a two-day period and bought one. Our life was a whirlwind all of a sudden.

Less than two weeks later we said our good byes to our Houston family, friends and the people of Oceaneering and then, late one afternoon, we began to drive our two cars to Huntsville, Loa in one car and me in the other. We thought we would drive for a while and get a hotel room for the night. We did not realize there was a hurricane threatening New Orleans and lots of people were evacuating. We repeatedly stopped at hotels along the way asking for a room and each time we were told they had no rooms available. It became apparent we were not going to be able to find a room, so we kept driving. At interstate rest stops there were no parking places. Cars were lined up on the roads going in and out. We kept driving through the night with little to no sleep. When we crossed over the Tennessee River going into Huntsville, the sun was coming over the horizon and my spirits were lifted as I listened to the Hallelujah Chorus on the radio. I definitely had the feeling God had a plan for us in this new place!

I arrived for my first day of work at Marshall Space Flight Center bright and early on September 21, 1998, and held my first expanded staff meeting. It was quite an experience for me. People looked at me as if I was either "all knowing" or as if they wondered, "What are you going to do with or to us." The first thing I said was, "I have not come here to bring in my own team. I have great respect for the people and management team of MSFC whom I have worked with for years. I look forward to getting to know each of you, visiting your respective organizations and learning about what each organization does in support of Marshall's mission. I am not saying there will be no organizational changes. I will listen and learn and then make decisions about how we are organized." I did not share with them that Dan Goldin had told me to bring in my own team and to re-organize the Center. In the end, I only hired one senior person whom I brought in as "my team" and that was Bob Sackheim, a nationally known propulsion engineer who had worked with at TRW. Sure, I hired a few others to come to Marshall as jobs opened up, but they were not people I knew before arriving at MSFC and all were already working for the government before coming to Marshall.

My first All Hands meeting was a great opportunity to share more about my positive view of Marshall Space Flight Center's future. I was combating hallway conversations that Dan Goldin, having repeatedly criticized Marshall in the year before I came, wanted me to close down the Center. This was just not true, and I set out to convince folks at Marshall that we had an important role in NASA's missions. I said I liked Marshall's Mission statement, *We Bring People to Space and Bring Space to People.* I talked about the fact that we are the world leaders in providing human access to space and the use of space for microgravity research and development to benefit humanity. I talked about the importance of the Center's X-Ray Observatory, due to be launched in the coming year. I talked about our world class Space Optics Manufacturing and Test Technology. I talked about our advanced space transportation role funding NASA's X-plane development programs. And I talked about MSFC's major role on the International Space Station program, performing module testing in our world-class test facilities. My closing remark was, "We have the missions. We have the goals. We don't have enough money, but we will get it. There is nothing Dan Goldin wants to do more than go to Mars……. How do you get to Mars? We get to Mars riding on Marshall Launch Vehicles. I quoted Earle Nightengale, 'Success is defined as the progressive realization of a worthy goal.' I said we have worthy goals and we are progressing."

Less than two weeks after I arrived at Marshall, NASA celebrated its 40th anniversary. What that meant for me was I was called upon to MC a large Marshall celebration including astronauts and the surviving Wernher von Braun team members as well as to give a speech. I was handed a speech that had been written for me to read. I have to admit I was in the slow reading group all my elementary school years. When I read it, I mispronounced the town of Tuscumbia. When everyone laughed, I quickly said, "I am from Texas and California and I am just learning to speak 'Alabamian.'" That brought more crowd laughter.

I was amazed as I discovered what the job of a Center Director entails. Of course, there were technical, business and personnel reviews and decisions to be made from managing the civil servant budget allocation to managing the $2.3B Marshall annual budget that paid for our on-site support contractors and contractors around the U.S. working on MSFC programs. I learned about the many meetings that took place at NASA headquarters that I was asked to attend, and I learned more about rivalries between NASA Centers.

I also learned there was a convenient barbershop on-site at the Center where I gladly got a haircut and did get my hair cut there for the rest of my time at Marshall. I never had to wait long for a haircut and another benefit was the barber filled me in on hallway rumors. What better place to hear what the folks at Marshall were really saying? Things were really quite different for me at NASA compared to Oceaneering and TRW.

Speaking of things being different one morning just after I had arrived at Marshall, I was rushing around in my office because I had a flight to catch, my first flight after becoming Center Director. My administrative assistant, Beth Partain, who was a tremendous help in familiarizing me with the Center and the way things worked, calmly came into my office and said, "Art, they will wait for you.... the plane is your airplane." I had just not put that together. Since the days of von Braun, Marshall had a Gulfstream I prop-jet airplane for use by the Center Director and accompanying employees and teams like the Shuttle team, to fly to business related destinations. We had pilots standing by to fly the airplane. By the time I arrived at Marshall this airplane was a real classic and wherever we went heads turned to look at this old relic airplane as we taxied to or from the runway. Just before the infamous 9/11 tragic day, Marshall took delivery of a Gulfstream III, a modern business Jet, having traded in the old prop-jet. This airplane served us well for the remainder of my time at NASA and beyond.

I found out early-on that Marshall leadership, in some cases, asked the Center Director to make what they considered critical decisions. One day I found myself sitting in a room full of people being briefed on a technical problem. After presenting the problem and the alternative paths going forward, the leader of the group turned to me and said, "Which alternative should we pursue?" I thought about it and realized, yes, if it were me, I would pick one of the alternatives, but I caught myself realizing some managers at

Marshall subscribed to the idea that the Center Director should be asked to make the final decision on what were considered pivotal technical decisions. My response came after a long pause. I said, "You all are the most knowledgeable people regarding this problem. Go off and think about this situation, look at the alternatives again, and come back tomorrow and give me your recommendation for the best path forward and why you would choose that path. Don't look to me to make decisions you are most qualified to make. I appreciate being consulted and want you to come forward with key decisions that have major impacts on our programs but don't come again without a recommendation and your rationale for making that recommendation. If I choose to ask questions or think more thought should be given to the recommendation, I will certainly make that clear." The word spread across the Center and I don't think I was approached again to make technical or business decisions without an accompanying recommendation unless I had requested a decision meeting where I specifically wanted to weigh in on the decision. They were empowered to make decisions. Now, I must say, I don't believe this practice was at all Center-wide. The X-Ray Observatory team, Shuttle team, and a number of other technical teams would not have come to me asking for my decision on technical matters on their programs. They were highly qualified to make their own decisions and did a great job technically managing their programs. I wanted to help and one type of problem I did get involved with was when big contractors like Boeing got into cost overruns and expected MSFC to just swallow the overrun. One Boeing Executive, some years later, told me about a time when "He got his head handed to him." He had held a meeting with me, at my request, to explain a big overrun on one of our programs. I had told him to come back in a week and tell me how, by the end of the fiscal year, he was going to have this contract back on budget. And he did come back and not only that but by the end of the fiscal year the contract was back on budget.

Not long after I arrived, I often heard how impressed everyone was with Wernher von Braun, whose desk I had the honor of sitting at and whose bust I passed every time I entered or exited my office. Well-meaning people would say, "Von Braun did it this way. Why don't you do it the way he did?" After hearing this comment too many times I politely said, "You know Wernher von Braun was the best von Braun ever. I can't be von Braun very well. I want to be the best Art Stephenson I can be."

A few weeks after I officially started in my new job, I found myself in front of big audiences. One such occasion was at a Huntsville Chamber of Commerce reception for Loa and me at the U.S. Space and Rocket Center, Marshall's welcome center and museum in town. What a warm welcome it was with the Mayors of Huntsville and Madison cities and business leaders attending. Dan Goldin returned for this occasion and local U.S. Congressman, Bud Cramer, attended. Not long after that I was asked to be the keynote speaker at the annual von Braun Dinner. This was a big dinner drawing about 1,000 people from across the aerospace industry. This introvert had to adjust to all of this. I was pleased to have our daughter Kristin and her husband, Mark, and our son, John and his wife, Amy, attend this event.

One month after I arrived there was a naming ceremony for Interstate highway I-565 in honor of Astronaut Alan Shepard, America's first astronaut launched into space on the Redstone Rocket designed and built by von Braun's team. This interstate highway is about eight miles long going from I-65 to downtown Huntsville. There is nothing like having powerful state representatives in the U.S Congress able to obtain funds for this excellent but short highway. An interesting thing happened at that naming ceremony. The Governor of Alabama's staff had asked for an advanced copy of my speech. When I

Huntsville welcomed Loa and me at the same time NASA was celebrating its 40$^{th}$ Anniversary. Sitting (right to left) is Loa, U.S. Congressman Bud Cramer, NASA Administrator Dan Goldin, USSRC Director Mike Wing, President of the Marshall Alumni Association Gerald Smith, and Huntsville Mayor Loretta Spencer
--- Credit: NASA Photo

got to the event the Governor gave his speech just before mine. He delivered a story I had intended to talk about in my speech.

The story was that Alan was an avid golfer and he took a golf ball and club to the moon and attempted to hit the longest four iron shot in history. As you know, the moon's gravity is 1/6$^{th}$ that of the earth's gravity so, yes, he probably did hit that golf ball a long way. Governors get to do whatever they want. Fortunately, I had two things to talk about and the second one was most important. I read a letter Alan Shepard's daughter wrote about her dad she had sent to me. It was a special privilege for me to be able to read that letter at this gathering to honor America's first astronaut in space.

I thoroughly enjoyed getting to know the people of Marshall. Each organization held All Hands meetings to introduce me to their organization. They provided very informative information and to illustrate they also included some fun things like humorous skits. I quickly came to the conclusion that, by far, most NASA MSFC civil servants and contractors are dedicated to NASA's mission and they come to work to make a difference. My introduction to Marshall and the civic and education leaders in town could not have been better and I felt fortunate to be a part of a great NASA Center as well as a great community.

******

## Chapter 14

# John Glenn's Return to Space

*"If there is one thing I've learned in my years on this planet, it's that the happiest and most fulfilled people I've known are those who devoted themselves to something bigger and more profound than merely their own self-interest."*
--- John Glenn

I had attended three Shuttle launches while working for Oceaneering before joining NASA but always as a spectator at the Banana Creek Viewing Site. My first Shuttle launch in my new job occurred on October 29, 1998, six weeks after I arrived at Marshall Space Flight Center. This launch was significant because one of the crewmembers was Senator John Glenn, the first U.S. astronaut to be launched into orbit around the earth. This STS-95 launch occurred 36 years after John Glenn's launch on the Redstone Rocket designed, built and launched by the von Braun team. Apollo 11 astronauts, Neil Armstrong and Buzz Aldrin, were not given an opportunity to go to space again after their historic mission. John Glenn had also been denied a second launch. Some have said that these astronauts were such high-profile heroes, NASA was not willing to risk losing them on another launch. John Glenn openly campaigned for an opportunity to fly again on the Shuttle. Dan Goldin talked about struggling with his decision whether or not to give Senator Glenn, a seat on a Shuttle mission. When he did approve of Glenn's participation, he reasoned NASA could study the effects of age comparing his medical condition in space at the age of 77 with his medical records from his launch 36 years earlier.

A first for me was attending the 1 ½ day Flight Readiness Review (FRR) held routinely two weeks prior to each Shuttle launch. This review walked through briefings on every part of the Shuttle system addressing flight readiness of each and any issues or problems identified on prior flights. I was one of 10 senior NASA managers sitting at a conference table in the center of the large FRR conference room. We were surrounded by about 80 other NASA and contractor technical experts and managers associated with the Shuttle program or payload for this particular mission. In addition, teams at JSC and MSFC were participating in the meeting by teleconference. Sitting at the conference table seemed to add importance to my role but it was clear to me I was largely relying on the highly skilled MSFC Shuttle team to do their jobs. During my roughly five years at NASA, they did an outstanding job dealing with every technical propulsion related issue that arose prior to a Shuttle launch. And there were always issues leading up to every Shuttle flight.

When the launch day came it was quite the experience to sit with other NASA leaders in the Launch Control Center Firing Room at Kennedy Space Center listening to the communications between the Shuttle team leaders prior to launch. During the countdown leading up to the launch, the Shuttle Launch Director polls the leaders of each Shuttle major element as well as the Air Force Range Safety Officer who spoke for weather conditions and radar monitoring the launch range. Marshall Shuttle element leaders and Safety and Mission Assurance speak for the Shuttle Orbiter Main Engines, the External Tank, and the Solid Rocket Motors. With everyone saying they are "go for launch," the launch continues, and liftoff occurs if the launch team does not identify any issues or automatic safety checks are not activated during the rest of the countdown.

This was my first time to be in the Launch Control Center (LCC) Firing Room. This room and a backup room are where engineers sat at consoles monitoring the health of each Shuttle element. The LCC Firing Room also had a row of desks up front where NASA's top managers sat looking out over the launch team at their consoles sitting below them. Sitting at these desks were four Center Directors (JSC, MSFC, KSC and Stennis Space Center), the Shuttle Program manager, NASA Associate Administrators, the Payload Manager and the Launch Director. My understanding was that I was to leave all decisions to the launch team. With the other Center and program managers I monitored the proceedings, listened in on communications between the Launch Director, the element leaders and the crew on-board the Shuttle. I was only to take action if there was a catastrophic event that required my coordination of specified actions Marshall Space Flight Center was to undertake.

About two hours prior to the STS-95 launch President Clinton and first Lady, Hilary, landed on the nearby Shuttle Landing Facility runway and, with many others in their motorcade vehicles, drove out near the fully fueled Shuttle on the launch pad with astronauts sitting in their seats atop the launch vehicle ready to go. This was something never done before, but I guess the President said, "Let's take a drive out to see the Shuttle up close." So, they did before driving over to the Launch Control Center and being escorted to the roof to view the launch with host, Dan Goldin, who by the way, reported directly to the President. They joined the families of the STS-95 crew. About that time, those of us listening on the communications network heard a statement by the Air Force Range Safety Officer that incoming aircraft had been spotted and multiple military jet aircraft had been dispatched to head them off. It sounded to me like there was a terrorist attack coming on the Launch

Control Center (LCC) with the President on the roof of the building. We learned some minutes later there were several private aircraft that had drifted into the "no-fly-zone" and they were quickly diverted away. The same thing happened at sea where several pleasure boats, wanting to see the launch up close, came too near the launch pad and were also diverted away by patrol boats. Thousands of people lined every road around Cape Canaveral/Kennedy Space Center, the biggest attendance recorded for any launch from KSC. Amazing how a national hero, first U.S. man to orbit the earth, and a sitting U.S. Senator can generate such interest in his second launch to orbit 36 years after his historic first launch.

      The STS-95 Shuttle mission was a success. Like all Shuttle missions, after their flight, the crew came to Huntsville, Alabama to thank the Marshall Shuttle team and

STS-95 Launch
--- Credit: NASA Photo

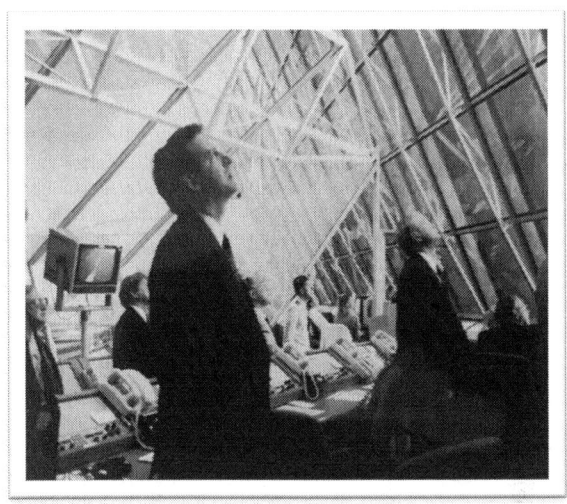

Viewing Launch from LCC
--- Credit: NASA Photo

all of the NASA Marshall employees and contractors who supported the Marshall Shuttle team for successfully launching them. This mission involved microgravity experiments and so the crew also thanked the Marshall Microgravity team that trained them to perform microgravity experiments on their mission. Each Shuttle crew came to the Center to share stories and pictures of their mission in an All Hands, televised meeting. When I was in town, I always had the pleasure of hosting their presentations in our auditorium and thus had the opportunity to greet many of our nation's astronaut heroes. News came that the STS-95 crew were coming to MSFC in December to thank Marshall for launching them and to share stories and pictures from their mission just like other mission crew visits. Some of our public relations team came to my office to share an idea they wanted to implement. It was based on a prior special event in Huntsville. After the Apollo 11 landing on the moon, the city of Huntsville held a parade to celebrate Marshall's role.

STS-95 Crew: Seated are astronauts Curtis L. Brown Jr. (right), mission commander; and Steven W. Lindsey, pilot. Standing, from the left, are Scott F. Parazynski and Stephen K. Robinson, both mission specialists; Chiaki Mukai, payload specialist representing Japan's National Space Development Agency (NASDA); Pedro Duque, mission specialist representing the European Space Agency (ESA); and U.S. Sen. John H. Glenn Jr., payload specialist.
--- Credit: NASA Photo

They made a big deal of this occasion. They closed all of the Huntsville schools and children, parents and other interested people lined the parade route. Following a parade through the streets of Huntsville some of the NASA employees carried Wernher von Braun on their shoulders up the steps of city hall where he gave a speech to the cheers of the people of Huntsville. The public relations team was recommending we hold a parade again, this time treating Senator Glenn in the same way. City officials wanted to have a ceremony in the Von Braun Center in downtown Huntsville and they thought it would be great to conduct a parade after that.

My response was:

- Are you all serious? I was surprised by this request.
- If we do this, I still want the crew to come to the Marshall Center first and share with our employees just like any other crew visit.
- I am OK with the downtown ceremony at the Von Braun Center and parade if the city officials want to do that.
- However, I know John Glenn a little and from what I have read about him I don't want anyone carrying him up the stairs of city hall. He would really not want to do that.
- Lastly, I need to know that the STS-95 crew and particularly the commander are OK with doing all of this.

Before you could "shake a stick" all of the plans were in place. On the day of the event, December 15, 1998, the STS-95 crew came to Marshall in the morning and we had our typical ceremony. I had received feedback that the crew was OK with the plan, but I made sure by pulling the commander, Curt Brown, aside and asking him if he was OK with what was about to happen downtown, not that I could change anything at this point. Thankfully, he told me the crew was well aware of the unique position they were in with Senator John Glenn attracting most of the attention on their crew visits and everyone on his crew were very happy to have John recognized. Curt and his crew demonstrated this throughout the day.

The celebration in the Von Braun Center was held in the same hall where the Houston Symphony performed with seating for about 1800 people. Every seat was taken and there were people standing. The city showed up for this free event with the Huntsville Mayor and U.S Congressman Bud Cramer participating. I was surprised after the Von Braun

John Glenn at ceremony at the Von Braun Center
--- Credit: NASA Photo

Center event to be shown to a 1957 Ford Thunderbird convertible that I sat in for the parade like some movie star. I think they did not tell me about that ahead of time because they figured, rightfully so, that I would have tried to beg off. The STS-95 crew was treated likewise. Schools were closed for the afternoon and the streets of the parade route were lined with school children, their parents and other interested people waving U.S. flags. Bands played as they marched. At the end of the parade we walked through Youth members of a Junior ROTC (Reserve Officer Training Corps.), in their dress uniforms with swords drawn on both sides of the path, and then up the steps of City Hall where a podium was placed for speakers to address the gathered crowd. I was more than impressed with John Glenn, with whom I had the privilege of spending most of the day, as I watched as he stopped in the midst of the walk to the city hall steps and knelt down and shook a small boy's hand and spoke some words to him. He did this after he told me he was running late and needed to leave soon. He still had to go through the ceremony we had planned where the Mayor and I were to say some words followed by John addressing the very large crowd that waited patiently, not to hear me or the mayor but to hear John's remarks. John's response to this small boy reminds me of a story I heard I can't resist sharing.

*"A couple of years ago I read a story that has taken on great metaphorical significance for me. The setting is Christmas Eve in Chicago in the 1920's, before the stock market crash. Two businessmen are rushing to catch the 6:00 P.M. commuter train for home. On the train platform a young handicapped boy is selling papers and other goods he can pick up and resell for a bargain at a small stand. The first man emerges on the platform. He runs into the boy, knocking him and his stand over. Hurling a few choice curse words at the boy, the man continues on to catch his train. A few seconds later the second man emerges on the platform. He sees the boy and his stand knocked down. He immediately helps the boy up and tries to gather up some of his goods. The man reaches in his billfold and pulls out a five-dollar bill. He gives it to the boy, saying he hopes it will help cover part of the boy's losses. Wishing the boy, a 'Merry Christmas,' he turns to catch his train. The boy yells after him, 'Say, Mister, are you Jesus Christ?' Red-faced and embarrassed, the man answers, 'No but I try to be like him.'"*
--- From "Climbing a Sycamore Tree" by Ann Hagmann

    I believe John Glenn was like Jesus Christ to this little boy at that moment and he was a witness to all of us, no matter what lofty position we might hold in life, we can never stop taking the time to care about people, even in our busiest moments. Oh, how I fail to do this so many times. Do you?

******

## Chapter 15

# MSFC Management Challenges

*"Change can be frightening, and the temptation is often to resist it. But change almost always provides opportunities - to learn new things, to rethink tired processes, and to improve the way we work."*
--- Klaus Schwab

In late November 1998, two months after my arrival at NASA, George Abbey, Director of Johnson Space Center (JSC), in Houston, Texas, asked me if I wanted to go to Moscow and then on to Russia's launch complex Kazakhstan to witness the launch of the first element of the International Space Station, the "Zarya" Module. I flew on a commercial flight to Moscow and, with little sleep, joined the American group, including Dan Goldin, for a 2,000 mile night flight to Kazakhstan, where I had gone with the AIAA years before. The successful launch took place not long after we arrived early in the morning. We stood outdoors in the cold as the sun came up just prior to launch. We were much closer to the launch vehicle than anyone would be allowed to stand for a U.S. launch. Besides being impressed with the simplicity of the launch and the brute force of Russia's workhorse launch vehicle, the thing I remember most about this time was going to a breakfast after the launch where they served caviar and vodka and then took us to an auditorium where televised press interviews were conducted with Russian and U.S. leaders. I was most concerned because I was beyond tired and a TV camera kept scanning the room as I struggled to keep my eyes open and not fall asleep. I could feel my head dipping from time to time. I pictured MSFC people watching this event back home saying, "Hey, there is Art and he can't stay awake for this historic event?"

George had JSC purchase an old Boeing 737 plane to fly NASA folks back and forth from Houston to Moscow during this busy time. The operation of the new International Space Station was to be under joint control – from Russia's Star City Control Center and from Johnson Space Center's Control Center. JSC people were required to spend a lot of time in Russia. He believed he was saving the government money. After flying back to Moscow from Kazakhstan the next day, we flew to Houston on "Abbey Air" stopping in Greenland for refueling and Washington DC to let Dan Goldin and company deplane. On the way back from Moscow, Dan Goldin asked me to come forward and sit with him and we proceeded to talk about Marshall Space Flight Center for the next two hours. The first thing Dan asked me was, "Have you re-organized Marshall yet? I want to see your re-organization plan." I told him I was close to finishing a reorganization plan and would get it to him within two weeks. He advised me on several aspects of such a plan including sharing his view of the engineering organization at Marshall. Out of 2700 civil servants about 1500 reported to the Director of Engineering. Dan said, "You are not the Center Director (CD), your Director of Engineering is the CD." Frankly I had already come to this conclusion long before coming to Marshall. He went on to say he wanted to "Blacken the skies with Marshall X launch vehicles." Marshall was already responsible for contracting for the development of three such vehicles --- "X" meaning "experimental vehicles." Three Marshall contractors, Boeing, Lockheed Martin, and Orbital Sciences Corporation were developing these vehicles. Dan impressed upon me the importance of success of these vehicles even though the contractors were given fixed price contracts, specifically stating that NASA was to have little to do with directing these developments. Having come from TRW and believing NASA caused more problems and cost growth than they should, he had created these hands-off contracts, yet he was clear with me these programs should succeed. I will talk more about X launch vehicles in a later chapter.

Throughout my first year Dan Goldin would occasionally call me and offer his counsel on the X vehicles as they encountered development difficulties. He did not hesitate to offer advice on a number of other topics. I appreciated him doing this, as I was in a learning mode. After all, I had asked for his support when I took the job. I greatly appreciated that he did not publicly criticize Marshall as he had been doing during the couple of years before I arrived and this was noticed by Marshall's employees and those who supported Marshall like the Marshall Retiree Association, city officials, and the Alabama state and U.S. congressmen and Senators. This fact greatly helped me interface successfully with these MSFC stakeholders.

The launch of the International Space Station Russian Zarya first element was quickly followed by the Space Transportation System (STS-88) Shuttle launch of the U.S. Unity module December 4, 1998. The STS 88 crew docked the two modules together on orbit. I was in the Launch Control Center "Firing Room" at Kennedy Space Center to support this launch. Everything went according to plan. I hoped and prayed this would be the case every time we launched a Shuttle.

On January 29, 1999, a little over four months after arriving, I announced a Marshall Center re-organization having previously obtained NASA Headquarters approval. All of the NASA Associate Administrators and Dan Goldin had approved this re-organization. My experience in Industry led me to adopt a customer focused program organization while retaining the Engineering Directorate to

Astronauts on Space Shuttle mission STS-88 work on the embryonic International Space Station, hours after connecting the first element -- the Russian-built Zarya FGB control module with the US-built Node 1 Unity module in December 1998.
--- Credit: NASA Photo

maintain engineering disciplines and providing engineers to support the various projects and programs led from the other new Directorates. The Engineering Directorate no longer oversaw the Marshall programs and thus was a smaller organization. I set up a Space Transportation Directorate to oversee all launch vehicle programs except the Shuttle program office that continued to report directly to me, a Science Directorate to oversee all earth and space science programs, and a Flight Projects Directorate to oversee the International Space Station Program. I won't go into the details of this re-organization and the rationale for it. If you want to know more about this reorganization you can read about it in the February 3, 1999 issue of the "Marshall Star," Marshall's internal weekly news publication (simply Google

"Marshall Star Archive"). I was dismantling an organization set up by von Braun himself. The engineering organization had not been appreciably changed in the 25 years since von Braun. I asked the Customer and Employee Relations Directorate, with the support of the Center Operations Directorate, to coordinate a move of nearly 50% of the Center employees and support contractors. Roughly 3,100 people needed to move in order to be collocated with their new organization. They came back to me and said the move would take six months to complete. My opinion was that people needed to be collocated with their new teams and it would be very disruptive if it took six months. My response was: Please go back and come up with a plan that accomplishes the move within two weeks. And they did! But they proposed doing the move over a 4-day period, not two weeks. They set up a 2-day training event on Thursday and Friday one week in downtown Huntsville at the Von Braun Convention Center for the entire Marshall Center population. They brought in about 30 instructors to run appropriate seminars that needed to be addressed that normally would have happened over a much longer period of time. Thus, the Center was deserted those two days allowing movers to do their jobs without interference. They hired every moving company in the Huntsville area to move each affected employee's and contractor's boxed up belongings and their computer to their new location over the four days --- Thursday through Sunday. When the employees came to work on Monday, they found their belongings and computer at their new desk location and a Hershey's Kiss candy on top of each computer! This was a clear demonstration of the Earle Nightengale principle I had adopted a long time ago: "What the mind of man [or woman] can conceive and believe, it can achieve." I was proud of our team who made this happen and suggested they send this large government directed move to the

Guinness Book of Records. Sadly, I don't think you will find this amazing government world record move there.

It did not take long after I arrived at Marshall to realize there was a "war" going on between MSFC and the NASA Stennis Space Center in Mississippi. About a year before I arrived Dan Goldin decided that all propulsion testing should be done at Stennis Space Center (SSC). Wernher von Braun had set up the SSC test site in the first place to test the large Saturn rocket engines. He did this after windows across the city of Huntsville kept breaking with his engine test firings at Marshall. The Stennis test site was later designated a separate NASA Center. MSFC was not arguing about the big test stands, as they knew those tests were appropriately conducted at Stennis. The argument was over smaller engine test stands. After the Goldin announcement, I was told trucks from Stennis had shown up at the entrance gate of MSFC to haul away all of MSFC's small engine test stands and they had been turned away. I am not sure this story was actually true but when I met with the propulsion folks, they told me they still worried about Stennis coming back for their test stands. Long story short, I talked to the Stennis Space Center Director, Roy Estes, whom I sat next to during Shuttle launches in the Launch Control Center and we came to an agreement that MSFC would retain small engine test capability and the matter was settled. Roy and I also agreed to send one of Marshall's test people to work with Stennis to help develop better relations between these two rocket engine test groups. The person we sent to Stennis was Robert Lightfoot. He was just the right person for this assignment. He eventually became MSFC Center Director, went to NASA headquarters as NASA's Chief Engineer, and finished his NASA career as acting NASA Administrator in 2018.

Another "turf battle" between NASA Centers was bubbling below the surface. This battle, like the test stand battle came about as a result of another decision by Dan

Goldin. He had decided all NASA Space and Earth scientists should report to Goddard Space Flight Center in Greenbelt, Maryland. His reasoning was based on the way industry companies were organized. Goddard was the NASA lead Center for science just as Marshall was the lead NASA Center for propulsion. Having come from TRW he saw no reason not to have people of similar backgrounds and disciplines report to one NASA Center – a typical industry practice where geographical location was not a factor. Dan believed all scientists should report to Goddard. Propulsion engineers should report to MSFC and so on. Dan did not account for the political impact of this decision. Marshall Space Flight Center had approximately 150 earth and space scientists at the Center and they did not want to report to Goddard Space Flight Center. This "re-badging" of Marshall employees was viewed by Alabama's most senior U.S. Senator, Richard Shelby, as the first step in just moving Marshall scientists to Goddard Space Center in Maryland. The result would be moving 150 engineers to Maryland and a like number of associated support people in Huntsville to Maryland. Alabama congressmen and senators are all about increasing and protecting jobs in the state. Our scientists picked up on that idea and they doubled down on not being assigned to Goddard even though Dan Goldin said they would not have to be moved and could remain at MSFC.

I thanked God more than once for giving me a good relationship with Dan Goldin before I came to NASA. I set up a one-on-one meeting with Dan in his office at NASA headquarters in Washington DC. With prayers lifted up, I told him I did not want to move the Marshall scientists or badge them to Goddard. The NASA Associate Administrator for Space Science, Ed Weiler, had disagreed with me on this point. He said he believed the Marshall scientists could not compete for "peer reviewed" science project funding and that Marshall was not properly competing for science funding. They were getting work out of an entitlement mind set in NASA and not based on merit. Peer review means unbiased scientists, if that is possible, with expertise in a science subject area from all over the U.S. were given proposals to read, evaluate and, as a group, select for award. I had told Ed the MSFC scientists were world class scientists and they could compete and win legitimate competitions for science work. Talking to Dan, I said, "If the Marshall scientists cannot compete as Ed Weiler maintained, then they will die a natural death as a result of legitimately competing for and losing their funding. If Ed was wrong and I was correct, the Marshall scientists will continue to win their fair share of science projects." This still did not convince Dan. On other occasions Dan had told me Senator Shelby was one of the most powerful and influential Senators in the Senate implying he had to pay attention to the opinions of the Senator. So, I said, "Dan, I have a meeting with Senator Shelby in two hours [and I was not lying]. He has made it very clear he does not agree with moving or assigning Marshall scientists to Goddard. Do you want me to tell him we are going to move the reporting of Marshall scientists to Goddard Space Flight Center?" Dan thought about it for a few seconds and then yelled out to his administrative assistant in the outer office to get Ed Weiler and Ghassem Asrar, the Associate Administrator for Earth Science, up to his office immediately. When they arrived, Dan explained to both that the scientists at Marshall would remain as MSFC employees and not be re-assigned to Goddard. He also told them the deal I had struck with him was the Marshall scientists would compete fairly for peer reviewed science funding and if they could not compete successfully, they would gradually lose their jobs anyway. Years later Ed Weiler told me he was wrong, that the Marshall scientists were consistently winning peer reviewed competitive proposals and they were the world class scientists I had told him they were.

      When I shared the outcome of this meeting with our

Marshall scientists, I told them we would help them compete by helping them keep their proposal bid costs down. Some of the earth scientists had already moved off-site, away from MSFC, to keep their bid costs down. I agreed we would allow them to have a separate cost structure apart from MSFC burdened labor rates as NASA moved, as planned, toward full cost accounting which means every dollar spent is accounted for in the appropriate organization. The best thing we could do was to move all of our scientists off-site to get their bid costs down. Not all of the scientists liked this idea. They liked having their offices with the rest of the NASA employees, so my decision was not popular with many of the scientists who had not moved off-site at this point. People always resist change even if it keeps their jobs. Someone once told me, always try to replace the word *change* with the word, *improvement*, when trying to sell an idea or action. One needs to share the benefits or improvements that come from changing something.

Based on the decision to move the scientists off-site we then needed an off-site facility for them. We did not want to rent a building, preferring to buy one. Some of our State representatives proposed using state funds to buy a building. With some effort we gained the support for this idea from,
(1) representatives of the Huntsville city Chamber of Commerce, (2) the Presidents of the University of Alabama, Huntsville (UAH) and the Alabama A&M University, (3) local representatives in the Alabama State House and Senate, (4) Alabama U.S. senators Shelby and Sessions and (5) Congressman Bud Cramer. I accompanied a Huntsville delegation to meet with the Governor of Alabama, Don Siegelman, in Montgomery, Alabama. We asked the Governor to allocate $5 Million in his next fiscal year budget to buy a building across from the University of Alabama, Huntsville that would house Huntsville's scientists from MSFC, UAH and Alabama A&M. The idea was to have

for peer reviewed competitive science projects. The Governor signed an agreement to do just that and we were off and running knowing we had support in the Alabama House and Senate. When the state government passed funding into law, Governor Sieglman came to Marshall to present the funding in an All Hands meeting.

The National Space Science and Technology Center (NSSTC) in Huntsville was opened for business about a year later. MSFC moved all of the Center scientists over to this new Center when the building modifications were completed after the purchase of the building. I later heard many of the scientists say they loved being off-site and would never want to move back to MSFC located on the Army's Redstone Arsenal behind security gates.

Huntsville and Madison city officials as well as the many businesses that support Marshall were very concerned

National Space Science and Technology Center,
a joint research venture between NASA
and seven research universities
--- Credit: NASA Photo

about the future of Marshall Space Flight Center at the time of my arrival. They constantly heard rumors about shutting down NASA Centers, with Marshall being one of them and re-directing Marshall work to other NASA Centers. Hearing all of this I decided to hold periodic "Marshall Community Breakfasts" inviting city and industry leaders as well as the leaders of the three local universities to come to a hotel in town, have breakfast in a banquet room, and get an update briefing from me on the state of MSFC. This was designed to improve communications. We held this breakfast two times per year. I was highly motivated to do this to quell the ongoing uninformed rumor mill. I believe this initiative along with frequent All Hands meetings at MSFC went a long way toward settling people's nervous feelings. I told them I would only share what I knew and that was all. I was not making anything up or guessing about outcomes. These initiatives also helped stop the Huntsville Chamber of Commerce and the Marshall Retiree Association from going to Washington DC and holding meetings with the Alabama delegation and with the NASA Administrator asking them for favors and legislative *earmarks* without the knowledge of the Marshall Center Director. The definition of an earmark is a funding line added to a NASA authorization bill to fund some pet project that is passed by the houses of congress into law. Congressmen and Senators laid claim to these earmarks each year and they sometimes could come up with some very poor ideas that used NASA money without helping NASA's mission. I told folks in town, "If you have something you want done with the help of the NASA federal budget like earmarks that become law, bring it to me and I will listen but from now on MSFC will set the legislative agenda for our supporters in Washington DC on NASA related matters. Amazingly this worked. From then on, with the help of MSFC's legislative folks, MSFC was the decision point for earmarks and the negotiator with our Alabama

Congressmen and Senators. Of course, we did not always get our way, but we won more battles than we lost. One excellent earmark that was funded was to build a badly needed new MSFC Propulsion Research Center. Congressman Bud Cramer, after seeing the poor state of our propulsion research labs, supported this $30M earmark and this new facility was built on site at MSFC.

Another example of this earmark issue came up in discussions with the Director of the U.S. Space and Rocket Center (USS&RC). Larry Capps wanted to talk to Bud Cramer about putting an earmark in the next year's funding legislation, like he had done in previous years, to build a new dormitory for his Space Camp. He did as I had asked and brought this idea to me for approval. It seemed to me, after some discussion about the dormitory idea, there was a greater need for an Educator Training Facility. MSFC had inadequate facilities on-site to conduct training classes. Also, NASA's Educator Resource Center, located at the USS&RC, was wholly inadequate and needed to be upgraded and expanded. This Center was available to teachers wanting NASA materials to teach students Science, Technology, Engineering, and Math (STEM). The U.S. Space and Rocket Center could use this new building for training, and educator meetings and Marshall could use it for training and an improved Educator Resource Center. He agreed and so, we took the idea to Bud Cramer. The construction of the Educator Training Facility completed the following year with earmarked NASA funds.

When I came to Marshall in 1998 the security at the Redstone Arsenal gates was laughable. By that I mean very casual. I remember one time I had taken my truck in for servicing in town and the dealer's courtesy driver was taking me to my office on site within the arsenal gates. The driver just waved a piece of paper at the guard at the gate and kept on driving. Dan Goldin, while visiting, observed the same casual behavior. He told me to get this fixed. I had a good relationship with the Redstone Arsenal Commanding General (we had played golf together several times on the Arsenal golf course). I talked to him about tightening up the Army managed security at the gates. Nothing much changed. So, I told him if things did not get a lot better soon NASA/MSFC, which had nearly 1800 acres of land within the much larger arsenal, would enclose our property with a fence and set up security of our own at our gates. That got his attention and soon after this we had much tighter security. When 9/11/01 happened, everyone was happy to have this better security already in place ready to support the even more intense security processes that were implemented the day after this national tragedy.

As I settled into the job, four important management emphasis points surfaced for our management team: *Safety, Management by Values, Open Communications,* and *Diversity.*

Of course, *Safety* of flight was highest on NASA's list. After the tragic loss of Shuttle Challenger and its crew, NASA adopted more rigorous flight safety reviews and rules. Every engineer in the Launch Control Center Firing Room at Kennedy Space Center in Florida was authorized to stop a launch if they saw something that was out of specified limits. From my time at Oceaneering, I realized that safety must be conscientiously addressed in all aspects of our lives, not just at work. One way industry measured safety was by keeping track of consecutive days of operation with no loss of an employees' work time from an accident on the job. I wanted to extend that thinking to address no accidents at home as well as at work. One of the MSFC employees was considered a top safety conscious person at work but one day while working in his boathouse on an electrical problem he electrocuted himself. So, I talked to our Marshall employees saying, we will know we have the right attitude about safety at work when we take the same safety conscious attitude home. We initiated safety moments at the beginning of all of our staff meetings across the Center. We used stories to motivate people like a picture of someone's sun glasses with a screw lodged half way through them with a caption, "Think you don't need safety glasses working in your yard? Think again." This was not a made-up story, it actually happened.

I talked about safety a lot. I had learned what the CEO of an organization thinks is important can have a big impact on the employees of that organization. The CEO has to walk the talk. The biggest workplace safety hazards, I had learned, were slips, trips and falls. So, I asked all of our employees to hold onto the handrail going up and down

Safety moment example. Credit: NASA Photo

stairs. I said let this be a sign we are being safety conscious. I asked people, if you see someone not holding on to the handrail, please politely point that out. One time, after many months talking about holding on to a handrail, I hopped up two steps to a platform in front of a lot of people to speak. After I finished speaking an employee came up to me and said, "You didn't hold on to the hand rail." I was embarrassed but I thanked him. You can bet that helped me do better from then on. Now, after leaving Marshall 15 years ago, I still can't walk up or down stairs without thinking about and holding onto the handrail. We talked and wrote about safety often in All Hands meetings and in our weekly Marshall Star publications.

One time Loa and I were in our car and we got lost in a residential area in Huntsville. We saw a young lady I did not recognize in her yard gardening and pulled over, rolled down the window and before we could ask for directions, she looked at us and said, "Oh, Mister Stephenson, am I doing something unsafe?" I knew then, at least with some employees and contractors, the message was getting into their DNA.

Jan Davis, a three-time Shuttle astronaut who was our Flight Projects Directorate Chief, suggested we form a combined NASA/Industry Safety group to meet regularly and consider ways we could improve safety in our programs and in our workplace. Jan and Amanda Goodson, Director of Safety and Mission Assurance, teamed up to form this NASA/Industry Safety group. It proved to be highly effective. We learned from our contractors. This safety group also helped our contractors take safety back to their companies in a new way. I was very pleased with how safety conscious our MSFC NASA and Contractor employees became.

The second management emphasis point was *Management by Values*. When I arrived at the Center the management team was already working on defining a Center Mission Statement and Values. As I mentioned earlier, I had adopted the concept of Managing by Values in my management approach at Oceaneering. Not only is it good to publish values, but if they are to mean anything they need to serve as guideposts in managing the enterprise. As I did at Oceaneering, I shared with the management team that I intended to manage by our values and asked them to consider the values as guideposts when making business decisions. I asked them to hold me accountable to do what I said. When issues came up in staff meetings, I tried to ask how our values would influence decisions on these issues.

With encouragement from our Director of Customer and Employee Relations, I initiated an effort over a number of months to personally address every MSFC employee in a meeting with the goal of establishing a culture of managing by values. I wanted to explain what I meant by this and so we conducted these sessions. Our five values were: *People, Innovation, Customers, Teamwork and Excellence.* I used an example to illustrate what I meant by managing by values. Let's say an employee had promised to deliver a laboratory test report to another NASA Center (in this case the customer) by a particular date. If we have a deadline to meet that we had promised a customer and our *Customer Value* said, "We do what we say we will do," then we needed, in this example, to deliver a quality report on time. Let's say we made a commitment to deliver the laboratory test report by next Monday and today is Wednesday. The employee who is key to achieving this milestone has a son graduating from college this coming weekend on Saturday and he has to travel on Friday to be there. It becomes clear that the test will have to go on into the weekend and the report will have to be written on the weekend to make the Monday deadline. The *People Value* says we honor our employees and support them by offering them a balanced life between work and family. To honor our *Customer Value* and our *People Value*, in this case, we need to call on our *Teamwork Value.* The right thinking involves addressing more than one value at a time. In this case, if a supervisor just looks at the *Customer Value* he would say to the employee, sorry, you have to cancel your trip to the graduation and stay and work on the test to make the customer deadline. By looking at all of the values, the supervisor would say to the employee, based on looking at our *Teamwork Value,* let's work to have some other person step in to complete the test and the report while you go to the graduation. In this example the solution came from looking at three of the five values rather than just one.

The third management emphasis point was *Open Communications*. We held a weekly expanded staff meeting on Monday mornings, following a long-established tradition at the Center. The latest NASA news, particularly from NASA Headquarters in Washington DC was routinely shared in these meetings. It seemed I was attending a meeting at headquarters each month or more often where NASA leadership, together with and at the direction of the NASA Administrator, made key decisions related to program funding, agency budgets, new program initiation, civil servant hiring policy, etc. By sharing these things with the expanded staff these managers then shared with their staff, so the Center employees got weekly updates. Also, I did my best to inform the Center on the status of various events like the status of Y2K when we transitioned out of the last Century. MSFC was responsible for making sure the NASA computing systems did not crash. Also, when the agency transitioned to a new accounting system, MSFC was responsible for leading that transition across NASA affecting every NASA Center. Dan Goldin seemed to like asking MSFC's very talented team to lead these important efforts. In addition to the weekly large or expanded staff meeting, I held All Hands meetings when needed, typically about once a month. My goal was to head off rumors and tell the workforce what I knew to keep them from having to speculate. I encouraged our top team to do the same with their teams. If a leader does not tell people what is going on folks will make things up and this misinformation spreads.

One of the things I had started at Oceaneering were skip-level lunch meetings. These meetings were designed to allow me to hear directly from people 2, 3, or 4 levels down in the organization. I asked the approximately 15 participants in each skip level lunch meeting to write down their thoughts in response to two questions: 1) What do you see at the Center that is going well and we should keep doing? and 2) What do you see at the Center that is not going well and what suggestion do you have to make this better? After a period of silent reflection, I would poll the group one at a time to record their responses on the white board on the wall. After we had all the ideas up on the board, each person received three vote stickers and they would place their stickers next to the ideas they thought most important. In that way we all learned what items the total group considered most important. I told them the management would address their concerns, particularly the most important issues.

Communications are most important during times of crisis. When the Shuttle Columbia Orbiter was destroyed and its crew lost on re-entry, at first I communicated on Center-wide TV almost daily. In this case I believed I could not over-communicate. For this introvert, like Moses, I felt God was regularly asking me to be in places that were foreign to my nature, but times dictate what we do because it is what we have to do, comfortable or not.

The fourth management emphasis point was workforce *Diversity*. When I arrived and looked at the make-up of the Marshall management team, I saw mostly white males. We had a long way to go to correct this situation. Due to affirmative action emphasis in the government, the Center was taking on minorities at the entry level, but they tended to stay at that level. While there were three African American managers reporting directly to me, the management people below that level down to first line managers were predominately, almost exclusively, white and mostly males. I came to believe this happened because of the process used to give people the most challenging jobs. It seemed to me the most difficult job assignments went to people who looked like, talked like, and thought like the supervisor. I think this was not necessarily prejudice working. It might well have been just the supervisor picking the person they were most comfortable with. When it came time to promote people, logically, the strongest candidate was selected based on work experience. Thus, the promotions continued to be given predominantly to white males who had successfully performed on the most challenging assignments. I did what I could to encourage managers to give people with different gender or race a chance at working the hardest jobs. We had more diversity in our management team when I left than when I arrived, but it was a very slow process and still had a long way to go when my time was up.

During my years at NASA the opportunities I had to meet really impressive, famous people I had admired from a distance were amazing. One day Sally Ride, the first U.S. woman astronaut to fly in space visited me in my office. We talked about an organization she co-founded to encourage girls to enter professions in science, technology engineering, and mathematics (STEM). Another time I met in my office with the man who was the last person on the moon, Gene Cernan. We spent an hour talking about his experiences as an astronaut. Like many astronauts, Gene was a fun-loving guy, which led to interesting stories. At the end of our meeting, when Gene was scheduled to address our Marshall team in the auditorium and on Center-wide TV in an All Hands meeting, I asked him what he was going to talk about. He said I want to thank your people for launching me on a fantastic journey to the moon on the Saturn V and share some of my impressions from being on the moon. I said I think it would be great if, in addition to thanking the Marshall people and sharing your moon experience, you share some of the stories you have been telling me. He did do that and held his audience spellbound for an hour. I received numerous comments on how much they loved hearing Gene's stories they had not heard before. Another time Gene returned to the Center with Harrison Schmitt to celebrate their $30^{th}$ anniversary of walking on the moon. Harrison was the only scientist, a geologist, of the 12 men who have been on the moon. They covered 22 miles in the Lunar Roving Vehicle collecting geologic samples, the most

Left to right: Gene Cernan, Art, Jan Davis, Harrison Schmitt
--- Credit: NASA Photo

of any Apollo mission that would shed light on the moon's early history.

Then there were times when some of my favorite astronaut heroes came to Marshall including Eileen Collins, John Young and Bob Crippen. Eileen came twice, once with her crew on a crew visit and once to accept an award and talk to us about safety. John and Bob came to celebrate the 20$^{th}$ anniversary of STS 1, when they flew the first Shuttle to orbit and made the first re-entry from space to a landing in California. The amazing thing to me was they were riding on a launch vehicle system --- Orbiter with External Tank and Solid Rocket Boosters --- all working together for the first time. The risk of this decision was enormous, and the Shuttle Orbiter had no escape system in case of failure during launch or re-entry. With launch vehicles the standard approach is to launch first without people on board. I felt privileged to be able to have casual conversations with these space pioneers getting to know them in ways few others had the privilege to experience. During the 100-year anniversary celebration of the first flight of the Wright brothers in Dayton, Ohio, Loa and I attended an American Institute of Astronautics and Aeronautics (AIAA) dinner. We were invited to sit at a table of eight with astronaut, Neil Armstrong, and his wife. Loa still talks about how she sat next to Neil. Our impression was that he was a very nice and unassuming man who remained relatively quiet. This was quite an honor for us to be able to sit with and talk to the first human to step foot onto the moon who many say will go down in history as the most famous person in the 20$^{th}$ Century.

In September 1999, Loa and I travelled to Europe to participate in an American Institute of Aeronautics of Astronautics (AIAA) invited group tour to see the European propulsion company capabilities. We travelled with 15 other industry and government leaders and their spouses to France and Germany.

Toward the end of the European Propulsion tour, in the middle of the night, I received an unexpected call. Dan Goldin woke us up to tell me the Mars '98 Climate Orbiter Spacecraft had just been lost as it entered the vicinity of Mars. They were not sure what happened, but he said he wanted me to lead the NASA accident investigation board to determine the root cause behind this NASA disaster.

The mission was a Jet Propulsion Laboratory (JPL) mission. When I got home, after working with NASA Center Directors to draft investigation board members, the new board met at JPL in Pasadena, California and started our investigation. Our findings showed the program navigation experts at JPL and prime contractor Martin Marietta were confused about use of English or Metric units in their navigation calculations. They had used different units in their calculations. Trajectory correction burns were in error as a result. Because of this the spacecraft was not where it needed to be as it approached Mars and rather than going into orbit around Mars it flew right by Mars and headed out into space lost forever. Our board was also asked by the NASA Administrator to assess the likelihood of success of the Mars Polar Lander that was due to land on Mars less than three months later. Our investigation came to the conclusion that, although we found propulsion elements on the Lander that could freeze, these issues could be corrected by turning on thruster heating elements and orienting the spacecraft toward the sun. However, based on other potential issues identified, I had the unhappy job of telling Dan Goldin, our investigative team believed the Mars Polar Lander probability of successfully landing was 50 percent. I went out to JPL to join the JPL team observing the automated landing and, with the world watching, the spacecraft crash landed on Mars and was lost. A subsequent investigation by another mishap investigation board uncovered the cause of the crash. The spacecraft's three legs, deployed as the vehicle descended toward Mars, opened with a bang. Sensors on board the spacecraft had been designed to detect contact of the legs on the surface of Mars. When the legs unfolded and locked into place with a jolt as the Lander was descending but still at considerable altitude, the spacecraft sensors concluded that the vehicle had landed and shut off the retro rockets that were to provide a soft landing. A prelaunch test to see the vehicle's response when the legs were deployed was never conducted. Had that test been conducted this issue could have easily been discovered and the problem easily fixed.

As I write these words today, November 26, 2018, the news just broke that NASA's Insight Spacecraft successfully landed on Mars today. I turned on the TV and watched the cheers and high 5s of the JPL team in their mission control room, which is more like an observation room since the landing is all automated. This was in stark contrast to what happened in that same room when Mars

Polar Lander failed to report after what was to have been a good landing. I felt so sorry for that team back then. Good to see the celebration today!

When I returned to MSFC after this full-time investigation I asked our Engineering Directorate and program directorates, based on the Mars '98 findings and published failure reports, to undertake a review of all of Marshall's programs to ensure they had the proper amount of oversight and insight to make sure we did not under test or lack needed tests or analyses specified on our programs. I asked the Engineering Directorate to make sure the verification process by analysis or test was adequate on each of Marshall's programs.

I was asked to testify in the U.S. Senate on the loss of the Mars Climate Orbiter along with the chairman of the investigation board that had conducted the investigation of the loss of the Mars Polar Lander. The Senators, including John McCain, took NASA to task for these failures. They listened to our explanation of the failures and criticized NASA repeatedly. This was not a good day for NASA and particularly not a good day for Dan Goldin. It was not a fun day for me either.

Coming from TRW to become the NASA Administrator, Dan was convinced NASA was spending too much money to design, manufacture and test planetary mission spacecraft. And it turned out, with Dan's direction, NASA was able to spend much less and be successful on the first Mars mission, the Mars Pathfinder mission, after Dan arrived. This Mars mission preceded the two Mars '98 missions and was a tremendous success. The cost of this mission was 50% less than the previous Mars mission. This was accomplished by cutting staffing and testing requirements. After this Pathfinder success Dan asked the Jet Propulsion Laboratory in Pasadena, California to cut costs again on the two Mars '98 missions that ultimately failed.

Like Dan Goldin's first "Faster, Better, Cheaper" successful Mars Pathfinder mission, the next two Mars mission programs cut staffing and testing even more. After the Mars '98 mission failures, Dan told me, we found the edge of the cost cliff so now we should know how to back away from it and be successful. The Jet Propulsion Laboratory Director resigned after the Mars '98 failures. NASA did increase funding for Mars missions going forward.

When I arrived at Marshall in the fall of 1998, the first program I was briefed on was the Advance X-Ray Astrophysics Facility or what I will call for ease, the X-Ray Observatory program. It had just experienced a serious test failure and the cause was a mystery. In addition, the program was over budget and the overrun increased daily. The contractor responsible for this observatory design, development, manufacturing and test was my old company, TRW. The test failure problem occurred during thermal vacuum testing when the air is pumped out of the sealed test chamber containing the Observatory to create a space like vacuum, and the temperature is raised and lowered to maximum projected temperatures anticipated while in space. The Sunshade Door, protecting the front of the X-Ray Observatory to avoid contamination during ground processing and during the launch as well as shading instruments from the sun while in orbit, did not open at the colder temperature. If this happened on orbit the mission would obviously be lost. Try as they might, the TRW designers and test engineers, working with the company that developed the mechanism that opened this protective cover, could not find the cause of the failure.

The cost overruns were mounting as the test program anomaly investigation continued with a large program team at TRW supporting the program. In addition, the ground station control and data downlink Center in Cambridge, Massachusetts was a long way from completing needed software development and verification. The MSFC X-Ray Observatory program office folks were blaming TRW for the cost overruns placing a lot of pressure on TRW's management team to cut costs. When I looked at the situation, my conclusion was first and foremost, we needed to make sure the government/industry team did not race to launch this $1.5B observatory to save cost and in so doing cause a failure on orbit rendering the observatory a piece of space junk.

With MSFC's Program Manager I went out to TRW in California to meet with TRW management. Going in, I knew TRW's practice was to assign and hold an engineer (called the "Responsible Design Engineer") responsible for every hardware component in the spacecraft from design through manufacturing and the same for every software product. I told TRW's top managers I wanted every Responsible Design Engineer on the program to sign a document saying everything had been done that needed to be done before the Observatory was shipped to Kennedy Space Center for integration with the Orbiter prior to launch. Thus, I was asking TRW to be sure they had done everything possible to make their hardware and software ready for launch. The message was, "Do the right things to be successful." I told them I would take the heat coming from NASA Headquarters for any additional costs incurred as a result. I think they all breathed a sigh of relief. When I was a young employee at TRW, the company had a slogan – *TRW – The Right Way*. I knew not taking shortcuts was imbedded in the culture there. TRW Management thanked me for adopting this approach.

Then I went to NASA Headquarters with the top MSFC program team and met with the Associate Administrator for Space Science, Ed Weiler, and his X-Ray Observatory team. Ed and his team were most concerned about the state of the ground station software development at the Smithsonian Astrophysical Observatory in

Chandra X-Ray Observatory Artist's rendition
--- Credit: NASA

Cambridge, Massachusetts. We agreed to send one of TRW's best mangers, who was a well-respected software expert, up to Cambridge for the next six months, or whatever it took, to get this software properly finished and certified.

The observatory cover door opening issue never was satisfactorily resolved. The test was repeated multiple times and each time the cover opened as required. The physics of the opening mechanism was analyzed, and it was agreed that it should consistently work over the required temperature range. Based on these tests and analyses we decided we would move forward with preparations to launch the Observatory. It was delivered to Kennedy Space Center, integrated with the Air Force Inertial Upper Stage, inserted into the Orbiter bay with the Orbiter in the vertical launch position, and after all the checks completed, declared ready for launch. As the launch date approached NASA Headquarters announced the X-Ray Observatory would be officially named the "Chandra X-Ray Observatory," named in honor of Nobel Prize-winning Indian-American, astrophysicist Subrahmanyan Chandrasekhar. I looked forward to a successful Chandra X-Ray Observatory launch and successful operations on orbit.

Being a NASA Center Director was full of surprises and for an introvert like me it seemed God was determined to have me out front and center and out of my comfort zone every day and almost every hour.

******

# Chapter 16

# Events Surrounding the Chandra Launch

*"The heavens proclaim the glory of God. The skies display his craftmanship. Day after day they continue to speak; night after night they make him known."*
--- Psalm 19:1-2 (NLT)

My sister Lynn's husband, Fred Riffle, upon hearing about some of my experiences in NASA encouraged me to write down some of my memories. He said, "When you do, share your thoughts and feelings about those experiences. You engineers never talk about how you feel." Responding to Fred's urgings, I wrote the following notes after a particularly amazing, intense, tightly scheduled 11 days.

-----------------------------------------------------------------------

I am writing this as I fly to San Jose, California, on July 28, 1999, to attend a Shuttle Upgrades Conference for the rest of the week. It will be nice to fly directly home Saturday, the 31st, with Marshall folks on the Marshall plane rather than taking commercial flights like I am doing today. We are flying over the Rockies now and I am reminded that I never get tired of flying when I can look out of the window.

The Rockies are an awesome display of God's grandeur.

Saturday, July 17, 1999

Since becoming Center Director at Marshall Space Flight Center in Huntsville, Alabama, in September of 1998, I have had many experiences that would have been interesting to record (e.g. my first launch --- John Glenn; Russian trip for first element launch of the International Space Station; First U.S. International Space Station element launch; John Glenn visit and parades in Huntsville). Maybe someday I will go back over them and write about some, but right now I want to capture the last 11 days.

Eleven days ago, on July 17, we celebrated the 30th anniversary of the Apollo landing on the moon. It was a busy day for me --- exciting, yet very taxing. We started out with MSFC's annual picnic and a torch relay with runners passing the torch from old timers to younger Marshall folks. I started the race by handing the first runner the torch. At the end of the run (1.5 miles) I took the torch back and made a couple of remarks. We then had a children's parade into the picnic area from the parking lot to kick off the picnic. This picnic is an annual event that we decided to combine with the 30th celebration. Marshall Civil Servants and support contractors and their families attended with lots to eat and lots to do for the kids. I managed to avoid the dunking booth this year but will probably not be able to avoid it next year.

*Thoughts & Feelings: It is a funny feeling to be the center of attention at such an event. People seem to want to have someone as their leader. Even if I have nothing intelligent to say it does not seem to matter. I enjoyed talking to the kids and seeing their excitement.*

Not long after the children's parade, Loa and I left for the Redstone airport to meet NASA Administrator Dan

Goldin's airplane. With him were his wife, Joe Rothenberg, my boss, and a number of other headquarters folks. We went from the airport to the U.S. Space and Rocket Center (US&SRC) in Huntsville to a dedication ceremony of the new, full size Saturn V Rocket Mockup identical in appearance to the rocket that launched men to the moon. I spoke at the event and introduced Bud Cramer, the local U.S. Congressman, who introduced Dan Goldin. Dan and I dedicated the Rocket. You can see the plaque to that effect at the base of the Rocket.

*Thoughts & Feelings: I never thought my name would be on anything. This was an experience from someone else's life. I just don't think I am the person who should be doing all of this, but it is fun, although stressful at times.*

We (Loa and I and Dan Goldin's party) went from the USS&RC Saturn V Rocket Mockup dedication to the picnic, had barbecue for lunch and then we escorted Dan and his wife, Judy, around for an hour and a half. Dan just wanted to talk to people.

*Thoughts & Feelings: It is awkward escorting Dan and his party around the picnic area. I kept thinking how nice it would be for me if I could just walk around myself without having to worry about the boss.*

After saying goodbye to Goldin's entourage, I was left with a few minutes to prepare for the next event, which was a 3 to 5 P.M. formal ceremony to commemorate the 30$^{th}$ Anniversary of the moon landing. Loa, Joe and I went to my office to prepare for the event. I was to be the MC and Joe was the Keynote speaker.

*Thoughts & Feelings: A stressful time --- I was trying to gather myself to read a speech for the ceremony that I had been given and it was a long script.*

We then went over to another building where we met the four Apollo astronauts who came to attend this ceremony --- Buzz Aldrin, Dick Gordon, Walter Cunningham, and Charley Duke. Beginning the ceremony, I read the script I had been given including introducing many people in the audience and each of the astronauts. Then I introduced Joe Rothenberg who is responsible for NASA's Shuttle and Space Station Programs and he gave his speech. Then each of the Apollo astronauts spoke about their experience on or near the moon. Buzz Aldrin had to leave in the middle of the ceremony, so we interrupted the proceedings so he could imprint his boot in the sand that will be bronzed and put into a park in the middle of the Center main buildings where this took place. We then finished up by unveiling and dedicating a new fountain to commemorate this occasion.

*<u>Thoughts & Feelings</u>: I was very nervous about reading a long script but surprisingly I pulled it off pretty well I thought without stumbling over too many words. Scared at first, I became more comfortable as I went through the speech. It was amazing for me to introduce these national heroes who had played a major role in our nation's history.*

After completing the ceremony at the Center at about 5 P.M., I then shifted into getting ready for my speech to be delivered at the Von Braun Center in downtown Huntsville. This event at 7 P.M. was a kickoff to the yearlong Von Braun Celebration of Arts and Sciences. I am a co-chair (with three others). It was an event that people bought tickets to – about 1300 people I would guess. A local TV station hosted it and they put together a documentary on the history of Huntsville beginning with the arrival of the Germans led by Wernher von Braun. I spoke about the future of MSFC before the video was shown. That was followed by a neat dance presentation that depicted in abstract form Marshall's history. The evening ended up with Willard Scott (Good Morning America weatherman) who entertained everyone with his unique humor.

*Thoughts & Feelings:* It was scary being a part of a semiprofessional show. I wrote my own speech for this and did a pretty good job I thought.

At the reception afterward, Loa and I met Willard Scott – an interesting and funny guy. It was good to finish the day, but tomorrow was not far off.

Sunday morning, July 18, 1999
We left on the NASA Marshall plane bright and early Sunday morning for Kennedy Space Center (KSC). Loa had to fly commercially since only government people were allowed to fly on a government plane, so she drove to Birmingham and then took Southwest Airlines to Orlando and drove to KSC. I wanted to meet the crew of Shuttle Transportation System launch (STS-93) that would be launching the Chandra Observatory so I made everyone get up early including my boss, Joe. We got down there with no time to spare as the crew were going to sleep at 11 A.M. I had a quick required physical after getting lost finding the place and then only had about five minutes with the crew including the first female Shuttle commander, Eileen Collins. They were all very kind and said they were looking forward to launching Marshall's Chandra X-Ray Observatory, the heaviest and largest payload ever launched by Shuttle when you include the weight of the upper stage used to get Chandra into a higher orbit.

Eileen Collins, mission commander; Steven A. Hawley, mission specialist; Jeffrey S. Ashby, pilot; Michel Tognini and Catherine G. Coleman, both mission specialists.
--- Credit: NASA Photo

<u>Thoughts & Feelings</u>: *It is a special experience to meet one-on-one with a shuttle crew about to be launched into space. Of course, they are very smart and capable, but at the same time, normal people. I was honored to be able to meet with them at that time.*

That afternoon I attended the Launch minus 2-day readiness, technical review meeting with about 90 other NASA and contractor employees responsible for the launch to make sure all was ready for launch. This review took place before every launch. I had attended a Flight Readiness Review (FRR) held at KSC two weeks earlier. The FRR is conducted prior to each Shuttle launch over a 1 ½ day period. After that review I was privileged to go out to the launch pad and look into the cockpit and payload bay seeing Chandra and the attached IUS ready to go. What a beautiful Shuttle Columbia launch vehicle and Chandra spacecraft.

Chandra & IUS in Columbia Orbiter Bay
--- Credit: NASA Photo

Sunday night, July 18, 1999
Loa and I attended a Marshall Space Flight Awareness reception and dinner. This event is to honor men and women who have worked a long time for NASA as a NASA employee or contractor giving them the chance to see a Shuttle launch. It is also designed to make sure we never forget that safety is above all else as we do our jobs for NASA. About 40 MSFC civil servant and contractor honorees and their families or friends attended. I was the keynote speaker. I was invited to join three astronauts for a picture with each honoree.

*Thoughts & Feelings:* It was a lot of fun honoring those NASA and contractor employees who have worked in the space program at Marshall for years, most having never seen a Shuttle launch. I again feel honored to be able to do what I do.

Monday, July 19, 1999
I started the day early (7A.M.) by flying from the Air Force Cape Canaveral airport (known as the Skid Strip) on Johnson Space Center's plane with George Abbey (JSC Center Director), Joe Rothenberg (Associate Administrator for Space Flight), Bill Ready (Astronaut and Joe's deputy), Kathy Nado (Joe's assistant) and the STS 96 Astronaut commander, Ken Rominger, up to Washington DC to attend a budget meeting at headquarters and the funeral of Apollo Astronaut Pete Conrad at Arlington Cemetery. He had died in a motorcycle accident the week before. It was attended by an amazing group of famous people. I sat in a pew in the chapel right behind some of the most famous astronauts; two of the original seven astronauts---John Glenn and Wally Schirra; first humans to step onto the moon---Neil Armstrong and Buzz Aldrin; first two to go into orbit and return on the Shuttle---John Young and Bob Crippen; last man on the moon---Gene Cernan; and other Apollo astronauts---Dick Gordon, Joe Allen, Tom Stafford, Charley Duke, Walter Cunningham, and the list went on. Speakers included Dan Goldin, Neil Armstrong, and Dick Gordon. Willie Nelson surprised everyone as he walked out in front and sang *Amazing Grace* a cappella. The graveside service following the memorial service in the chapel was conducted military style. A horse drawn carriage was used to transport the casket causing all of us who followed to watch our step. Military stood at attention in endless rows and gave a four-gun salute. A military band played and four F14s flew overhead with one splitting off and going straight up to signify the departure of one of the corps.

*Thoughts & Feelings:* It was an amazing experience to be at an event to honor Pete Conrad and be in the presence of all these famous astronauts who pioneered human space travel and went to the moon and first flew the Shuttle. One cannot help but feel goose bumps at such an occasion remembering and honoring one of the pioneering astronauts.

    I was amazed to find Senator John Glenn standing alone on one of the cemetery streets with no one within a hundred yards. When I walked toward him, he remembered me from his time seven months earlier in Huntsville and said, "Hi, Art" before I had a chance to remind him of my name. We talked for 10 minutes or so about Pete Conrad's funeral ceremony and the celebration/parade following his October Shuttle flight we had in Huntsville last December. He spoke about the Huntsville visit as special for him. It was weird having to say good-bye because my ride was scheduled to leave. How awkward and torn I felt as I cut our conversation short and walked away from the first U.S. astronaut to orbit the earth. As I got some distance away, I turned around and there he was still standing alone. Perhaps he was thinking about Pete Conrad and some experience they had together or perhaps he was thinking about his first flight on Marshall's Redstone Rocket to orbit the earth or perhaps he was saying a prayer for all astronauts who risk their lives to move humans beyond earth's bonds. I don't know but I sensed that he was comfortable being alone and decided he was an introvert (like me). He proved that even an introvert could leave his private, solitary place and do amazing things in life as a test pilot, astronaut and U.S. Senator. Not long after that day John retired from the Senate.

------------------------------------------------------

*Editorial Note:* I can't adequately share how impressed I was with this great man. For me he was someone who seemed to do things right throughout his life. He adopted an approach to life that is aligned with today's standards for astronauts. He did not join in on wild parties typical of test pilots in those days. Most importantly, he stood up against extreme political pressures when he felt he should. An example of this was when he was getting ready for his flight and President Johnson called him asking him to ask his wife, who struggled with stuttering and a fear of the press, to go out and meet with the hordes of press people in her front yard. He politely told the president, "No." He always seemed to take the high road.

---

After leaving John Glenn I rejoined my group in the awaiting van and went to a reception for a little while. I spoke with Judy and Dan Goldin at the reception. Judy spoke warmly of her visit to Huntsville, the Marshall Picnic and meeting Loa.

We returned to Florida in time for a big reception sponsored by TRW and MSFC. I was hosting this event although TRW paid for it. We were launching Chandra that had been designed and manufactured by TRW with oversight by MSFC. It was great to gather with my family, personal friends, TRW friends I had worked with for years, and my NASA and contractor friends. I gave another speech about Shuttle and Chandra but frankly right now I don't remember what I said. The wife of the scientist for whom the Chandra X-Ray Telescope was named in absentia was there and I enjoyed visiting with her. I invited her to go to the Chandra ground station at the Smithsonian Astrophysical Observatory in Cambridge, Massachusetts. She said she would like to do that.

Tuesday, July 20, 1999
The first launch attempt occurred at 12:30 A.M. We counted

down to 8 seconds from liftoff with no problems and then suddenly an abort was called. I was surprised like everyone else. One of the engineers had detected what he thought was a leak in the aft engine compartment I had viewed two weeks before. It turned out to be a "burp" in a ground pump and nothing more, but the launch had been scrubbed. Any engineer on console in the Launch Control Center, can call out a concern and stop the launch. Safety is front and center. As always thousands of people showed up to witness the launch. The first lady, Hillary Clinton, and the World Cup woman's Soccer team had flown in to see the launch but were denied.

*<u>Thoughts & Feelings</u>: The feeling of being responsible for the Shuttle propulsion is overwhelming. Two minutes on the solid rockets and three main engines followed by another six and one-half minutes with the main engines continuing to burn was a long time to hold one's breath and was accompanied by a lot of prayers on my part. I take it very seriously because if something goes wrong, we could have another "Challenger" type accident and MSFC would have to answer to the world. These launches have been the tensest eight and one-half minutes in my life experience and I will be repeating it every time there is a Shuttle launch while I remain in this position. With every launch I pray for the safety of the astronauts going from earth to orbit in eight and one-half minutes.*

After the late night/early morning, I slept some and took most of Tuesday off visiting with good friends (Klinkers, Finleys, Longs, and Mehls). It was good to see them, and I enjoyed the casual interaction. They were real troupers and decided to stay for the next launch attempt scheduled for two days hence.

Wednesday, July 21, 1999.
Back to work – I met with the main engine folks from Rocketdyne, visited the Solid Rocket Booster facility and toured the operations there that Marshall is responsible for.

Thursday, July 22, 1999
We got an early start with another launch attempt planned for about the same time – 12:30 A.M. Hillary Clinton came back for it from Washington. This time weather was a factor and we wound up not launching again. A cloud cell seemed to hover in the area holding us up. We all thought it would move out of the way at first but then it did not move as fast as predicted and grew in size. Toward the end of the planned launch window time, the Marshall Chandra team said they could handle a larger launch window but that turned out not to be enough and once again the launch was scrubbed.

*Thoughts & Feelings: I felt helpless to make it happen and embarrassed that our Chandra team had not figured out and made available the maximum launch window to begin with.*

Dan Goldin, I found out later, was upset because he was led to believe we could have launched if MSFC had used the new criterion. We will not really know if we could have launched but I was in trouble with Dan because of our team's recalculation of the launch window. Delaying the launch cost the program over an estimated $1M.

Each time we had a launch delay after sleeping for a few hours I went running and then took a swim in the Atlantic Ocean. That evening I went to dinner with friends and then headed for the Launch Control Center while our friends went to the Banana Creek Viewing area hoping the third time would be the launch everyone was anxious to see.

Friday, July 23, 1999
Like the earlier launch attempts, this one was also scheduled

for 12:30 AM. Would the third attempt go? This time the launch countdown went per the plan. However immediately after liftoff STS-93 commander, Eileen Collins, was on the intercom talking about a problem. This being my fourth launch in the Launch Control Center (LCC) Firing Room, I had never heard any problems having to be addressed from Shuttle commanders or pilots on the way to orbit because all had gone well on my previous launches. Something was wrong. I was praying like never before. Everything after liftoff is automatic except the crew can switch to backup systems. A short on the main power bus took out controllers in Main Engines #1 and #3 (there are only three engines)

STS-93 Columbia Launch
--- Credit: NASA Photo

but the backup controllers did their job when the crew switched Main Engine power to the backup system. As we held our breath, Columbia, the oldest orbiter, made it to orbit but a little under speed and seven miles below the planned orbit altitude. We ran out of liquid Oxygen. There was a second problem we did not hear about during launch. I was told after the launch one of the engines was running 100 degrees hotter than normal. In reviewing video, they determined the next day that there was likely a leak in the engine nozzle – a serious situation. This was caused by a plug pin in one of many engine oxidizer injection posts coming loose during engine ignition and hitting the nozzle cutting three cooling tubes in the nozzle. There had been two malfunctions on this flight but Eileen and her pilot initially only knew about the electrical short. Columbia arrived on orbit a bit lower than planned but these two failures did not jeopardize the mission.

*Thoughts & Feeling: Very scary with two propulsion problems on the way up. I was not sure what the problems were at the time. If I had known about them in more detail, I would have been even more concerned.*

After Columbia successfully reached orbit, three of us went from the Launch Control Center to the Vertical Assembly Building over on the Air Force side of Cape Canaveral to witness the deployment of the Chandra X-Ray Observatory out of the Orbiter payload bay – no sleep tonight. I got there as the Payload bay doors on the Orbiter opened and could see the Chandra connected to the Air Force's Inertial Upper Stage (IUS) inside the bay. We watched through the night as the Chandra was turned on and then eventually tilted up and deployed out of the Shuttle bay. The Shuttle backed away a number of miles from the Chandra/IUS. The IUS was then commanded, from an Air Force ground station, to execute ignition and its two required burns. Sitting next to MSFC's Program Manager and the Chandra Chief Scientist, who had spent over 20 years on the program, we all were nervous as we waited to hear how the IUS performed during its two required burns. The last time this upper stage propulsion system had been used it failed causing the loss of the satellite it was boosting to a higher orbit. MSFC had participated in the investigation with the Air Force and we were convinced the investigation team had found and fixed the problem. Nevertheless, this stage is very complex and if it did not work, we would lose the $1.5B observatory. We were supposed to get telemetry through a ground station in Diego Garcia (an island south of India in the Indian Ocean) but they reported they had not gotten any telemetry signal throughout the planned time period for the two burns. We pushed back feelings of panic. Again, for the second time today, I was praying for delivery to the desired orbit. Finally, after way too long (and we had all turned blue), we heard another ground station in England say they received a signal from Chandra/IUS, and Chandra's orbit had been altered to a highly elliptical orbit as expected with both IUS stages burning as prescribed. I found out 4 days later that the ground station in Diego Garcia had been improperly configured with a switch out of place and that is why they did not pick up the expected downlinked telemetry signal.

*Thoughts & Feeling: Major, Big Relief*

After that the Chandra Solar Arrays deployed perfectly, the Inertial Upper Stage separated from Chandra and we celebrated before heading for a bed at 10 A.M.

*Thoughts & Feelings: Joy and relief – a great feeling of team success.*

Before going to bed I called MSFC in Huntsville and asked to go on the PA system to tell all 6,400 people there that the Chandra launch was successful and congratulated them all for their part in achieving this great Center-wide success. While engineers directly involved in the Shuttle and Chandra programs are key players, everyone including support organizations played a part in this success. It was a big day for NASA and for Marshall Space Flight Center. After I made this announcement recognizing years and years of work by the MSFC team, TRW and many other contractors, I received numerous emails from employees thanking me for letting them know about the successful Chandra deployment in orbit. They were not getting any feedback until this announcement. They had heard the STS-93 launch was successful during the night but not about the IUS orbit insertion. It was a great day for MSFC. Flying home was a lot of fun later that day after we got a couple hours of sleep!

*Thoughts & Feelings: Absolute joy for our Chandra and Shuttle teams and the whole Center as everyone contributed in their own way.*

Monday, July 26, 1999
I was in Washington DC for meetings at NASA Headquarters and at the end of the day I joined Dan Goldin and several others as we flew to Kennedy Space Center to witness the STS 93 Columbia Orbiter landing. With MSFC not being involved in Shuttle Orbiter landings this was to be my first time to witness a landing. We arrived only to discover the landing would be postponed due to Florida weather. Columbia had not started its de-orbit burns so it remained in orbit. We flew back to Washington DC and I caught a flight back to Huntsville, Alabama determined to see Eileen Collins land the Orbiter on the next attempt.

Wednesday, July 28, 1999
I flew to Orlando on a commercial airline and drove a rented car to Kennedy Space Center intending to tour the Solid Rocket Booster refurbishment facility where the boosters, having landed in the ocean, are towed back by boats, cleaned and disassembled. I would then attend the landing of STS 93

that evening. News broke during the day that NASA's budget for fiscal year 2000 was being cut by 11 % relative to 1999 ($1.4B) by the House subcommittee. Dan Goldin, in a press release let it be known that if this budget passed in both houses of Congress, he would consider closing 1 to 3 NASA Centers and would have to lay off a number of civil servants. I knew this would pique the interest of the Alabama Senators and Congressmen. When I got to Florida, I got on the phone for 3 hours and talked to the Alabama delegation in Washington DC (two Senators and two Congressmen) as well as local officials in Huntsville and Madison (two mayors, County Commissioner, Chamber of Commerce Chair) to let them know I was joining Goldin in fighting for the budget that the President had asked for in January following his state of the union message and to thank them for their support. After that I was able to go through the Solid Rocket Booster refurbishment facility. It was interesting seeing the two Solid Rocket Boosters (SRBs) that I had seen on the launch pad ready to go three weeks before and then watched them burn for two minutes getting the Shuttle up to over 5,000 miles per hour and 250,000 feet in elevation. They were charred by the Booster Separation Rockets to move them away from the Orbiter and big orange main engine fuel tank called the External Tank. They were also charred from the aerodynamic heating during re-entry. Water impact caused one of the rings on the booster to tear apart. They showed me the big blown-apart nuts (12" round X 6" thick) that held down the entire Shuttle stack (Orbiter, External Tank, and two SRBs) on the launch pad (four per SRB or eight total). They said the astronauts keep them as souvenirs. (Re-reading this later on, it is interesting to note that the SRB team took note of my interest in these nuts and had one cleaned, chromed and mounted on a plaque and gave it to me – a very nice memento.)

*Thoughts & Feelings: Once again I was amazed at the wide*

*range of things that go on under the direction of Marshall (Orbiter Main Engines, External Tank, and Solid Rocket Boosters).*

The Orbiter retrofitting/processing between flights occurs at KSC. The External Tank, having been manufactured in Louisiana and shipped to KSC, burns up after separation from the Orbiter nine minutes after launch when the Orbiter main engines have used all or nearly all of its liquid oxygen and hydrogen. After disassembly at KSC, the SRB's four segments are sent back by train to Thiokol in Utah to be refurbished and reused on another flight.

<u>Now to the Landing</u>: I met Roy Bridges, Director of Kennedy Space Center, in his office at 9:30 P.M. as planned. We drove out to the Skid Strip and awaited Administrator Dan Goldin's plane from Washington DC. His flight from Washington DC had been delayed and operators at the Air Force controlled landing strip at Cape Canaveral where KSC is located were denying requests to land. The area had been restricted because the Orbiter was expected to land soon. I guess Dan threatened to call the President or something, but they finally allowed his plane to land. I rode with Dan and Roy in Roy's car while Dan's entourage rode in a van behind us. Goldin's late arrival caused the need for a police escort at 70 mph to get over to the Shuttle Landing Facility runway – with five minutes to spare. As we got out of the car, we could hear the Shuttle Communication link chatter on loud speakers. Commander Eileen Collins said a few words as the unpowered Columbia Orbiter rapidly descended passing through 50,000 feet elevation. The first female commander was at the controls of the Orbiter. We could hear the Orbiter before we could see it as it approached the runway in the dark. It sounded like an approaching freight train. The noise was caused by air rushing over the very hot underbody of the Orbiter that had been heated to 2000 degrees F by

aerodynamic heating during re-entry into the atmosphere. This being a night landing, we finally saw the Shuttle flash into the halogen lights as it shot past the end of the runway and made a perfect landing and roll out passing in front of a grandstand crowd with rousing applause.

After the excitement of the landing the Orbiter had to cool down before the crew could emerge from the vehicle. We waited while Dan conducted numerous press interviews. We then drove over to the KSC Crew Quarters that are about 10 minutes away to greet the immediate family of the astronauts who were waiting there for the crew. Of course, they were relieved and very happy for their loved one's safe return. After a short while we drove back out onto the landing strip and drove up next to the Orbiter, bathed in lights and still cracking with sounds as it cooled down. We awaited the emergence of the astronauts and their walk down the steps of the tall ramp that had been rolled up to the Orbiter with a medical unit on top. The crew would pass through it before coming down the ramp to the runway. I was standing next to Administrator Dan Goldin. We greeted them reception lineup style. I thanked each for their good work in deploying Marshall's Chandra X-Ray Telescope. They all expressed their excitement having played their part in making history with the launch of this historic observatory. We then walked around the Orbiter Vehicle and I thoroughly enjoyed listening to the Crew's comments about how beautiful a ship Columbia is and comments like kidding Eileen that she had missed the center line by six inches to which she responded that the runway lights were offset six inches and she hit the line of the lights perfectly. Eileen impressed me. She was very real. When I asked her how she felt right after launch when the anomalies occurred, she said she was not nervous during the launch when things were not going well as the engine Digital Controllers failed and they had to rely on the backup units. She said they had practiced this exact failure many times and it just seemed natural to switch to the backup electrical system. She explained her relief when, on the way up to orbit, she was told they could make it to a landing in Africa and then, later, with more altitude gain, they heard they could make it to orbit even if one engine failed. (These notifications happened on every Shuttle launch, but this launch was different because of the power bus failure.) Her feelings about these events along the timeline were like mine as I remember standing in the firing room. However, I was firmly standing on the ground and she was riding on and in charge of the Orbiter. She said that although she was not nervous "going up-hill" she was nervous coming down to the landing. She said, "Explain that one." I thought, no male Commander would admit being nervous about anything but here was a woman who was totally honest with me. She said, "How embarrassed I would be if I did not land perfectly!" For those who may not know this, the Orbiter has very small wings compared to a commercial airliner and flies like a rock so to speak. It comes down to the runway at a much steeper angle and the vehicle, being unpowered (called dead stick) has only one shot at flaring to make a landing. There is no room for error.

     I spent time talking to another member of the crew, Cady Coleman, who was the astronaut responsible for deploying Chandra/IUS out of the Orbiter payload bay using the Canadian robotic arm. She wanted to know how the video had come out. I was surprised to find out the crew had not seen the video as we did on the ground following the deployment. I told her during deployment the sun reflected off the spacecraft in a way that created the shape of a perfect Cross. We both got a little teary eyed about that. I also had some time to talk to Steve Hawley who was the flight engineer astronaut on this mission. He talked about how beautiful it was to see Chandra fly out of the bay of the Orbiter. At some point along the way I invited Cady and Steve to MSFC and also to the Chandra X-Ray Center in

Cambridge, Mass. They all seemed eager to meet the teams that had put the Chandra together and will operate it.

Joining up with Eileen again, I looked on as the astronauts were looking at the tires. The Orbiter comes in at about 200 knots so the tires smoke as they hit the ground. The right tire was shredded a bit. We then walked back to the rear of the vehicle to view the Orbiter Main Engine nozzles and see where the leak was in Engine 3 that caused the Orbiter to run out of liquid Oxygen prematurely placing the Orbiter in a 7-mile lower orbit than planned (143 mi. vs. 150 mi. orbit altitude). With field glasses we could see that the engine nozzle on the inside had a rip across three tubes that was caused by the loose plug pin as the engines ignited on the launch pad.

On the way back to the "Skid Strip" to say goodbye to Dan Goldin and company, I called Loa to relay what a wonderful experience this had been. She said yours truly was on national TV. It is fun to be a part of history in what really was a small way.

Goldin and I talked about a lot of business things during the course of the evening but when we were waiting for the STS 93 crew to come out of the Medical Unit and down the steps, he turned to me and said, "Art, you couldn't do this at Oceaneering." After I agreed, he said, "This is a wonderful thing to be doing and being in NASA is the only way to do it."

*Thoughts & Feelings: This is working out well, thank God. After only 8 months with NASA I was ready to pinch myself. I might pay a lot to do what I just did but instead I get paid to do it. Wow!*

---

Three months after launching Chandra I was talking to our pastor, Larry Dill, one morning at church (Trinity United Methodist Church) after services and I was sharing with him the experience of seeing a brilliant light reflecting off the Chandra observatory in the shape of a Cross as it was lifted out of the Orbiter bay. He asked me to write an article for publication. Here is what I wrote for the March 5 – 11, 2000 church newsletter called "The Trinity Times."

*Title: "Discovering God's Universe with God as a Partner"*

*We are taught as engineers and scientists that the natural laws govern and that if we study them and live within them, we will understand and be able to positively shape our world and our understanding of the larger universe that surrounds us. And so, we go about our business day to day designing and building and flying spacecraft that will further our knowledge and it is all very logical and explainable.*

*But then something happens when we stand at Kennedy Space Center and view the launch of a Space Shuttle; and the experience of blinding light and body buffeting noise brings out feelings that are emotional and we explain to others afterward that it was a Spiritual experience, that God must be a part of this awesome event. Those of us that are involved in the Space Shuttle program know that the vast complexity of the Shuttle Space Transportation system makes it vulnerable to failure and so we do everything we can possibly think of to ensure that everything is right with the Shuttle hardware and software and then, as the clock ticks down to zero and the engines light off, we turn to God and pray for another successful liftoff as the Shuttle rises from the launch pad and eight and one half minutes later it is in orbit travelling at over 17,000 mph.*

*Oh yes, I pray asking God for a successful launch every time I sit in the Launch Control Center at Kennedy Space Center representing Marshall Space Flight Center and the Shuttle propulsion elements for which we are responsible. Although we like to think we have total control* of the situation, we know from events that occur too often that this business is dangerous, and we don't have all of the answers.

This past summer was a high point in many careers for employees at Marshall Space Flight Center and our prime contractor, TRW. We successfully launched the Chandra X-Ray Observatory. People had been working on this program for more than 20 years. A few hours following a challenging launch, I was in the Air Force Payload Operations Center watching the video monitor of the Chandra being deployed from the Shuttle Orbiter. We were listening to Cady Coleman, the astronaut deploying the Chandra/IUS, as she raised the vehicle at an angle in the cargo bay and then pushed a button that sent a command to release it from a spring-loaded mechanism. As the Chandra/IUS slowly moved away from the Orbiter, I experienced something I never expected to see.

Cady was talking about how beautiful the Chandra was as the sun glanced off of the highly reflective mylar insulation material. She was also talking about its awesome mission to catch and resolve faint x-rays emitted from exploding stars thousands of years before that were at such large distances from earth that the X-rays, travelling at the speed of light (186,000 miles per second) were just arriving at the earth. Suddenly the light reflection off of the telescope became extremely bright and formed into the distinct shape of a Cross and held this image for what seemed like a long time.

It struck me then that we were sending this new telescope out to view the universe but by the grace of God and in His time. God is with us, but he is also a long way out in front of us, guiding, revealing, and in so doing, loving us as a parent loves a newborn child but with intensity we can't imagine.

Space launch and exploration are not only the application of engineering and science as we have learned *through trial and experience. This business is about a partnership with God that is really happening with His loving oversight. We cannot go forward without it.*

*Art Stephenson*
*Director, Marshall Space Flight Center*

Writing today in December 2018 I remember Chandra had some initial on-orbit issues but those were successfully addressed, and the Observatory has been successfully operating ever since.

Dan Goldin asked me to accept an award recognizing the Chandra team's accomplishment. On November 9, 2000 I had the honor of accepting the National Air and Space Museum's prestigious 2000 Trophy for Current Achievement awarded to the Chandra X-Ray Observatory team at a black-tie event at the Museum in Washington DC. This award recognizes the individual who or team that had achieved what was considered the most outstanding accomplishment in space that year. I wish all of the MSFC, TRW and Smithsonian Astrophysical Observatory Chandra team members could have been there to receive this award for they are the ones who were being recognized, certainly not me.

## Chapter 17

# MSFC Space Program Challenges

*"Whatever you do, work at it with your whole heart.... It is the Lord Christ you are serving."*
--- Colossians 3:23, 24 (NIV)

In addition to the challenges on the X-Ray Observatory, I found MSFC had difficult challenges on just about every program at the Center. This is not unusual based on the type of technically challenging programs NASA regularly undertakes. Our oversight of the International Space Station (ISS) Italian modules caused me to make a trip to Italy to address cost issues and the resulting delivery delays. Also, the ISS Standard Equipment Rack contract with Boeing had cost overrun challenges. Technical issues are a part of NASA programs because NASA works on cutting edge technology. Our project to recycle astronaut urine and waste water to be used as drinking water onboard the ISS was a difficult cutting-edge technical challenge that took far longer than expected but eventually has been successfully implemented on the ISS.

From the beginning of the Shuttle program the top program safety of flight risk was the Shuttle Main Engines. During development of these engines there were numerous tests that resulted in catastrophic failures on the test stand.

The engines operate at extremely high pressure (5,500 psi) and temperatures (1,500 degrees F). In 1986 NASA initiated an upgrade program to redesign the high-pressure Liquid Oxygen and Liquid Hydrogen pumps. The Oxygen pump upgrade was successfully completed before I arrived at NASA, but the Hydrogen pump was having manufacturing problems at Pratt & Whitney. Two weeks after I took the reins of Marshall Space Flight Center, I received a call from Dan Goldin. He started the conversation by saying something like, "You are going to kill astronauts aboard Shuttle if you don't finish the redesign of the Main Engine high pressure, liquid hydrogen, fuel pump. Get on it." Within a couple of days after that call I was on a plane headed for Pratt & Whitney with the Shuttle Main Engine team. The new pump manufacturing process was causing cracks in the walls of the pump. The inspection process at Pratt and Whitney, was not adequate. Over the next three months, MSFC helped them develop improved inspection techniques. We initiated an investigation and after some effort working with Pratt and Whitney, the cracking problem was resolved. Two years later, after extensive testing, the first new Hydrogen pump was flown on a Shuttle mission and proved very successful. This improved fuel pump along with the improved liquid oxygen pump resulted in more than doubling the reliability of the Orbiter Main Engines.

I went to view an upgraded Shuttle Orbiter Main Engine test firing at Stennis Space Center. It just so happened John Young, my hero, the commander of the first Shuttle flight into space, was also there to view the engine test. I asked him to join me as we watched this magnificent event. Before we went out on the roof of the test control center building, I was given a large umbrella with word that if the plume from the 8 ½ minute rocket engine firing headed our way due to winds we would need the umbrella. You see the main engines burn liquid oxygen and liquid hydrogen

Observing Upgraded Shuttle Orbiter Main Engine test firing with John Young at Stennis Space Center
--- Credit: NASA Photo

STS Orbiter Main Engine Test Firing
--- Credit: NASA Photo

and guess what --- it produces H2O or water. And the water plume came right at us. The umbrella I held for John and me was not enough to keep us from getting wet. After this experience I thought --- Wow, I just stood with my hero, John Young, and watched one of the three engines that propelled this man into space on the first Shuttle flight!

Another Shuttle Space Transportation System issue was foam coming off the External Tank. According to analyses performed by Johnson Space Center experts, the foam was not a flight safety issue but only a maintenance issue. Foam had been coming off the External Tank from the beginning of the program and it would hit the underside of the Orbiter on the heat shield ceramic tiles damaging them but not causing a safety of flight issue.

Over the course of my time, NASA launched 22 Shuttle missions. I was in the Launch Control Center Firing Room for every launch except two. When I could not be there my deputy would fill in for me.

The X vehicles MSFC was overseeing in 2000 were struggling. The contracts were written in such a way that Marshall could not direct the work. Marshall was powerless to help the prime contractors other than to seek more funding for these programs. Frankly, we were not motivated to seek more funding since the contractors had signed fixed price contracts. Marshall's role was to provide testing support to the X vehicle prime contractors per agreements signed when the contracts were let and that was all MSFC was to do.

As mentioned earlier, MSFC was responsible for three Experimental (X) launch vehicles contracts: Lockheed Martin for X-33, Orbital Sciences Corporation for X-34, and Boeing for X-37.

Lockheed Martin's X-33 was to be a demonstrator for the future "Venture Star" single stage to orbit launch vehicle. The test vehicle being designed and built by Lockheed Martin, smaller than the final Venture Star configuration, was to demonstrate key new, revolutionary technology including a new aerospike propulsion engine and a lightweight composite tank technology. The vehicle flight goal was to fly to an altitude of 250,000 feet and land 450 miles away from the launch site thereby demonstrating the feasibility of ultimately achieving single stage to orbit with the larger vehicle. During my first year at MSFC I went to Lockheed Martin's Sunnyvale, California, plant to observe the composite tank under construction. I also went to Rocketdyne in Canoga Park, California, to learn about their aerospike engine under development for the X-33.

The goal of the X-33 program was to develop and demonstrate technologies that would lead to a reduction in cost of launching payloads to orbit from $10,000/lbs. to $1000/lbs. If successful, this breakthrough would greatly increase access to space. While in test at Marshall the X-33 composite tank cracked. At that point the program explored the use of lightweight aluminum tanks instead of composite tanks, but the weight of these tanks was judged to be too high

Artist's rendition of Lockheed Martin's
Venture Star in low earth orbit.
--- Credit: NASA Photo

to achieve single stage to orbit. The aerospike rocket engine was also experiencing development problems at the same time. Lockheed Martin was experiencing cost growth issues and had asked NASA for more funding to continue the development.

Orbital Sciences Corporation's X-34 vehicle was to serve as a test bed for space launch technologies that could be evaluated when flown to an altitude of about 250,000 feet before returning to land on an airport runway. The plan was to launch the vehicle off an aircraft carrier vehicle at about 40,000 feet altitude, flying out of Edwards Air Force base in California. The vehicle was designed with only one set of flight control avionics. When the development was well along, Dan Goldin surprised us when he called me and said he wanted the vehicle to have a second set of avionics. He was concerned for the safety of people below the flight path if a failure occurred and insisted on adding a backup set of avionics. Unfortunately, the vehicle did not have room in the avionics compartment for a redundant set of avionics.

A third X vehicle, X-37, was being designed and manufactured by Boeing under a fixed price contract with MSFC. This vehicle was to be launched on an expendable launch vehicle and have the capability to stay for long periods of time in orbit using a deployed solar array. The vehicle was to return from orbit and land on a runway. This program also encountered development issues requiring additional funding.

While these development issues were coming to light Congress approved a $5B new program led by MSFC to advance launch vehicle capabilities encompassing a wide range of associated component and subsystem technologies and new launch vehicle concepts including two stage to orbit concepts with the first stage returning to land on a runway. We had worked for a year to sell this program to the President and Congress. The idea for this new program,

Orbital Science's X-34 Mockup
--- Credit: NASA Photo

Artist's rendition of Boeing's X-37
--- Credit: NASA Photo

known as the Space Launch Initiative (SLI), came out of Marshall's Space Transportation Directorate. I took the concept to Dan Goldin and asked him for support in selling it to the President's Office of Management and Budget (OMB) and to Congress. OMB works with the President to put together the President's budget that goes to the Congress following the President's State of the Union message to Congress each February. In addition to OMB, I asked Dan for his approval to let us approach multiple Senators and Congressmen and their staffs to gain congressional support for this program. Surprisingly, Dan said go ahead. It was unusual for any NASA Center Director to interface directly with a member of the U.S. House or Senate other than his or her own state representatives. The Alabama delegation helped me gain an audience with a number of key members of the House and Senate. While I was the only one seeing members of the House and Senate, the Space Transportation Directorate SLI team, with the help of the Customer and Employee Relations Directorate, played a major role by briefing OMB and congressional member staffs. Members of Congress viewed the new launch technology that would come from this program as critical for competing in commercial space launch on a world stage and also keeping our military launch capability ahead of our country's adversaries. The OMB office personnel I briefed, with the help of SLI program manager, Dennis Smith, convinced the President to back the program. When the President decided to adopt this program, Dan Goldin asked me to represent NASA and join the President's Science Advisor in announcing the Space Launch Initiative program at a conference in Washington D.C. After the President put the program funding in his proposed FY2000 budget, submitted to Congress in February 1999, we worked with members of Congress to obtain approval of the program and support for passage of the bill that authorized SLI funds in the FY2000 budget. With the government fiscal year starting in October, we issued requests for proposals from industry in November 1999 and began awarding contracts in February 2000. As I mentioned earlier, the X-33, X-34 and X-37 prime contractors were requesting additional funds from NASA. They were told they could only receive additional funding for their programs by winning proposals submitted in response to MSFC's Space Launch Initiative (SLI) requests for proposals (RFPs). The RFPs addressed wide-ranging technologies that would advance Launch vehicle system and subsystem technologies. Also, RFPs addressed system level launch vehicle concepts. As I recall when the SLI proposals were evaluated, including proposals submitted by Lockheed Martin for X-33 follow-on and Orbital Sciences for X-34 follow-on, the proposal evaluation teams, convened by Marshall with technical experts from multiple NASA Centers, did not recommend awarding contracts submitted by the X-33 or X-34 contractors. I had the unhappy job of telling the NASA Administrator neither program was selected for further funding. The X launch vehicle programs were his invention and he expressed his sadness in seeing both of these programs terminated. He turned to me and said you will be the one to announce NASA's decision to terminate both programs. So, one unhappy day soon thereafter, sitting with a phone in NASA Headquarters in Washington DC, I announced these program cancellations on a conference phone call to a group of twenty-some interested members of the press and took their questions. The X-33, and to a lesser extent, X-34 program were highly publicized programs and cancellation of these programs received nationwide press coverage. It was the first time and the last I would hear myself talking on a taxi's radio as I was driven to the Washington National airport to fly home that evening.

The Boeing's X-37 demonstrator vehicle was adopted by the Air Force when NASA did not continue funding for it, and it went on to be launched to orbit numerous times by expendable launch vehicles and operated in space for months at a time. The objective of these Air Force missions has never been revealed to my knowledge.

Nearly $1B in Space Launch Initiative contracts were awarded over the next year, but like the MLV launch vehicle program proposal I managed at TRW, the champion for the program, Dan Goldin, moved on, retiring from NASA in 2001. His replacement, Sean O'Keefe, decided to move in a different direction. He cancelled the Space Launch Initiative program. My many experiences working on government programs that were cancelled, leaves me with a sad feeling. Had Dan Goldin remained as the NASA Administrator I am convinced the SLI program would have developed component and subsystem technologies and revealed new reusable launch vehicle concepts that would have greatly assisted this nation's space launch capabilities. Rather than NASA leading the way to new launch concepts, over a longer period of time, commercial launch vehicles, such as Space X, and more recently, Blue Origin, are causing the revolution in launch vehicle technology we at NASA were advocating.

Another MSFC program had a very interesting history. It was the longest running development program in NASA's history --- 40 years. Gravity Probe B was to be an earth orbiting spacecraft designed to test two unverified predictions of Einstein's general relativity: the geodetic effect and frame-dragging. This was to be accomplished by measuring tiny changes in the direction of spin of four gyroscopes contained in an Earth orbiting satellite crossing directly over the poles at a 400-mile altitude. If you don't understand the previous two sentences you are not alone. The significance of the reference to four gyros was that these gyros needed to be maintained at a very low temperature. The gyroscopes were housed in a dewar of helium to maintain a temperature near absolute zero (0 degrees Kelvin or minus 456 degrees F). Precise required measurements accurate to 1 part in 10,000 was no small feat. Placing the Dewar on a spacecraft and launching it into space while keeping the gyros at a temperature near absolute zero for the one-year mission was very challenging for designers. The program was managed by Stanford University with Lockheed Martin as the subcontractor to manufacture the spacecraft.

Rex Geveden was the NASA Gravity Probe B program manager at MSFC. He joked that the program was older than he was having been in development for nearly 40 years. The Gravity Probe B Principle Investigator was Francis Everitt. He had dedicated his entire career to this mission. He came to my office asking me to support his efforts to keep his program going every year. The Space Science arm at NASA headquarters recommended cancellation of the program year after year. Every year Francis went to Congress and managed to have them reinstate the program with a minimum amount of NASA funding which kept the program alive with a small staff but resulted in delay after delay stretching the program completion out in time. Each year NASA had to redirect funds from other programs to support this program they always tried to cancel. The only reason the program had not been cancelled, I am convinced, was because of Francis' efforts to keep it alive. I did what I could, through the Alabama delegation in Congress, to keep this MSFC program going.

As I mentioned earlier, as a result of the Mars Climate Orbiter Investigation, I had directed our Marshall Engineering Directorate to review every MSFC program to ensure NASA had the right amount of oversight and insight into the requirements verification process to ensure program success. This meant our engineers were to look into the proper amount of testing and analysis on each of our programs. The deployment of the legs on the Mars Polar Lander spacecraft caused the spacecraft to prematurely shut down the landing retro-reactor thrusters used to slow the rate of descent of the spacecraft as it approached the surface of Mars. The result was the spacecraft was destroyed as it crashed into the Mars surface. As discussed earlier if the proper test had been conducted this failure could have been easily detected and corrected.

The Gravity Probe B program was one that had limited MSFC oversight and almost no technical insight. Historically Gravity Probe B (GPB) was set up to run with little involvement by Marshall engineers. In response to the review I had requested of each of Marshall's programs, the engineers looking into the GPB requirement verification processes went to Stanford University and asked the GPB program office to provide analyses or test results showing compliance with each GPB component, subsystem and system performance requirement. The GPB team at Stanford knew they had run most of the requested analyses and tests at the component, subsystem and system level, but due to turnover in personnel and a lack of a rigorous process to retain records of compliance, they could not provide all of the requested analyses and test results. The MSFC engineers said, if you don't have this information, you need to perform the missing analyses and tests. This would have caused a massive effort by a small team at Stanford. That is when I received a call from Francis Everett who told me about the impossible situation I had created. I met with the Marshall team looking into the GPB verification process to understand the situation. The GPB team at Stanford, I was told, did not have the human resources or time to give the MSFC team what they wanted. After hearing this, I re-directed the MSFC engineering team to look at the planned testing going forward to see what those tests would verify or not verify in terms of each requirement. This should eliminate the need to go back and verify those requirements that would be verified by the upcoming system level tests. After that, given the list of requirements still needing to be verified, I asked the team to determine what analyses and tests needed to be done to ensure program success. When they did this the list of analyses and tests needed was drastically reduced and the Stanford/Lockheed Martin Team agreed to do this needed work.

When the Gravity Probe B spacecraft was in final thermal vacuum test, I got the news Ed Weiler, NASA Associate Administrator for Space Science, was holding a review of the program and the member of his staff overseeing Gravity Probe B was recommending, once again, the program be cancelled. She wanted to cancel with the final thermal vacuum system test in process. I found this to be incredible. I went to the meeting at NASA Headquarters with Rex Geveden. Ed agreed to wait for the results of the thermal vacuum test. We agreed that if a major issue was revealed during this final test the program could be cancelled. The final system test was successful and finally

Artist's rendition of Gravity Probe B in low earth orbit.
--- Credit: NASA Photo

the spacecraft, after more than 40 years in development, headed to the launch pad at Vandenberg Launch facility on the West coast.

In 2004, six months after I left NASA, I got a call. It was Rex calling to say he had just watched the successful launch of the Gravity Probe B spacecraft. It was good to celebrate this long-awaited milestone with Rex.

After operating successfully on orbit for its planned mission life of one year, Francis Everett called me one day when I was working at Northrop Grumman and told me the spacecraft experiment had successfully confirmed Einstein's theory of general relativity. Francis was a happy man.

The successful implementation of the MSFC Payload Operations Center (POC) was a great success during my time at Marshall. This Center was set up to train astronauts to operate ISS onboard science experiments and to schedule astronaut conducted experiments accounting for

First official call to International Space Station by Art Stephenson and Dan Mulville on February 3, 2001.
---Credit: The Huntsville Times

limited power available to experiments. This Operations Center looks very much like the ISS Mission Control Center in Houston at Johnson Space Center. Operators at consoles in the POC are monitoring space science payloads in test and the associated power, temperature, etc. The POC team sets up schedules for the astronauts to perform experiments and works with them to conduct the experiments. Dan Mulville, NASA's Chief Engineer, and I had the privilege of making the first official call to the International Space Station crew from the POC. Since that call in 2001, with full-time occupation of the ISS, the POC continues to operate 24 hours a day, 365 days a year.

Successful implementation of Marshall's space programs is the basis for the existence of the Center. Since the retirement of the Space Shuttle Transportation System in 2011, Marshall Space Flight Center has been working on a next generation launch vehicle called the Space Launch System with MSFC's prime contractors. This launch vehicle program will initially provide a smaller launch vehicle compared to the Apollo Saturn V launch vehicle but will eventually, as a result of upgrades, provide the same payload weight-to-orbit capability as the Apollo Saturn V launch vehicle. This new Saturn V class launch vehicle will once again support missions back to the moon and eventually support missions to Mars. Marshall continues to have an exciting future.

******

Chapter 18

# Columbia

*"O Lord, the night is so dark and my light so dim. Stay with me through the dark night; bring me to a new and brighter day."*
--- Rueben P. Job

Prior to the launch of STS 107 in January 2003, NASA conducted the routine day and one half Flight Review (FRR) at Kennedy Space Center (KSC). As mentioned earlier, this review was conducted on every Shuttle mission about two weeks prior to the planned launch date. I was there. The Shuttle team went over every aspect of the vehicle to make sure everything that could be done had been done to achieve a safe, successful mission. One of the issues raised was a long-standing concern about insulating foam coming loose from the External Tank and potentially hitting the leading edge of the Orbiter wing. Foam had come off the External Tank during every launch since the beginning of the Shuttle launches, in August 1977, nearly 26 years running. This foam had never hit the leading edge of the Orbiter but consistently hit the underside of the Orbiter requiring some of the thermal tiles to be replaced after every mission. Some chunks of foam were seen coming off of the tank under the nose of the Orbiter where it attached to the tank on the two Shuttle launches prior to STS 107. The MSFC External Tank team had briefed me on this before we left Huntsville to attend the FRR at Kennedy Space Center. Like previous FRRs, Johnson Space Center (JSC) system engineers, who were responsible for the analysis of potential damage to the Orbiter from foam coming off the External Tank, stated at the review, once again, the loose foam was not considered a safety of flight issue. The analysis concluded the foam could not reach the carbon heat shielding panels on the leading edge of the Orbiter but would only strike the underside of the Orbiter causing damage but not catastrophic damage to the Orbiter underside heat shield tiles. Again, this phenomenon had been observed on numerous flights and was only considered a post mission maintenance issue. Unfortunately, everyone who considered this problem was wrong and STS 107 mission would prove they were wrong.

About a year after I joined NASA the agency had adopted a sign off process whereby eight top NASA officials representing the Shuttle program office, the payload, and the four human space flight centers (KSC, JSC, MSFC and Stennis Space Center) all signed a document approving the launch. I signed the STS 107 document along with seven other senior NASA managers. As one of the FRR reviewers, I have often wished I had asked the questions during the FRR the Investigation Board asked after the accident. Hindsight can be so clear.

As I said in Chapter 1, I was surprised by the Saturday morning call from my deputy, Dave King, informing me that the Orbiter was breaking up over Texas. Fifteen days earlier we had launched Columbia successfully and had gone home after another successful Shuttle launch. Our job was to get the Orbiter to orbit. After that Johnson Space Center was responsible for the on-orbit mission and the landing at the end of the mission. We went home pleased with the successful launch. I don't recall being told that foam had been observed hitting the leading edge of the Orbiter. Had I known, I would have been much more concerned about damage to the wing. I expected to hear the landing was successful as always at work Monday morning.

After Dave's Saturday morning call, I asked for all MSFC senior staff and Shuttle managers to join me in our Marshall headquarters ninth floor Conference room one hour later. I recall feeling really low as I drove to the Center and seeing a very sad group of people come together for that meeting. We started the meeting with a silent prayer. I prayed for the families of the crew, for the NASA workforce and for guidance as to what to do going forward with the failure investigation. We then discussed the situation. I was informed at that time that the foam coming off the External Tank actually was observed, via the launch pad high resolution cameras, hitting the leading edge of the Orbiter during launch soon after it lifted off the launch pad.

Some days later I learned JSC (Johnson Space Center) and NASA Headquarters Shuttle managers wrestled with what the condition of the Columbia Orbiter wing might be after being hit by the foam coming off the External Tank. It was something JSC's analyses had not considered since their analysis concluded this would not happen. Looking at the situation while the 15-day mission was in progress, they believed the velocity of the foam when it hit the wing would not be high enough to cause damage to the wing leading edge heat shield panels. The JSC Shuttle leadership held the view that foam coming off the External Tank was like a car going down a highway hitting an empty lightweight Styrofoam cooler coming out of the back of a pickup truck ahead of the car and, as we all know, this would not cause severe, if any, damage to the car because the speed of the foam and car at impact would be close to the same. Thus, the wing condition should be OK. After the disaster I learned that the NASA Headquarters and JSC managers dealing with this situation determined that even if the wing was damaged, which they doubted, there was nothing that could be done to rescue the crew as they waited on-orbit for recovery before their

Orbiter life support systems were exhausted. This assessment was based on the fact that the Columbia on-orbit stay time was not sufficient to be able to move another Shuttle to the launch pad and launch it in time to make a rescue. I don't know and never heard whether or not launching Russian Soyuz launch vehicle(s) was considered as a rescue option.

The STS 107 mission did not go to the ISS as its mission was a microgravity mission with no need to go to the ISS. The last 16 Shuttle launches, going back to February 2000, two years before, had all been International Space Station (ISS) assembly missions with the exception of the Hubble Space Telescope servicing mission in March 2002, nearly a year before STS 107. Had this happened on a mission to the ISS, the wing damage would have been observed and, in that case, the crew could have remained on board the ISS until an Orbiter could be launched to rescue them.

The crew of STS 107 was never told about the foam hitting the leading edge of the Orbiter wing. Their last televised transmission, just minutes before entering the blackout period during re-entry into the atmosphere, was a joyous time with astronauts happily talking about a great mission and coming home.

This mission was a MSFC payload mission to conduct microgravity experiments in the SpaceHab module mounted in the Orbiter cargo bay. This module was a laboratory that astronauts could pass into via a connecting tube from the Orbiter lower crew compartment located below the cockpit. MSFC microgravity experiment engineers had worked closely with the Columbia astronauts preparing them to conduct the mission science experiments and knew the crew first hand. Folks at Marshall were really grieving the loss of the crew. Many had worked directly with them training them for the mission.

When I walked into the Center the Monday morning after the Saturday disaster, I held an early morning All Hands, Center-wide TV broadcasted meeting. I shared what I knew about the situation, which was very little, and said NASA will get to the bottom of this failure and MSFC and Lockheed Martin, the External Tank manufacturer, will correct the cause of the foam coming off the External Tank. The Shuttle launches will resume safely after that. I talked about how low I was feeling about the accident. I could tell how everyone else was feeling by the way his or her head hung low. I said this was the first time since the day I came to Marshall I had not been greeted with warm hellos and smiles. We were all feeling the loss and there was nothing wrong with that. However, I asked people to move beyond mourning if possible and please smile when they see me, as I needed their smiles. I encouraged them to share smiles too if they could. This was a serious time, but I felt the STS 107 crew would not want us to be saddened by this. They knew the risks that come with space flight. The crew would want us to get to work and solve the problem that led to the loss of their spaceship and not stay in a place of sadness.

The loss of the Columbia's crew was a major shock to NASA and particularly a shock to JSC and MSFC. Marshall's Solid Rocket Booster failure during the Challenger launch in 1986 caused the loss of the Challenger crew and there was significant stress on Marshall employees after that disaster. Now, Marshall Shuttle employees, particularly the External Tank team, were wondering if they were at fault for this accident. NASA launched an investigation setting up a Columbia Accident Investigation Review Board.

The Chairman of the Columbia Accident Investigation Board, Harold Gehman Jr, a retired U.S. Navy Admiral, came to MSFC and met with me to describe the investigation process he intended to follow. Harold said the investigation would involve interviews with a number of

Marshall employees and these were conducted over the next two months. I expected to be interviewed but was never asked to do so.

My first concern was for the welfare of Marshall civil servants and contractor personnel. I believed then and, looking back on that time, I continue to believe God placed me at MSFC to deal with this most difficult time. The Customer and Employee Relations Directorate brought in counselors to be available to meet with employees dealing with this difficult situation. I went on Center-wide TV every week to encourage people to take advantage of these counselors, to have someone to talk to about the feelings they were experiencing. I met with a counselor myself and told the employees and contractors that I was doing this. Center-wide TV weekly broadcasts allowed me to let people know what the Accident Investigation Board was doing and what our Shuttle team was doing. I am glad to say we had no threats of suicide and I was told people were able to deal with the situation in a better way than they did after the Challenger accident.

The local and national media were eager to interview us. The first interview with the External Tank program manager did not go well as they seemed eager to talk about who was to blame. After that we decided Marshall employees would refer all media inquiries to the Accident Investigation Board to avoid getting out in front of the board with the news media.

I heard the External Tank manufacturing people at the Michoud Assembly plant in Mississippi were worrying about being at fault, many not able to sleep. I contacted the Shuttle Program manager at JSC, Ron Dittemore, and asked if he would join me at the Michoud assembly plant to address the people there about this situation. We went and my message to them was if they followed specified procedures while applying the foam insulation on the tank, they had nothing to worry about. If they did not, then there may be a problem. They knew they had followed the specified procedures and so I think they were relieved. I said no one was out to find fault that I knew about. The review would go forward as directed by the Accident Investigation Board.

The investigation board, besides launching an extensive interview process with JSC and MSFC Shuttle personnel, started to look at the physics of the effect of the foam hitting the leading edge of the Orbiter. They conducted impact tests in a laboratory recreating the situation during launch. What this investigation revealed was, due to the acceleration of the vehicle lifting off the launch pad, the velocity of the foam at impact was much higher than previous analyses assumed. Between the time the foam broke loose from the tank and hit the Orbiter wing, the high acceleration of the vehicle resulted in a much higher impact speed than the previous analyses had concluded. Also, previous JSC analyses had stated the foam would not ever reach the leading edge of the wing. The investigation team discovered, by analysis and test, air pockets between the insulating foam and the aluminum tank expanding due to the rapid altitude change, could cause an explosive ejection of the foam that could result in the foam reaching the leading edge of the wing.

People asked, after the failure, why did NASA not have a way to 1) observe the front edge of the wing upon reaching orbit and 2) have a way to fix a failure on the heat shield panels on the leading edge of the Orbiter wing if there was damage? Good questions in hindsight. Techniques were developed to do both during the return to flight development efforts prior to the next Shuttle launch.

I won't try to explain more details about the findings of the Columbia Accident Investigation Board. This is readily available on line. The Board report does address the safety culture at NASA. After the loss of Challenger and her crew, NASA implemented some very good processes designed to improve safety. The Columbia accident report

Space Shuttle Columbia STS 107 crew. From left to right are mission specialist David Brown, commander Rick Husband, mission specialist Laurel Clark, mission specialist Kalpana Chawla, mission specialist Michael Anderson, pilot William McCool, and Israeli payload specialist Ilan Ramon.
--- Credit NASA Photo

suggested additional changes to improve safety and these were also implemented by NASA. I can attest to the fact that MSFC already had an excellent safety culture at the time of the Columbia accident. I believe MSFC never lost sight of the importance of safety not only in being responsible for the Shuttle propulsion elements but also safety in the workplace and at home. While the responsibility for understanding whether or not foam could reach the leading edge of the Orbiter, and, whether or not it could do damage was the responsibility of JSC, one could argue, MSFC should have independently done our own assessment. Perhaps we would have come to a different conclusion than JSC did. If I had a second chance at it, I would ask the MSFC team to make an independent study of the foam issue. The Columbia

Accident Investigation Board did recommend, and NASA did implement the establishment of a separate, new safety and engineering center organization reporting to a non-human space flight center, Langley Research Center, to independently assess all aspects of the Shuttle safety prior to each Shuttle mission.

A group of us from Marshall flew to Houston on the morning of the STS 107 crew memorial service held on the Johnson Space Center grounds. A very large crowd had gathered in the middle of the Center, outdoors between buildings. President George W. Bush spoke along with many others, including Sean O'Keefe, NASA Administrator. It was a blur to me. I just remember feeling so sorry for the families that had lost their loved ones.

A few days later the town of Huntsville, Alabama held our memorial service for the STS 107 crew in Huntsville's Von Braun Center Music Hall. There was standing room only. Those of us, who spoke, spoke from the heart. The speakers, in the order they spoke were:

1. Tereasa Washington, Director of MSFC Customer and Employee Relations
2. Rabbi Jeffry Ballon, Temple B'Nai Shalom
3. Loretta Spencer, Mayor of Huntsville
4. Art Stephenson, MSFC Director
5. Dr. Jan Davis, Director of MSFC Flight Projects
6. Courtney Stadd, Chief of Staff to NASA Administrator
7. Bud Cramer, U.S. Congressman
8. Bob Riley, Governor of Alabama
9. Dr. Gary Bradley, Minister of Mayfair Church of Christ
10. Dr. Bhagabat Sahu, Chairperson, Hindu Cultural Center of North America
11. Mark Daniel, Member of NASA Advisory Committee

12. Rev. Dr. Julius R. Scruggs, Pastor, First Missionary Baptist Church.

As these speakers gathered backstage before the memorial service, I asked that we gather in a circle, hold hands, and pray together, honoring our respective religious faiths, in support of the Columbia crew families and asking God to guide us as we spoke, offering people attending some comfort knowing God's love prevails. It was a special moment for me to pray with government, civic, religious, and political leaders. I felt the presence of the Holy Spirit in that moment. When bad things happen, people come together to support one another, and take time to look to God for strength.

Jan Davis, Shuttle astronaut on three missions, gave a memorable testimony. She spoke about flying in space, circling the earth every 90 minutes with close friends who had done the hard training to be there, and deep friendships that come from that experience. She spoke of her friends that were lost on this mission with tears in her eyes. She spoke from her heart about the knowledge every astronaut has about the risks of space flight. And she spoke about what the STS 107 crew would say to us now about getting to work to return to flight. It was a testimony and moment I will never forget.

Sean O'Keefe, the NASA Administrator, was pressured by Congress to fire some people. Sean took the position no one was to be blamed --- no one intentionally did anything wrong to cause this failure. I believe some people were reassigned to other jobs as a result of this tragedy but as far as I know no one was fired. The Columbia Accident Investigation Board did not recommend anyone be relieved of their job.

As I said earlier, I have consistently moved on to a new job after about 5 years. After that period of time I noticed in the past that my fresh ideas diminished, my ability to make a difference was reduced, and my sense of being able to have a beneficial impact on the organization was declining. People seemed to know what I was going to say before I said it. I would become restless somehow. At four and one half years in the job when the Columbia accident occurred I was not aware of those feelings yet and I had not thought about leaving the Marshall Center Director job. I really enjoyed working with the folks at Marshall and was still energized to keep working to improve our Center culture to more fully embrace our values as we conducted our business.

I also wanted to do more with diversity in our management ranks, giving more opportunities for our minority population. However, after the loss of STS 107, I began to think about leaving, turning over the leadership of MSFC to another person to head the daunting task of overseeing the Shuttle return to flight effort. Discussions with Bill Ready, my boss, NASA Associate Administrator for Human Space Flight, led to a decision for me to step aside as Marshall Space Flight Center Director on June 15, 2003. I shared this decision with the Marshall Team and local press on May 20. I told Bill I wanted to retire at the end of 2003 after more than 5 years with NASA but for the benefit of the Center we agreed I would step down on June 15 to allow a new Center Director to be in place for the six months leading up to the first Shuttle "return to flight" launch which was estimated at that time to be January 2004. (Actually, the next Shuttle launch did not occur until 2 ½ years later in July 2005.) After I announced I would be stepping down as the Center Director, the press immediately asked if I was being forced out as a result of the Columbia loss. My response was, no, that was not the case and it was consistent with my long-standing pattern of moving on after five years in a job. The new Director, I said, needed to be in place during the Shuttle return to flight effort and well beyond the first post Columbia Shuttle flight.

Bill Ready and I agreed I would report to Adena Loston, the Associate Administrator for Education, from June 15 until my planned retirement date of January 9, 2004. My main focus was to support the advancement of the National Space Science and Technology Center (NSSTC) and, in general, to promote NASA STEM (Science, Technology, Engineering and Math) education initiatives. I moved my office to the NSSTC in Huntsville to make it clear to all I was no longer involved in the MSFC business.

(Marshall Star article on my departure: https://marshallstar.msfc.nasa.gov/5-22-03.pdf)

After leaving MSFC I was pleased to read a news release entitled, "Marshall Best Place for Federal Workers." To quote the Huntsville Times article, "A first-ever survey of employee satisfaction in the federal government has pegged Marshall Space Flight Center in Huntsville as the best place to work...... Besides listing Marshall as the best federal sub-agency, the Partnership for Public Service ranked NASA as the top overall federal agency.... The data were drawn from May to August of 2002."

Chapter 19

# MSFC Education Programs

*"Intelligence plus character --- that is the goal of true education."*
--- Martin Luther King. Jr.

Throughout my time at Marshall I was passionate about supporting education initiatives. I believe teachers are the unsung heroes of our nation. They are the ones who shape the future of our nation by inspiring the next generation to pursue their dreams through education. When I first arrived and was introduced to the university and college educators in Huntsville and Madison, I was fascinated with their efforts to encourage young people to grow academically, particularly toward STEM (Science, Technology, Engineering and Mathematics) related subjects/professions. I thought the week-long Space Camps conducted at the U.S. Space and Rocket Center were great motivators for kids to want to be involved in STEM professions. Our oldest grandson, Paul, was a repeating space camper who chose engineering as a profession after attending space camps. The future of NASA and our National Defense is dependent on talented young people wanting to enter technical professions.

Not long after I came to Marshall, I was introduced to a great MSFC-sponsored education program Marshall employees had developed called the Great Moon Buggy Race, conducted at the U.S. Space and Rocket Center. This annual event was for high school and college teams that designed, built and raced human powered vehicles like the Apollo vehicle that astronauts on the moon rode across the landscape. Marshall engineers had developed the fold up moon buggies for the Apollo program. Like the Apollo buggies these student buggies had to fold up into a 4 ft. by 4 ft. space as if to be launched. The time it takes to deploy the buggy from this position into an operational state plus the time it takes to run the obstacle course at the U.S. Space & Rocket Center determines the winner. The 4-wheel buggies have to be powered by one man and one woman and usually the wheels are powered by elaborate chain and peddle systems. The two contestants sit side by side or back to back or one behind the other. Typically, 25 high school teams competed on Friday and about the same number of college teams competed on Saturday. Teams come to Huntsville for the weekend competition from all over the United States and,

North Dakota State University students enter
first obstacle on the course.
--- Credit: NASA Photo

when I was involved, one team from Russia and one from Puerto Rico participated. The winners are announced in a ceremony Saturday evening. I loved watching the excitement the teams brought to their task. During these two days Marshall engineers set up a machine/welding shop in the parking lot where all of the teams assemble their buggies. If they have a breakdown on the rough obstacle course on their first run, they can repair their buggy and still do well as the best run between two runs is the one that is used to determine their finishing place. NASA MSFC's media team uses the Marshall TV truck to film interviews with the contestants and send each team's race attempts and interviews to their hometown news outlet.

I could go on and on about my passion for education initiatives and efforts to educate the public on NASA related work that benefit our daily lives. Our MSFC Education department often attended public gatherings to promote NASA's missions and hand out Education materials available to teachers.

One morning I was on my daily run in the neighborhood where we lived and got an idea "out of the blue" to start another annual program to copy the Great Moon Buggy Race but with high school and college teams designing and building solid fueled rockets and microgravity payloads to be launched on these rockets.

The name of this student program would be Student Launch Initiative, the same acronym as the Space Launch Initiative our Center was leading to advance launch technology. The goal was to launch a rocket with a microgravity payload to a height of one mile above the launch pad, deploy the microgravity payload and recover the payload after safely landing. The rocket part of this mission was to connect to MSFC's role in advanced space transportation and the microgravity payload was to connect

Annual MSFC Student Launch Competition draws high school and college teams from across the nation
--- Credit: NASA Photo

to MSFC's agency leadership role in conducting microgravity experiments in space. Marshall's Education

Department did all of the hard work to find funds they did not have to do this event and do all of the work of advertising the opportunity and running the event. My guess is they really were not happy with the boss' idea but never said so and made it happen with joyful perfection. This event has been held annually ever since just like the Great Moon Buggy Race. Forty-five college teams and fifteen high school and middle school teams competed in the Student Launch Competition in 2018.

Every year the U.S. Space and Rocket Center (USS&RC) hosts the "National Teachers of the Year" for a weeklong "Space Camp." Each state (all 50 states plus a couple of U.S. Territories) selects a "best educator" to participate in a number of activities including visiting the President in the Oval Office. The Space Camp is one of their events during their year as "Teacher of the Year" for their state or territory. At the USS&RC they fly in simulators, conduct Shuttle or ISS missions inside mock-ups and launch homemade rockets. They are just kids for a week. I loved going to the opening ceremony and coming back for the closing ceremony. These teachers were just wonderful people --- so excited and motivated to teach their students from what they learned at Space Camp. The second year I was at the Center, at the end of the closing ceremony, I announced they were all invited to attend a Shuttle launch. Marshall would host them at Kennedy Space Center. The catch was, we would provide the buses from their hotel to the VIP viewing area, but they had to pay their travel, room, and board for the trip. They absolutely loved the idea and about half of that first group made it to a launch during the following year. We continued to offer this opportunity to the National Teachers of the Year for all of the remaining years I was Center Director. One of the privileges I had in my position was to be able to invite anyone I chose to attend a launch. Our Customer and Employee Relations Directorate took care of everyone I invited to a launch in a very hospitable way.

I enjoyed my last six months with NASA working on NASA's education team. To be honest I missed working with the Marshall people out at the Center, but I believe the decision to step aside was the right one. One of the things I did was teach a master's level course in "Leadership" at Alabama A&M University. I created this course based on my own experience and relied on many of the leadership books I had read over the years and tried to apply in my practice of leading. I found I loved to teach, enjoying the student interactions. It was fun to bring my own creative ideas to teaching this class. I am sure some students thought I was crazy at times, but we had fun while learning.

During my short time with NASA in the Education office I was able to address the question, "What do I do now?" I was too young (61) to stop working and we needed money to pay the bills. My next career step turned out to be a return to industry.

## Chapter 20

## Back to Industry

*"For I have learned to be content, whatever the circumstances.... I can do all things through Christ who strengthens me."* Philippians 4:11, 13 (NIV)

About a month after stepping down as Director of MSFC, I received a call "out of the blue." from an old friend at Northrop Grumman Corporation. Northrop Grumman had purchased the Space part of TRW, my old company, the one where I worked for 28 years before going to work for Oceaneering Inc. in Houston, Texas, eleven years before. I was offered an opportunity to be interviewed by Northrop Grumman Space Technology Sector executives to be considered for a position on an executive consulting group of three people they referred to as the Management Support Council (MSC). This group was to be comprised of a retired four-star Air Force General, Howell Estes, a retired Special Access programs executive, Al Munson, and a retired NASA Executive who he suggested might be me. Traveling to Redondo Beach, California, I interviewed with a number of Space Technology Sector Vice Presidents, Sector President Wes Bush, and Howell Estes who was the leader of the MSC. Some of the Sector VPs were old friends I had worked with when I was at TRW; others had joined the company since I left. I was very impressed with the Space Sector top team as well as Howell Estes, former Commander of the Air

Force Space Command in Colorado Springs, Colorado. I was pleased and excited to be offered the NASA consultant position on the MSC. God had opened another door for me.

    One concern I had was medical insurance for Loa and me. As a consultant we had no "company" insurance and so for a year I signed us up for Cobra insurance but after a year we would have to seek insurance on the open market since Cobra insurance was only available for a maximum of one year. Due to Loa's brain hemorrhage incident she was uninsurable. I asked Wes Bush to consider hiring me so we would have company insurance. The only offer he could come up with was much lower pay than the consultant pay, and we were not ready to move back to California and leave our family in Texas. So, I turned the offer down and took the consulting job knowing I would probably have to find full-time employment in a year just to have insurance for Loa.

    My last official day with NASA was Friday, January 9, 2004. I flew to Los Angeles the following Monday, January 12, to begin my consulting job with Northrop Grumman's Space Sector. The three of us on the Management Support Counsel went to Redondo Beach for one week each month. We did our best to offer Customer perspectives on the work the Space Sector was performing. We met with each of the Sector's Vice Presidents as well as others during our visits and listened to their challenges and offered whatever thoughts/advice that occurred to us that might help. We also reviewed and commented on the Sector Strategic Plan. We met monthly with Wes Bush to share what we could to help his Sector achieve its goals. We were trusted and invited to sit in on Wes' staff meetings. In effect we were members of Wes' staff, a very unusual situation for consultants to have.

    At the same time, I was consulting for Northrop Grumman (NG) I also consulted for two other companies, but NG was my main consulting customer.

In the summer of 2004 Northrop Space was bidding on a NASA/Jet Propulsion Laboratory competitive proposal to design and manufacture a nuclear propulsion powered spacecraft call "Project Prometheus." This program was supported by NASA Administrator, Sean O'Keefe, and appeared to some that this was to be a program he initiated and would be a cornerstone of his legacy. I was asked to be chairman of the Red Team Review of Northrop's proposal to Jet Propulsion Laboratory. This is a common approach used by aerospace companies to internally critique proposals before submittal to the customer. The Red Team is comprised of knowledgeable people not associated with the proposal who come together to act as the customer evaluation team. The Red Team reads the proposal, scores it, and offers suggestions to improve the proposal in verbal and written form. The review typically takes about three days culminating in a readout briefing to the proposal team and submittal of written comments and suggestions for improvement of the proposal. The proposal team then takes this information and finalizes the proposal that is submitted to the customer.

After Northrop's Prometheus proposal was submitted to JPL the company prepared for Orals at JPL. The term Orals refers to a time when each contractor's management team orally presents their proposal to the customer and then responds to real time questions on the company's proposal asked by the customer's (JPL's) Evaluation Board members. The Prometheus Orals at JPL were scheduled for two days for each competing company. These orals are critical to the success of the team's proposal. In this way the customer is gaining clarification of each company's proposal but also, they are evaluating the proposal team leaders as they respond to questions. This is important because the customer is looking at how they would be able to work with each company's management team.

I was asked to chair a mock Source Evaluation Board to act as if we were the JPL customer evaluation board. Northrop arranged to meet for this "practice orals" in the very room where the actual JPL orals would take place at a hotel near JPL across town in Pasadena. The day came and we assembled the mock Source Evaluation Board sitting at a table much like we assumed the JPL evaluation board would do. The Northrop Team orally presented their proposal followed by responses to questions we asked. Our mock board had developed questions ahead of time. We did our best to act as if we were the JPL evaluation board members in every respect. I acted in the role of the JPL board chair. Our mock board took breaks just like the JPL board would do and came back with additional questions just like we expected the JPL board would do. We concluded our one-day mock orals evaluation board activity by compiling a set of recommendations for the NG Prometheus team to consider.

When it came time for the real Oral meeting with JPL the Northrop Grumman team did an excellent job. The competitor's lead VP at Lockheed Martin, who was a former TRW VP and friend of many at Northrop Grumman, told us later on, their orals were a disaster. Northrop Grumman won the competition and was awarded this very large development contract with funding of about $250M in the first year of the contract (2005). When Wes Bush got the call from the Director of JPL saying NG won the contract, he asked the proposal/program team leaders to gather together in a large conference room, but he did not say why. Surprisingly the first person he called after that was me. He asked me to come up to his office and when I got there, he said, "Come with me. I am walking over to notify the proposal/program team we won the contract." I had the privilege of watching Wes play with the team a bit as he seriously said he had received a call from the JPL Director, paused for a moment with a straight face, and without giving away who had won, he said, "And, we won!" The room erupted in celebration!

Not long after NG won this contract, in September 2004, I received a surprise call "out of the blue" from Wes Bush's assistant who asked me to come up to Wes' office. He wanted to talk to me. I wondered what could this be about? When I sat down with Wes, he surprised me when he said he wanted to hire me as a full-time Vice President of Northrop Grumman. I would move from being a consultant to be an officer of the company. I must admit I had missed running an organization. I eagerly accepted his offer. I don't know if he remembered I needed to find full-time employment for insurance reasons, but I would not be surprised if that was a factor. Funny thing – I heard a back-story on this offer. Howell, who was knowledgeable of Wes' plans before me, told me Wes had gone to Northrop Grumman's President and CEO, Ron Sugar, telling him he wanted to hire me to lead a new Laser Division he was creating. Ron, who knew me well, responded by saying, "He is too old and would only have three years to work before reaching 65." That was Northrop's mandatory retirement age for officers of the company. Wes went back to Ron after this rejection not long after that and insisted he wanted to hire me. Ron agreed. Wes surprised me again when he made an exception to company policy and connected my 28 years from my earlier time with TRW to what would be my last three years of employment. God had opened another door for Loa and me. Now we had insurance and a much better retirement plan based on my highest three years of pay, which would now be based on my three years as a Vice President instead of a retirement based on what I was making in 1992 when I left the company. For the next 3 ½ years I commuted every week from Houston to Redondo Beach, California.

Wes asked me to head up the company's new Laser Division called Directed Energy Systems. Suddenly I went from managing only myself and offering advice often not accepted (no complaints --- that is just the way it is with consultants) to overseeing a large building full of about 200 folks who were designing and building state-of-the-art lasers used to shoot and destroy enemy missiles in various phases of flight. LASER stands for Light Amplification by Stimulated Emission of Radiation. Lasers destroy things by placing severe radiation energy on the target and basically burning through it. Learning about lasers was like drinking from a fire hose, as I knew nothing about lasers. My prior experience with lasers was writing a paper in college on the subject. I asked one of the laser experts to spend a couple of hours with me each week so I could learn the basics. The laser work at the company was situated in several different organizations before Wes decided to consolidate all of the laser work in one organization. I was back in the business of setting up a new organization, including selecting people to manage various parts of the business (e.g. engineering, marketing, business). This new organization supported three major laser programs.

The first program was a megawatt, chemical gas laser known as the Tactical High Energy Laser that had a long history of demonstrated success in tracking and shooting down multiple, simultaneous incoming large caliber rockets and mortars while in flight. The biggest need for such a system was to defend against rockets and mortars being launched into the U.S. Green Zone in Iraq where US troops were stationed. This laser was ready to be deployed. We were under contract to the U.S. Army for testing this laser and testing on the White Sands, New Mexico proving grounds was essentially complete. The first thing I faced was working to sell the Army on deploying this demonstrated system. It just so happened my good friend, General Larry Dodgen, previous commander of the Redstone Arsenal, was now overseeing this program as well as several others. I met him on the telephone the day following his swearing in ceremony as commander of Redstone. That day was the infamous 9/11/2001. He called me to get my opinion on whether or not to close the Army's Redstone Arsenal as MSFC's 6200 employees were working on NASA's 1800 acres of property located in the middle of the Arsenal. We agreed to close the Center and Arsenal. We worked together to share technology between our two organizations and had a very good relationship.

Larry Dodgen, Redstone Arsenal Commanding General giving me a plaque with a piece of the Pentagon destroyed when the plane, piloted by terrorists, hit the side of the Pentagon in Washington DC on 9/11/2001.
--- Credit: NASA Photo

I briefed General Dodgen and his staff a number of times returning often to address his concerns. After nearly a year of deliberations by the Army with a lot of technical exchanges with his command, General Dodgen just could not commit to deploying this very capable system. In a subsequent briefing I made to the Under Secretary of the Army it became apparent that Army staff had concluded the logistics of supplying required chemical gases for the laser was something the Army did not want to undertake in a war zone. Our contract funding was cut off and that was the end of this pursuit. Of course, this was a major disappointment and caused a number of people on this program to be let go or redeployed to other parts of the company.

The second laser program was the Air Force Airborne Laser. This was a megawatt-class chemical oxygen iodine gas laser mounted in a Boeing 747 aircraft. The Northrop Grumman laser filled the entire lower deck of this very large aircraft. It was an amazing feat just to get it integrated into the aircraft. In 2005 I flew with the TRW program manager to Lancaster, California, where the laser was undergoing testing. The program was constantly under threat of being cancelled and I found myself in regular quarterly meetings with partners Boeing (aircraft) and Lockheed Martin (atmospheric compensation laser). There were major issues still to be resolved. Five years later, in 2010, after I left Directed Energy Systems, this massive airborne laser successfully demonstrated its ability

Airborne Laser. Credit: U.S. Missile Defense Agency

by shooting down two test missiles while in flight off of the California coast. Only one airborne laser was built. In 2011 President Obama's Defense Secretary canceled the program after 16 years in development.

The third laser area was the High-Energy Solid-State lasers projects. The company was investing large sums of Independent Research and Development funds into these next generation lasers. We were also receiving development funding under contract to the Air Force for use in airborne applications. These lasers were considerably smaller and lighter than the chemical gas lasers and showed tremendous potential. Funding at the time I got involved was relatively small but was expected to grow with time. During my year leading Directed Energy Systems (DES) I spent a lot of time meeting with our Air Force Customers in Colorado Springs, Colorado.

While overseeing DES, the company also asked me to consult with the Integrated Systems Sector regarding their pursuit of NASA's Crew Exploration Module (CEV) later named the Orion Spacecraft. Northrop Grumman was the prime contractor and was teamed with Boeing Corporation in competition with Lockheed Martin to win this potential $10B program. I was very familiar with this competition from my days at NASA. Johnson Space Center was responsible for the program. The Integrated Systems Sector's business was to design and manufacture military aircraft like the T-38 trainer and the B2 Bomber, not space systems, yet they were proposing to be the prime contractor on this space vehicle. The Space Systems Sector, where I worked, supported the Integrated Systems sector in this pursuit. Scott Seymour was an aggressive Sector President and while I was Center Director of MSFC he had come to see me about bidding on the Space Launch Initiative (SLI) program. His sector wound up being awarded an SLI contract. When SLI was cancelled Scott decided to compete for CEV. One of the points I kept bringing up with the CEV team and Scott in my consulting role was they needed to promote their program manager to vice president and the program should report at a high level in the organization. I recommended the program report directly to Scott.

After a year as VP of Directed Energy Systems in the Space Sector, I was asked by the company to move over to the Integrated Systems Sector to head their pursuit of the *Constellation Program*. This program to go back to the moon required all of the elements needed to do that including an Apollo-like command module, a Lander and habitats on the moon. The first competition was for the CEV. They took my advice and named the CEV program manager, Doug Young, Vice President. I was brought in as his boss with a title of Sector Vice President. I did everything I could to help Doug win this competition, but it was too late to help formulate a new win strategy. When I asked what Northrop's discriminators were, necessary in my opinion to win, I was told the customer had "leveled the playing field" meaning the customer had specified the job so tightly there could be no discriminators. Five months after I arrived the proposal was submitted to JSC and in the fall of 2006 Lockheed Martin was awarded the contract. We had planned a big celebration hoping we would win. Some 200 people were assembled in a large hanger awaiting the announcement. Doug was in Washington DC ready to talk to the press had we won. I was with Scott when he got the call we had lost and went over to tell the folks waiting in the hanger. With Scott I told the team we had lost. It was a sad day for all, many of whom had worked for three years on this proposal effort. I remember the gracious call I received from Ron Sugar, CEO of Northrop Corporation, the day after we were notified the company had lost our bid. I had come home from Hawaii where my family was vacationing just to be there for the announcement. I was sitting in a plane waiting to taxi and take off for Hawaii feeling pretty low when Ron called me. He said he was sorry about the loss and then said we will learn from this and move forward to a better day. He could have been critical of us for losing. He did not have to make that call but he did and for that I admired him.

This was a tough year for me as I had been asked to lead an organization that was comprised of people who really did not understand Space Programs as they were airplane designers/builders. They certainly were not to blame. They worked hard and did their best. It was tough in that I did not think we could win for a number of reasons like not having discriminators. But I did have some fun with an education program I brought into being as part of our NASA public relations effort to show we supported education, a priority I knew NASA held, starting with the NASA Administrator, Sean O'Keefe. As I am still passionate about education and supporting teachers, I have to tell this story.

As part of our public relations effort we funded a program to offer teachers, in cities where Northrop facilities existed and in key NASA cities around the country, the opportunity to experience a commercial zero G flight (G meaning gravity). A commercial company, Zero Gravity Corporation, created a business to enable people to feel what it would be like to be on a Shuttle or space station in "zero G." A commercial jet was set up for this "adventure" with seats in half the interior and an open bay area in the other half. After flying to altitude, participants were invited to leave their seats and move into the open area as the airplane flew up and over the top of a roller coaster type loop. They experienced a zero G effect for about 30 seconds during the loop before the aircraft pulled out of a dive to recover with participants pinned to the floor during this 2 G pull out maneuver. They also experienced what it would be like to be on the moon with 1/6 earth's gravity or Mars with 1/3 earth's gravity. Not only did we offer to fly local teachers in those cities, but remembering the National Teachers of the Year, I offered to fly them at a designated site as well. Northrop paid the bill for all the teachers to have this experience. The

Credit: Creative Commons Attribution-Share Alike 4.0 International license

teachers conducted experiments on these flights and were able to share this experience with their students back home. The teachers loved it and I loved seeing their excitement as I went with them a couple of times. Many very happy teachers experienced zero G courtesy of Northrop Grumman.

  Getting back to my situation after the loss of CEV -- So now over two years I had held two different jobs in two different Northrop Sectors. I was a year away from retiring and qualifying for Social Security and I needed a job. One of Ron Sugar's messages to his senior management was "You got to where you are because you are a highly capable leader. If you fail at some endeavor, we will find you another job." I called Alexis Livanos, who had replaced Wes Bush as Sector President of Northrop Grumman Space Systems when Wes was promoted to Chief Operating Officer of Northrop Grumman reporting to Ron. Alexis invited me to return to his division and offered me the job of Deputy Program Manager on Space System's National Polar-

Orbiting Operational Environmental Satellite System (NPOESS). Northrop Grumman Space Systems had won this large satellite program three years earlier in competition with Lockheed Martin. The bad news was this program was in serious trouble. Vice President Al Gore had observed two Government organizations were building satellites to do the same thing, so he ordered the creation of a joint program office to build one satellite system to provide earth and atmospheric environmental data to both DoD (Department of Defense) and NOAA (National Oceanic and Atmospheric Agency). NASA had always helped NOAA by overseeing the design and manufacture of NOAA's environmental satellites. NOAA, NASA and DoD oversaw the joint program office and they did not get along. They proceeded to staff this office with inexperienced people, and this made for a difficult situation for Northrop Grumman who had competitively won the contract to build this multi-satellite system. I won't bother you with more details but suffice it to say the program was in deep trouble and the biggest concern was the Northrop Grumman relationship with NASA was toxic.

I went about trying to mend fences with NASA's Goddard Space Flight Center. The Goddard NPOESS program manager seemed "out to get" Northrop according to the Northrop team. I did everything I could to meet the program manager's demands and initially we got along and made progress mending fences but after a honeymoon period I found myself enduring accusations toward Northrop by this government program manager. I wound up going to the Goddard Center Director, a good friend of mine, who promised to help improve this program manager's behavior. Even that did not work. I arrived at a point where I was eager to retire and get away from, what seemed like, an impossible situation.

I was going through my files today and I came upon a letter that Ron Sugar had written days before I turned 65 stating the company policy regarding mandatory retirement at 65. The letter went on to say he was authorizing a delay in my retirement by six months, due to the company's NASA issues on NPOESS I was trying my best to help.

I will only say when my time came on April 1, 2008 to retire when I was 65 ½ I was very happy (no fooling) to move on. I felt sorry for the Northrop Grumman NPOESS team that performed admirably and were constantly under fire from the government. Two years later the program was cancelled under unhappy circumstances. In an effort to salvage the program, Wes Bush, having replaced Ron Sugar as Northrop Grumman CEO, made every effort with Northrop's Sector Vice President, Dave DeCarlo, to offer the government a really excellent three satellite constellation that met the space sensing environmental needs of NOAA and DoD at a very affordable price. This offer was rejected by the government. The bottom line, it seemed to me, was NOAA and DoD wanted a divorce at any cost. Both agencies started their own environmental satellite programs after NPOESS was cancelled.

About six months after I retired, I was asked by Dave DeCarlo to once again consult as a member of the Management Support Council. I enjoyed serving in this capacity for 7 more years until August 2015 when I fully retired.

# Chapter 21

# Supporting Angels

*"Alone we can do so little; together we can do so much."*
--- Helen Keller

I have already said the star "supporting angel" in my life is my wife, Loa. She has been there from the beginning doing all the chores and child rearing I did not have time to do while I was working. I will always be in debt to her.

From a personal standpoint, the supporting angels for most of us, hopefully, are a supportive family and close friends. Loa and I were blessed with parents and siblings who were there for us. My sister, Lynn, and I were close friends as we grew up and have continued that close relationship. My two brothers, Carl and David, were so much younger than I, and as a result we did not have the same supportive relationship in our growing up years until we became good friends as adults. As I mentioned before, we joined a small supportive Koinonia group in our church. Cathy and Larry Davis, June and Bob Diets, Roger and Georgia Klinkers, and others were there as our supporting angels. We can't express our thanks enough for how they were there for us. Later on, we were in other support groups whose members were also our supporting angels. I have maintained good friendships with four college fraternity brothers. Over these many years we have gotten together once a year for a guys' weekend catching up on each other's lives. These friends have been there for each other to offer support in the difficult times in life and to celebrate the good times. We certainly have been blessed to have caring friends.

From a professional standpoint, beginning with my first job, after graduating from the University of Redlands, when I was writing test procedures at Litton Industries, I depended on others for support. At Litton, I worked with other test procedure writers who helped me do my job. I asked them questions about the writing process they followed to learn how I could successfully execute my job. They were very helpful.

When I started work at Space Technology Laboratories on the Apollo program, I was learning on the job and I learned from others who took the time to teach me how to do my job. At one point a coworker said, "Just design a register to store that information." I had to ask, "How do you design a register?" He took the time to show me.

When I transferred to the Radio Frequency (RF) Laboratory and started work there the same thing happened. I was dependent on others to help me learn my job. Said another way, I had supporting angels standing beside me and behind me helping me succeed. The technician that had worked for my father and was assigned as my technician to help me was a supporting angel to me. He taught me basic laboratory techniques about RF circuit design. The three young engineers who sat with me in a large office had superior knowledge coming from technical engineering schools they attended compared to my mostly liberal arts education. They had more experience designing RF circuits and to a man they took time to teach me what I needed to know in order to execute my job.

When I was promoted to Section Head in the RF Lab and oversaw a group of engineers, I was able to hire a secretary. From the first day she supported me I was aware of how much I appreciated her help. Without doubt she made a difference in my ability to perform. As my responsibility increased as a Department Manager it became even more obvious that I accomplished nothing day to day on my own. Looking over what I have written in this book, I hope I have not made it look like I did this, and I did these things all on my own. This would be incorrect because I did very little on my own. The better way to look at my career, if anything, is *I learned to ask for and accept help from others. Also, I hope I learned from my mistakes.* In so doing, some might say I was successful.

When I transferred to the Space Vehicle Division at TRW, I was asked to lead new business pursuits which translate to working with customers to understand their requirements, likes and dislikes, and then to assemble a team to develop a win strategy and write and submit proposals to the government. I had some experience leading proposals back in the Electronics Division. Realizing I needed to know more about proposal preparation, I reached out to TRW "Proposal Operations" to understand proposal processes they recommended and took advantage of learning from proposal writing courses like the Hy Silver's Proposal Writing Course available outside the company. Proposal consultants from outside the company were a big help critiquing and helping us write improved proposals. Yes, I was successful in leading proposals and was associated with winning not because of some great talent, but because I was blessed to have many supporting angels. A lot of technical and administrative people contributed to every proposal. Steve Hart was head of Proposal Operations at TRW during my time there. He shared with me how frustrating it was to work with engineers who had great technical ideas but had no idea how to lead a proposal team. Because they came up with the great technical ideas, key to winning any proposal, company management assigned them the job of running the proposal, but Steve said they often would not follow the proposal operations processes and so they did not get the benefit from proposal operations available to them. As a result, Steve said things like lack of coordination across the proposal and thus contradicting statements and not enough time to rewrite the proposal after a red team review led to losing proposals they could have won. Steve and I got along really well. Why? Because I respected Steve and his team's opinions and tried my best to listen to their advice and follow it. We won a number of proposals. I say "we" because whatever we did was a team effort using everyone's expertise.

Key to winning a proposal is having a marketing person who is a specialist in understanding the customer and the competition, someone who could advise the proposal manager. I had the support of a number of very helpful marketing managers. One was Fred Brown who was a tremendous help in winning the TRW OMV proposal. Another was Roy Klusendorf at Oceaneering.

Let me talk about unsung heroes or supporting angels, who, in my opinion never get the thanks they deserve. I am talking about invaluable administrative assistants who kept me on track throughout my long career. I think of one of my first secretaries, as we called them back then, but what we now call administrative assistants. Sally Kobyashi was a wonderful assistant. Time and again she corrected my grammar and punctuation as assistants over my whole career did. She typed on an electronic typewriter, the latest and greatest technology, and used "white-out" to make changes with perfection. How hard it was back then when assistants did not have computers. Like all of my administrative assistants over the years, she answered the phone and kept my calendar and helped me be where I was supposed to be when I was supposed to be there. I think of Betty Johnson who was my administrative assistant for over five years when I was in the TRW Space Vehicle Division. She faithfully supported my efforts during our pursuit of solar array programs and the Orbital Maneuvering Vehicle.

Donna Domini was the administrative assistant to the former President of ILC Space Systems who became my administrative assistant at the new integrated Oceaneering Space Systems when we acquired ILC Space Systems. She came to me when we arrived and said, "Do you want me to support you or would you like to select someone else?" I said, "I really do want you to be my administrative assistant. You are invaluable to me because you can help me learn about the heritage ILC Space System's way of doing business that we spent a lot of money to acquire." Like the other aforementioned assistants, Donna was a wonderful, loyal assistant for the six years I was there. I have to mention Jane Robertson. She held a number of jobs at Oceaneering Space Systems when I arrived at the warehouse in Webster, Texas. She was my administrative assistant, Human Relations Manager, and also the business manager. When we took over ILC Space Systems she became the business manager for this new organization that included contracts and human resources management. She was extremely talented and carried out her multiple roles to perfection. I really appreciated her contributions.

Beth Partain, my administrative assistant at Marshall Space Flight Center for four years, was so helpful to me. Like Donna, she came to me on the first day I was there and said, "Do you want me to support you or do you have someone else you would like to support you?" I am very willing to go do something else." I said, "Beth, I need you to help me find my way here. I have never worked for the government and I did not grow up here at Marshall. I have a lot to learn and you are invaluable to me. Please stay and help me do this job." Beth was a wonderful administrative assistant and she taught this Californian that the southern way of going slow, paying attention to asking people about themselves, before proceeding to the business topic was the best way. I will admit, being a long time Californian, I sometimes forgot this great advice and dove right into the business at hand, but I know Beth's way was much better. Gail Ralls was there to help Beth and gave her all to help our office function effectively. Pat Fuller helped me by dealing with external correspondence, which seemed unending. When Beth retired, I asked Pat to take Beth's place. She was reluctant, worrying about her ability to fill in for Beth, but accepted the position and did an excellent job seeing me

NASA Administrative Assistants Gail, Pat, and Beth made my life much better day in and day out.
--- Credit: NASA Photo

through until I resigned. I think they would all not volunteer this but if they were honest, they would say I was "high maintenance."

When I went to Northrop Grumman, I had one administrative assistant after another as I moved every year into a different job. They were all extremely helpful and always worked to make my day the best it could be.

Clearly, administrative assistants throughout my career were so important to getting the job done. There are many other people in supporting roles in engineering organizations that I firmly believe are also unsung heroes and supporting angels. I will just talk about Marshall Space Flight Center supporting angels although I could just as well talk about those supporting angels at TRW, Oceaneering, or Northrop Grumman.

In a MSFC expanded staff meeting on a Monday morning involving about 80 people not more than a few weeks after I arrived at Marshall Space Flight Center, we were talking about Center employees and staffing needs. One of the engineering managers, in a way that was not disguised, pointed out that the engineers at MSFC are most important. My immediate response was to say, "Time out." I went on to say something like every employee at Marshall is equally important. We all have important jobs to do here. Engineers are very important and are the ones who create and sustain MSFC as part of NASA. We cannot go on without our engineers. But those who support the engineers are equally important to making our Center function. For example, the guard at the gate you say hi to every day when you come to work serves a key role. It could be a very bad day if that guard let the wrong people through that gate. The people who clean every night and pick up our trash are important. People in Center Operations and Customer and Employee Relations and Legal and Finance are all very important. They all help our engineers do their jobs. This was a break in the Marshall culture. Since the time of von Braun, engineers were viewed in a special honored way. People no longer talked around me about engineers being more important. My view was and is all of those who support the engineers in an engineering organization are supporting angels and should be held in high regard.

At Marshall, Sheila Cloud and her great Center Operations team kept the MSFC facilities working for all of us. She and her people went about keeping the power and air-conditioning going, the grass cut, the trash collected and on and on. They provided security staff, cafeteria workers, pilots for our airplane, bus drivers, and custodians and so many more important people that were so essential to making it all work at Marshall. They did their jobs in a way that made them transparent, not attracting attention because they did their jobs so well.

Dave Bates and his team kept the budgets and finances at Marshall humming along without attracting attention doing what was needed to satisfy a demanding NASA headquarters financial office.

Steve Beale and his procurement team changed the procurement culture at MSFC --- "to do what they said they would do when they said they would do it" --- a part of our Marshall *Customer* value. They consistently awarded contracts meeting the award dates they had announced months earlier.

Tereasa Washington and her excellent Customer and Employee Relations team helped us with human capital, media, education, government, and internal communications. She also was not afraid to tell me or others when we got out of line when it came to doing the right thing with our workforce. She was an advocate for conducting our business in line with our values.

Charles Scales and his Equal Opportunity office team helped us achieve diversity goals at the Center. Charles helped me connect with Oakwood College and Alabama A&M University, both schools attended primarily by minority students. He also led Center events to recognize the contributions of minority populations at the Center.

Bill Hicks and his Legal Counsel team kept us legally in line while helping us run proper procurements without any protests in my nearly five years.

Amanda Goodson and her Safety and Mission Assurance team helped us fly Shuttle safely, formed and led our safety council with Marshall contractors and led our workforce safety initiatives. They kept us looking at safety at work and at home.

My point is every one of these support organizations did work that enabled our programs and associated engineers to do their jobs without worrying about the many functions that are required to make any organization function smoothly. They are all unsung heroes.

In the military a general officer typically has a person who is always there to help that officer any way he or she can. While at Marshall I was privileged to have such a person. This person was typically a young engineer who was interested in being exposed to the daily activities of the Center Director, wanted to help, and by doing so was interested in learning from this experience. Their official title was *Technical Management Intern to the Center Director*. Each one who served in this role during my 5 years was very helpful to me. I want to thank Drew Smith, Roslin Hicks and Richard Sheppard for their excellent efforts to help me through each day.

From the bottom of my heart, I thank all those who spent their days helping me do my jobs along the way. I am sure I did not adequately thank people and for that I am sorry. Howell Estes, whom I had the privilege of working closely with as a consultant to Northrop Grumman for 8 years, makes every effort in his writings not to use the word "I." He does this to emphasize that each of us is not an island when it comes to accomplishing things. As he would say, it is not about "me" but about "us." We work and succeed only with the support of others.

******

## Chapter 22

## Titles or Testimony?

*"To thine own self be true. This means above all not to be hypnotized by what [you] have achieved but on the contrary to get clear of it, that is, to go on living and find renewal."*
--- Gabriel Mercel and Edward Robinson

When I was in leadership positions in industry and NASA I held position titles like Advanced Systems Manager, Vice President, Executive Vice President, Director and President. When I was younger, I thought how great it would be to be recognized with titles like these. When I was in these positions, I thought life was no better than when I was a Section Head. I do admit because of my personality makeup I enjoyed being in some leadership role because I loved working with people more than designing circuits, receivers, astronaut tools and spacecraft. I derived satisfaction from working with people who did those things. When we launched these things, I believe I got just as much satisfaction as those who were closer to the work. I liked to believe I helped them be successful and therefore I could claim to be part of that success.

All the time I worked in industry I can't remember receiving any awards. Maybe there was one, but I can't remember what it was. When I was a leader in government, as Director of NASA's Marshall Space Flight Center, I received many awards. To begin, NASA was generous with awards. I received the NASA Outstanding Leadership Medal, the NASA Group Achievement Award, and the NASA Exceptional Achievement Medal. It was nice to be recognized but when I thought about it, the tasks I was recognized for were about carrying out "duties as assigned." For example, the Outstanding Leadership Medal was given in recognition of MSFC campaigning for and getting congressional approval for the Space Launch Initiative program. Then there were awards that came my way, I think, because I was in a visible position. The American Society for Engineering Management selected me as the 2001 Engineering Manager of the Year. Also, in 2001, after giving the graduation speech, I received an Honorary Doctor of Science from the University of Alabama. I was named a Fellow member of the American Institute of Aeronautics and Astronautics while at MSFC. I received a Community Service Award from Oakwood College in Huntsville. And, as I mentioned earlier, my alma mater, the University of Redlands, recognized me with their annual Career Achievement Award. I am thankful to all who selected me for these awards. You honored me and I appreciated that very much.

So, during my career I had lofty titles and while at NASA I received impressive awards but as I look at these things, they are not what I want to be known for. I want to be known for the testimony I gave through what I said and more importantly through what I did. I want to be known for helping others and bringing people together to achieve worthy things.

Amongst all of the awards I received while working for NASA, there was one that I felt especially good about. This is the only award I hung on my office wall at Marshall and still is the only award on my office wall at home. It was the 2003 Martin Luther King Jr. Unity Award given to me by the Huntsville, Alabama, chapter of Alpha Phi Alpha

Fraternity. I want to share what I said upon receiving this award because I think it best captures some of what I tried to testify to while at Marshall.

Receiving the MLK Unity Award from Kirby Stevenson
--- Credit: NASA Photo

My acceptance speech at the Dr. Martin Luther King Jr. Huntsville breakfast on January 20, 2003:

*"Members of the Alpha Phi Alpha Fraternity and this great community please accept my heartfelt and deepest thanks for this award. I can think of no higher honor. When I was informed last Monday that I would be receiving this honor I was truly humbled. And it is only fitting that I use Dr. King's own words to describe how I feel.*

*'Occasionally in life there are those moments of un-utterable fulfillment which cannot be completely explained by those symbols called words. Their meanings can only be articulated by the inaudible language of the heart.'*

*This is one of those moments for me. And it is a moment when I think of the NASA/Marshall Civil Servant/Contractor team members, both individually and collectively, who share, with me, the common goal of "Inclusion" and "Unity." My sincere thanks to those who support me in this effort every day. I would not be standing here without you – You know who you are.*

*I have always tried to live my life by faith and fairness, believing in the value of all persons, and striving to treat each person with dignity and respect. I will be the first to admit that if this were easy for each of us as we all wish it were, it would not be a basic tenet or commandment of every religion in the world. Neither would there be so many laws on the subject. But while changing hearts and minds about others is sometimes an almost insurmountable challenge, changed behavior toward others can lead to changed hearts and minds. So we must at every opportunity seek to 'include.'*

*We all understand the need to produce excellent products or results with the least amount of effort and resources. We at NASA/Marshall have complex missions and issues and we never seem to have enough people to do the job. So, just from a practical standpoint, we cannot afford to leave one bit of talent untapped in accomplishing our work. No company or country can.*

*It is not about giving away something that belongs to the majority. It is about allowing and encouraging that which belongs to all of us – opportunity. It is about seeking our sameness to understand the ease with which we can come to 'love one another'....And it is about seeking and valuing our differences to understand the ease with which we can come to respect one another's potential for contribution. It is about knowing that different backgrounds and experiences bring perspectives and approaches that improve every final product. So, we have made the commitment to make a difference in how we value and promote diversity with the workforce at Marshall Space Flight Center and with our choice of partners outside the Center.*

*Sometimes I get impatient with our progress, and I will continue to do so because it is a cause worthy of impatience. When discouraged, I recall the words of the great Maya Angelou who said:*

*'Not everything you do is going to be a masterpiece, but you get out there and you try and sometimes it really happens. The other times you're simply stretching your soul.'*

*So, I know that my efforts are never futile because if I change some behaviors, and some minds, I will have helped to create the mosaic masterpiece we seek. If not, well, all of us can use a little soul stretching. It is for me simply a question of our ultimately being mediocre in our separateness – or being great in our unity. This annual breakfast reminds me of that... and it reminds us that Dr. King's incredible journey and passion must never be forgotten.*

*Thank you for this award and thanks for this opportunity to join with each of you in re-committing ourselves to 'Unity' as envisioned by the great Dr. Martin Luther King Jr."*

As I said, this award was really special to me. The folks that conducted the annual Dr. Martin Luther King Jr. breakfast did not have to give this award to me. And unlike some of the other awards I received I don't think they picked me for the award because of the lofty position I held in the Huntsville community. I like to think they picked me because they saw that I valued diversity in the Marshall workforce and did what I could to promote unity at the Center.

Titles or Testimony, which is more important to me? There is no doubt in my mind that I want to be known for the latter and don't care much about the former. What will people say about me – my legacy? What will Jesus say when I see him in heaven? Was I out for myself, to look good? Was I just interested in climbing the corporate ladder or was I interested in helping people accomplish their goals?

While working I focused on working and that took a lot of my energy and time. When I retired and began consulting, I was now able to address life without going to work every day during the week. When I stopped consulting and went to full-time retirement, I had more time to do as I would choose. Moving toward retirement the question before me was, "Now what do you do?"

## Chapter 23

## Giving Back

*"How does God's love abide in anyone who has the world's goods and sees a brother or sister in need and yet refuses to help? Little children, let us love, not in word or speech, but in truth and action."*
--- 1 John 3:17-18 (NRSV)

For a long time, I have been convinced I wanted to "give back" by helping others, particularly the poor, with my time, talent and finances. While working, like most hard-working people, I had little time to give to helping others outside of those I tried to help on the job, or through small groups I led in the church and United Christian Ashrams over the years. I had more time for giving back when I moved from full-time employment to part-time consulting and then to full retirement. We were blessed later in life with income that exceeded our needs and we have been able to support Christian organizations we are passionate about in addition to our church.

One Christian organization we became passionate about when I was at Marshall is the Harvest Youth Club (HYC) in Harvest, Alabama. When I met Melvin and Sylvia Allen I was impressed with their commitment to a ministry for at-risk children and youth. In 2000 they sold their middle-class home and used the proceeds to buy property a quarter mile from where Melvin grew up in a very poor

Melvin Allen, Director of Harvest Youth Club, with club members
--- Credit: HYC Photo

residential area in Harvest, Alabama, near Huntsville. They built a large youth clubhouse building on that property and purchased and installed a doublewide mobile home next to it to live in. They established a Christian after school program called the Harvest Youth Club (website: harvestyouthclub.com). They began working daily with 60 to 70 children and young people to share God's love and help them achieve better school grades and make available a safe, fun and encouraging environment for the kids as an alternative to hanging out in a neighborhood where drugs and alcohol were major issues in the community. When they started, they asked the children and youth to share their report cards. They discovered most were getting D's and F's. They incentivized the kids to do better by offering a $10 McDonalds gift card for those who made the "honor roll" by receiving report cards with only As, Bs, and Cs - no Ds or Fs. They tutored the children and youth in their school subjects telling them they could be successful. Pretty soon their grades got better and a majority of their children and youth made the honor roll. After over 90 percent of their students made the honor roll, they created a higher-level target to achieve only As and Bs. It did not take long for 75% of Harvest Youth Club (HYC) members to receive only As and Bs on their report cards. These are amazing results in a neighborhood where the norm was to do poorly in academic school work. Over the last 18 years, HYC children and youth have gone on to graduate from trade schools and colleges and are productive, successful members of society. Some of the HYC graduates have returned to help the next generation at the club. We have supported HYC financially since 2001. Our church in Houston, Texas sent teams to help build three buildings at HYC over the years.

When I retired from full-time work at Northrop Grumman, I questioned what my life would look like going forward. The day after I retired, I thought, Wow, I don't need to get up early, fight traffic, and work my tail off for five or six days every week. I can stay in my PJ's longer and do whatever I want. Someone once told me, "When you are retired every evening is Friday evening and every day is Saturday!" What a great life it will be!

I have always loved to play golf having started playing when I was 12. I never was a great golfer, but I had fun. If I shot a score of bogey, I was happy. Bogey for those who do not golf is on average a score of one over par per hole. One time when I was still working full-time, I was invited to play in a 3-day tournament --- Friday afternoon, Saturday, and Sunday. The first day was fun; the second day was fun but a bit tiring; the third day was beginning to feel like "work." From that tournament experience I confirmed I was only going to play golf occasionally in retirement. I found this to be true about any sport or hobby although I guess I will continue to be an avid Texans football and Astros baseball fan and continue to love to fly fish in the summer in Colorado. There was something missing and I knew what it was. I wanted to keep trying to make a positive difference in the lives of others. I wanted to be a part of building God's Kingdom here on earth. I wanted to offer others hope. And I wanted to keep alive hope in me to grow toward a deeper relationship with God day by day until He calls me home.

I believe God loves each of us unconditionally. We don't serve our neighbors in need to earn His love, we serve them because of His love. We are the hands and feet of Christ. We help others not because we are obligated but because we joyfully choose to do so in response to God's love for us.

Following my retirement, I talked to Betty Flanders, director of missions at our church, about an outreach to the homeless and poor in southeast Houston I had heard about. She told me where to go and I started volunteering there. This Christian organization started by asking the homeless what they needed. The first thing they said was they wanted to be able to take a shower, they wanted to be clean. The goal of Crossroads at Park Place (website: crossroadsatparkplace.org) is to help people to feel better about themselves when they leave at the end of that day of service than when they arrived. Crossroads serves about 180 homeless and poor people every Tuesday and Thursday mornings. They are served a hot breakfast and lunch. They receive hygiene, clothes, shoes, coats, backpacks, belts, hats, socks and underwear. Crossroads volunteers clean their clothes, offer showers, haircuts, a place to receive their mail if they have no address, and a place to hang out in air conditioning in the summer and a heated hall in the winter. Social service agencies come to Crossroads to arrange medical help, housing assistance and other referrals. Maybe the most important thing Crossroads does for people is offer them hope. Only the Executive Director and the kitchen manager are employed. Some of the clients are paid

Crossroads meeting hall at Servants of Christ Church in Houston

a small amount to help set up, clean up, and take down after lunch. Volunteers make it happen at Crossroads, volunteers like exuberant Carolyn, who organizes the clothing storage room and volunteer recognition events; kind Mary, who sorts and measures clothing; generous Courtney, who checks in the clients at the front desk; friendly Eddie, who oversees the computers for clients; sweet Kay, who serves clients and brings a box of cookies for clients and volunteers every week; and hard-working Kitty, who volunteers where needed. They, along with many others, show up week after week because they care about the people Crossroads serves.

I have been on the board of Crossroads the last eight years and served as chairman of the board for two of those years. The great thing about Crossroads is people feel welcomed, valued and they leave with an improved sense of dignity. In the Book of Matthew 25:35 we read that Jesus said, "I was hungry, and you gave me food, I was thirsty, and you gave me drink, I was a stranger and you welcomed me, I was naked, and you clothed me.... Truly I say to you, when

Art and Bruce at lunch at our favorite Chinese restaurant (Jan. 2019)

you did it to the least of these you did it to me." That is what Crossroads strives to do for the homeless and poor in southeast Houston. By volunteering I feel like I am making a difference, even though it may be small, in the lives of those we serve. Certainly, my life has been more fulfilling since I started volunteering at Crossroads.

    About nine years ago I met Bruce at Crossroads. At that time, he was homeless, living on a friend's back porch out in the open in the sun and in the rain. We became good friends and have continued that friendship ever since. We go out to lunch one to two times a month and usually talk about Texans football. He knows more about the Texans than I do. Several times Bruce has gone with me to Texans games. Bruce is a disabled longshoreman who had to quit working after being exposed to a chemical used to kill insects in the grain transported in the cargo bay of a freighter he was serving on. It was a mistake on the part of the captain to have his crew return to the ship before the chemical effect was gone. Bruce does a great job teaching Bible study with Sandy at Crossroads. I am happy to say about nine months ago he got an apartment and is no longer homeless. I cherish the friendships I have made as a volunteer with the good people who come to Crossroads and happen to be homeless or poor. Some people I know think the homeless and poor are lazy. This is not the case for most. Many are trapped in mental illness and have no one to care for them. Many are trapped in some sort of addiction, unable to make the commitment to beat their addiction. And many are just down on their luck. I have seen people get off the street like Bruce and that is encouraging. I pray he will never have to go back on the street again. Crossroads volunteers do their best to support the poor and homeless helping those willing to be helped.

Over the last 10 years since I retired from full-time work, I have volunteered and served on the boards of two other Houston organizations in addition to Crossroads that help to make life better for those they serve. One organization is Mission Milby Development Corporation (website: missionmilby.org), a ministry to a largely Hispanic community in southeast Houston. This organization has an after-school program for at-risk youth, providing positive Christian programs for them. Some of these youth enter the program as gang members. Mission Milby set up free Internet access for everyone living within a 5-mile radius and offers computer skills training in their on-site computer lab. ESL (English as a Second Language) classes are offered to local residents. It has a full-time "Justice for All" organization on site to help people gain citizenship. An AARP income tax service is offered the first three months of each year. Mission Milby also brings in instructors from the University of Houston and Rice University to teach subjects like finance and micro-industry methods. Some young people have come out of the Mission Milby youth programs and gone on to college. They were able to break the cycle of poverty.

Another organization I joined is Walk to Emmaus. This organization offers a 72-hour retreat experience for Christians ready to go deeper in their relationship with God. The Walks are organized as Women's walks and Men's walks. When Loa and I went on our Walks we came away with renewed excitement about our relationship with God. Our son and daughter and their spouses have said the same thing. I have enjoyed sponsoring many people as they went on their Walks. I have also enjoyed participating on the leadership team putting on these walks and being one of 15 speakers on some of the Men's walks. I can't tell you how gratifying it is to listen to people at the end of this weekend talk about the difference the weekend has made for them and how they have grown closer to God.

About the same time I retired 10 years ago our Clear Lake United Methodist Church started sending a work team every spring to the 175-acre campus of a Christian organization called Servants in Faith and Technology (SIFAT). About 15 to 20 people travel the 750 miles in April every year from Houston to this beautiful wooded campus in a remote area of Alabama near the town of Lineville. We build, repair, clean and paint facilities and just do what we can to help SIFAT improve their campus. One year we built an outdoor amphitheater, another year a fire escape on a two-story lodge, another year we put a new roof on the cafeteria, and another year we installed lighting, a sound system and built a hermetically sealed booth to protect sound system electronics from the humid air in the open-air SIFAT Quonset hut meeting hall. We have even sewn and installed curtains (not me). Loa and I were able to go 8 of those 10 years.

Why do we go each year? We go because we believe in what SIFAT (website: sifat.org) is doing to help the suffering poor in more than 90 countries around the world

SIFAT Leaders (left to right): Benjo Paredes (Bolivia Founder), Sarah Corson (Founder) & Tom Corson (SIFAT Executive Director) Sarah is interpreting for Benjo.

have a more abundant life. SIFAT's motto is *Sharing God's Love in Practical Ways*. Over the past 40 years SIFAT has trained indigenous leaders from poor communities in over 90 countries in appropriate technologies. SIFAT invites these leaders to come to the SIFAT campus in Alabama to learn about these technologies and community development techniques. Sarah and Ken Corson founded SIFAT after working as Christian missionaries with the poor in Cuba, Costa Rica, Puerto Rico, Haiti, Bolivia, Venezuela, Ecuador and in the United States – Indiana, New Jersey, Kentucky and Alabama.

In Ken's words, "God provided so that we could teach appropriate technologies to help some of the poorest people in the world find ways to meet their basic human needs of clean water, food, alternative energy, housing, health, education, and microenterprise for a livelihood." These SIFAT graduates return to their communities with the knowledge SIFAT has provided. Because they are trusted in their communities, people are open to these new ideas and poor people's lives all over the world are improved. SIFAT's goal is to help people help themselves. Graduates can propose projects for their communities asking SIFAT to help financially and/or help by sending teams from churches in the U.S. to build infrastructure. For example, for the past 5 years I have led a Clear Lake United Methodist Church Mission Team to Ecuador where we are one of 20 teams that go there, one after another, for a week every summer to build additional facilities for poor Christian churches. We do this because the churches and Compassion International, an organization that supports poor children, don't have the funds to build these additional facilities. For every floor a

SIFAT Clear Lake UMC team working on church facilities to enable a poor church in Ecuador to have more children in their Compassion International program.

church adds to a building they can add roughly 50 more Compassion International children to their program (website: compassion.com). A child in the Compassion program can be released from poverty as a result. Compassion children receive a school uniform required to attend public schools in most southern hemisphere countries. Many children can't go to school because their parent or parents can't afford to buy a uniform. Compassion children are given a hot lunch, medical aid, tutoring in school subjects, and a healthy Christian environment off the streets of the city where they are pulled into drugs and prostitution. Who funds these Compassion children? People like you and me. The cost is $38/month. Loa and I love our two Compassion children, Genesis in Ecuador (6) and Ashley (12) in Nicaragua. We exchange letters, pray for them, and share our faith in a loving God who sustains all of His children. I have a specific volunteer job in my role as a SIFAT board member. I am chairman of a committee of

Art holding Genesis, Art & Loa's Compassion child in Quito, Ecuador.

three and we receive and hopefully find a way to approve small project proposals graduates submit to SIFAT. These projects must meet certain criteria. They must have strong potential to improve the lives of people in the community they serve, and the projects must yield sustainable results within the time frame and funding of the project. By sustainable we mean the project results in an outcome that has permanently improved the lives of people in the community and also this improvement will go on for many years without the need for more funding from SIFAT. Over the last 2 years we have approved and funded 25 small graduate projects. The funding for these $3,000 to $5000 (occasionally as much as $15,000) projects does not come from the SIFAT budget. We go out and solicit donors without taking away donations from donors who support SIFAT's General Operating Fund. The ideas for projects come from the graduates, as they know what is most needed in their indigenous community and use what they have learned from SIFAT training to come up with a project. I would love to describe all of these graduate projects. They typically address issues Ken described like clean water, food, alternative energy, housing, health, education, and microenterprise for a livelihood. The projects are all exciting and life changing, enabling people to live more abundant lives. Let me share just one of these projects that addresses a unique need.

    In 2018 one of SIFAT's graduates (name not mentioned for his safety) proposed a project to build a structure with no walls, just poles holding up a metal roof. This place is needed so some of the 1 million Sudanese refugees, stuck in refugee camps in Uganda, can have a place where they can gather to worship Christ out of the hot sun and rain. They fled for their lives out of South Sudan and migrated to Uganda only to find themselves in refugee camps in Uganda with not enough food. The modest $3,500 proposal was to build the simple shelter and plant a garden

Worship Center for Sudanese in Uganda refugee camp

to grow food alongside it. The goal was to have a place to worship and have food for people to eat. I can't imagine such dire conditions. We take our places of worship and having food to eat for granted. It is a pleasure to give to such a worthy project.

SIFAT graduate projects are not SIFAT's projects but are the graduate community's projects. SIFAT celebrates success when the people of a poor community say, "We did it, we improved the lives of our people." Said another way, SIFAT tries to be enablers not doers. For those who go to help a graduate's community in other countries, that project offers an opportunity to serve and those who participate on such a SIFAT Short Term Mission Team always say they received far more than they gave. Lives are changed when people go on work teams to help others help themselves.

Loa and I are passionate about SIFAT. We feel called by God to support this mission organization. I am in my fourth year on the SIFAT board and hope to be helping SIFAT for many years to come.

If you want to read a great book that shares the story of the Corson family going into remote jungles in Bolivia, risking their lives to help people there help themselves, read *Risking Everything* by Sarah Corson available from sifat.org.

Hurricane Harvey in September 2017 was devastating for many households in Houston. As I write this in December 2018, over 15 months since the storm hit Houston, there are many people still living in homes that have not been repaired after the flood. Our church was overwhelmed by the outpouring of compassion from our members but also from church congregations around the country. As a result, our church, soon after the storm, had a budget of about $180,000 to help folks in homes flooded by Harvey. We have been working to restore homes ever since. Tomorrow, I will join a small team of retired men to work on a home. We are removing wallboard soaked by the water and replacing it with new wallboard and taping and floating the wallboard after that. Our church has also helped owners with donated funds to buy appliances and cabinets ruined by the flooding. We consistently hear how grateful people are for the help they receive. As we live comfortably in homes not flooded by Harvey, we can't help but reach out to these unfortunate people who didn't have insurance or the insurance they had was not enough to do needed repairs. People have lived "upstairs" or in a trailer in their front yard for, in some cases, well over a year waiting for help. We are pleased God has given us the opportunity to give back helping those flooded by hurricane Harvey.

John Wesley, the founder of the Methodist Church, said something we have tried to live by. I mentioned it earlier and will state it again because it has been so important to me. He said, "Earn all you can, give all you can, and save all you can." I understand, John Wesley wound up making a lot of money as a result of his book sales, yet he gave away his money to the needy with the goal of only having enough money for his burial when he died. Loa and I have had the good fortune of earning and saving a fair amount of money and we have the joy of sharing our resources with our church and organizations like those I have described here. The best use of the money God has trusted us with is to help those who are suffering to have the abundant lives God intended for them.

So where do I go from here? I know I am getting older and less capable physically and mentally. My hope is God will give me the ability to keep making a difference by giving back until the day I die. What a joy life is as we worship God, walk with Christ doing our best to follow Him by helping the "least of these" and experiencing the power of the Holy Spirit in our lives.

*"The opposite of love is not hate. The opposite of love is not caring."*
--- Ken Corson (SIFAT Founder)

Made in the USA
Columbia, SC
14 May 2019